Adaptive Leadership in a Global Economy

With the entire world experiencing the global pandemic and its aftermath, VUCA (Volatile, Uncertain, Complex, and Ambiguous) conditions have never been more extreme and the need for adaptive leadership never more urgent. But how is adaptive leadership applied outside Western cultures? How can it be taught through leadership development programs? Which tools enhance its practice and its teaching? How does adaptive leadership relate to other key theories and practices?

This volume answers these questions and more as it illustrates how adaptive leadership practices address some of the world's most pressing challenges—political and cultural division, remote work, crisis management across a variety of sectors. Adaptive leadership has been explained as a key leadership approach for dealing with adaptive, as distinguished from technical or predictable, problems, especially prevalent in complex environments. However, adaptive leadership scholarship has suffered from a lack of conceptual clarity and casual application of its core concepts. It remains solidly Western in its prescriptions. This book will expand readers' understanding of adaptive leadership and its potential to solve local and global adaptive challenges and will explore its relevance and application to cultures outside the United States.

Aiming to increase conceptual clarity about adaptive leadership to enhance future scholarship and application and illustrate novel approaches and perspectives, this book will be of interest to researchers, academics, practitioners, and students in the fields of leadership, strategy, and organizational studies.

Mohammed Raei is an Independent Leadership and Organization Development Consultant.

Harriette Thurber Rasmussen is an Assistant Clinical Professor at Drexel University's School of Education, USA.

Routledge Studies in Leadership Research

Critical Perspectives on Leadership
The Language of Corporate Power
Mark Learmonth and Kevin Morrell

Cognitive Automation and Organizational Psychology
Priming Goals as a New Source of Competitive Advantage
Alexander. D. Stajkovic and Kayla Sergent

Women's Leadership Development
Caring Environments and Paths to Transformation
Gelaye Debebe

Strategic Leadership and Systems Thinking
Peter S. DeLisi

Leadership, Gender and Ethics
Embodied Reason in Challenging Masculinities
David Knights

Digital Supply Chain Management
Reshaping Talent and Organizations
David B. Kurz and Muragan Anandarajan

Researching Leadership-As-Practice
The Reappearing Act of Leadership
Vasilisa Takoeva

Adaptive Leadership in a Global Economy
Perspectives for Application and Scholarship
Edited by Mohammed Raei and Harriette Thurber Rasmussen

For more information about this series please visit: https://www.routledge.com/Routledge-Studies-in-Leadership-Research/book-series/RSLR

Adaptive Leadership in a Global Economy

Perspectives for Application
and Scholarship

Edited by Mohammed Raei and
Harriette Thurber Rasmussen

NEW YORK AND LONDON

First published 2022
by Routledge
605 Third Avenue, New York, NY 10158

and by Routledge
2 Park Square, Milton Park, Abingdon, Oxon, OX14 4RN

*Routledge is an imprint of the Taylor & Francis Group, an
informa business*

Library of Congress Cataloging-in-Publication Data
Names: Raei, Mohammed, 1974- editor. | Rasmussen, Harriette
Thurber, 1954- editor.
Title: Adaptive leadership in a global economy : perspective for
application and scholarship / edited by Mohammed Raei, PhD and
Harriette Thurber Rasmussen, EdD.
Description: New York, NY : Routledge, 2022. | Series: Routledge
studies in leadership research | Includes bibliographical references
and index.
Identifiers: LCCN 2021037247 (print) | LCCN 2021037248
(ebook) | ISBN 9780367567149 (hbk) | ISBN 9780367567156
(pbk) | ISBN 9781003099109 (ebk)
Subjects: LCSH: Leadership.
Classification: LCC HD57.7 .A3134 2022 (print) | LCC HD57.7
(ebook) | DDC 658.4/092--dc23
LC record available at https://lccn.loc.gov/2021037247
LC ebook record available at https://lccn.loc.gov/2021037248

ISBN: 978-0-367-56714-9 (hbk)
ISBN: 978-0-367-56715-6 (pbk)
ISBN: 978-1-003-09910-9 (ebk)

DOI: 10.4324/9781003099109

Typeset in Sabon
by MPS Limited, Dehradun

Contents

Figures

Tables

Abbreviations

AL   Adaptive leadership
AST   Adaptive structuration theory
BRICS   Brazil, Russia, India, China, and South Africa
CAS   Complex adaptive system(s)
CL   Complexity leadership
DIAL   Democratic Indigenous Adaptive Leadership
FTF   Face-to-face
GDSS   Group decision support systems
GVT   Global virtual team
IPIs   Individuals in position of influence
IS   Improvement science
PDSA   Plan-do-study-act
VUCA   Volatility, uncertainty, complexity, and ambiguity
WFA   Work from anywhere

Glossary

Acting politically: Acting based on the assumption that no one acts only as an individual but represents a set of other party loyalties and expectations (Heifetz et al., 2009).

Adaptive challenge: Systemic challenges that have no immediate solution because in order to solve them, stakeholders have to change or set aside their habits, assumptions, behavior, or values. Solutions to these challenges are not easily created and require conflict, experimentation, unlearning of old habits/assumptions/values, and learning new ones (Heifetz, 1994).

Adaptive change: Change that requires some or all stakeholders to develop new habits, assumptions, values, or behaviors. This type of change is usually resisted both consciously and unconsciously (Heifetz, 1994).

Adaptive leadership: A set of practices that helps groups, organizations, and societies address and resolve adaptive challenges (Heifetz, 1994).

Adaptive leadership with authority: Adaptive leadership exercised from a position of power.

Adaptive leadership without authority: Adaptive leadership exercised while lacking positional power.

Adaptive work: "The learning required to address conflicts in the values people hold, or diminish the gap between the values people stand for and the reality they face. Adaptive work requires a change in values, beliefs, or behavior" (Heifetz, 1994, p. 22).

Authority: Authority that is tied to a formal position. Power is granted, or authorized, in exchange for service.

Elephants in the room: Sensitive and disruptive issues that a group avoids acknowledging and discussing.

Going to the balcony: Standing apart from daily activities and concerns to see the big picture (Laurie, 2000).

Holding environment: A place to hold the stress and distress of adaptive work and hold attention on adaptive challenges—a place where the conflicts between the different stakeholders are brought out into the open in a psychologically safe environment (Heifetz, 1994).

Orchestrating conflict: Creating and leading the process of getting parties
with differences to work through conflict (Heifetz et al., 2009).
Psychological safety: "A shared belief that [an environment] is safe for
interpersonal risk taking" (Edmondson, 1999, p. 354).
Technical challenge: Challenges that can be solved with existing
knowledge and do not require a change in values, assumptions, or
habits (Heifetz, 1994).

References

Edmondson, A. (1999). Psychological safety and learning behavior in work
teams. *Administrative Science Quarterly*, *44*(2), 350. https://doi.org/10.2307/
2666999
Heifetz, R. A. (1994). *Leadership without easy answers*. Harvard University
Press.
Heifetz, R. A., Grashow, A., & Linsky, M. (2009). *The practice of adaptive
leadership: Tools and tactics for changing your organization and the world*.
Harvard Business Press.
Laurie, D. L. (2000). *The real work of leaders: A report from the front lines of
management*. Basic Books.
Uhl-Bien, M., Marion, R., & McKelvey, B. (2007). Complexity leadership
theory: Shifting leadership from the Industrial Age to the knowledge era. *The
Leadership Quarterly*, *18*(4), 298–318. https://doi.org/10.1016/j.leaqua.
2007.04.002

Contributors

Lejla Bilal, manager of international product at McGraw Hill. Her extensive research into global virtual teams has made her a regular presenter at international conferences sharing her insights on adaptive leadership, professional learning communities, and team science. She is a co-founder of Transform•Ed Collaborative, an educational leadership collaborative. She holds a PhD in Leadership and Change from Antioch University.

Michael Christopher Boyce Senior Assistant Professor at the Hamamatsu University School of Medicine, Japan where he is actively involved in international service-learning program development and research. With a passion for global activism, his expertise and MA are in negotiation, conflict resolution, and peacebuilding. Moving from Canada to Japan in 1996, Michael lives and works on the coast of Shizuoka Prefecture. He is a doctoral candidate in organizational leadership education at Northeastern University.

Renee Charney, CEO and executive coach of Charney Consulting LLC. She is a founding faculty member of the Knowles Johnson Institute of Graduate Studies. She holds her clients as capable, whole, and resourceful, and helps them realize their capabilities for changing, adapting, and leading. Renee is a leadership researcher and thought-partner focused on shifting mindsets from fixed to growth, accessing potential and possibility, and unlocking capacities for learning and unlearning across multiple industries, including healthcare. She has presented internationally on topics that include adaptive, individual, and organizational leadership and learning.

Robert Crow is Associate Professor of Educational Research at Western Carolina University where he teaches in the masters and doctoral programs in educational leadership. Robert's research interests include improvement science and networked improvement communities of practice. He currently co-facilitates the Rural

Innovative School Leadership networked improvement community and is a Carnegie national faculty member for improvement science.

Jennifer Eggers is the founder of LeaderShift Insights®. She works with leadership teams facing disruption to increase their adaptive capacity. She is known for facilitating high-stakes meetings with challenging stakeholders, creating alignment, and impactful senior executive coaching. Jennifer was a partner with Cambridge Leadership Group, and has held senior roles at Bank of America, AutoZone, AlliedSignal, and Coca-Cola. Her book, *Resilience: It's Not About Bouncing Back* is an international bestseller.

Soyhan Egitim, EdD, is a full-time English lecturer at Toyo University in Japan. He completed his Doctor of Education degree at Northeastern University in 2020. As a multilingual expert in language education, research, and training (English, Turkish, Japanese), Dr. Egitim has promoted intercultural language education, leaderful language classroom practices, and collaborative leadership in diversity management through lectures, academic publications, presentations, and training workshops.

Lisa Gick, CEO and Founder of [curious]®, a leadership and change agency. A PhD candidate in Leadership and Change, she is a visiting instructor in the Business College at Mount St. Joseph University. She is a leadership researcher, coach, and organizational consultant in several industries, including healthcare, and enjoyed a 25-year career focused on the employee experience as an executive at Macy's, Inc. Lisa writes and presents regularly on leading in the modern workplace, including leader identity, organizational complexity and leading change.

Tomas Hancil (www.complexityguys.com) is an executive coach and organizational consultant based in the Czech Republic with more than 20 years of experience working with global organizations. He is a leader in the field of developmental leadership and is one of the leading thinkers, writers, and translators in the field of developmental psychology and complexity leadership in the region. He trained originally as a philosopher and holds a PhD from Princeton.

Jeffrey M. Hardesty, EdD serves his remote rural community in eastern Washington State as school superintendent. He began his career in education during the mid-90s as a teacher and co-developer of a new school for students struggling in the mainstream setting. This experience drove his curiosity about systemic barriers to meeting the needs of all students. Over the past 24 years, as a teacher, principal, and now superintendent, Dr. Hardesty has worked to inform instructional practice, policy development, and legislative decisions to address the systemic barriers that result in disproportionate student outcomes.

Jacqueline Hawkins, Special Populations Ed.D. Program Lead, Department of Educational Leadership and Policy Studies, University of Houston. Dr. Hawkins' research focus has been on prevention and intervention work for educators and parents who engage with students in applied contexts across the education pipeline. She engages a systems change approach to research professional development, transition support, and early interventions for students who strive for better outcomes. She also has provided evaluation coaching and evaluation support to various organizations in the Houston region and across the United States.

Four Arrows aka Don Trent Jacobs, Professor, Educational Leadership for Change, Fielding Graduate University, is a member of the Lakota Medicine Horse Tiospaye. He has doctorates in Health Psychology and in Curriculum. He has authored numerous publications that have been endorsed by such notables as Noam Chomsky, Vandana Shiva, Bill McKibben, and Henry Giroux. Recipient of a Martin Springer Institute Moral Courage Award for his activism and of recognition from several Canadian Aboriginal organizations, his most recent book is Sitting Bull's Words for a World in Crisis. He lives in Mexico and Canada. See fourarrowsbooks.com.

Magda Kaspary is a global human resources (SHRM-SCP certified) and organization development professional with more than 15 years of experience in different industries in South and North America, and Europe. Magda holds two master's degrees, in Social Psychology (PUC/RS Brazil) and Organizational Leadership (Pinchot University, Seattle/USA). Currently, Magda is a PhD student at Saybrook University. She is an Intercultural Development Inventory qualified administrator, ACC ICF coach, and Points of You® Certified.

Shannon Kenny, social entrepreneur and published author. She began her career as a historian and has worked as a freelance writer, editor, and educator in the fields of history, social sciences, and social justice for over 20 years. In 2018, Shannon founded technology startup Prontopia, to solve supply and distribution gaps in access to essential human services. Informed by the Indigenous women's leadership activism of her mother, Carolyn Kenny, Shannon's work seeks to restore balance to the interplay of technology and society by recognizing where technology companies have forsaken human connection to each other and to the land for short-term gains focused on minimizing human effort.

Deidre Le Fevre, Associate Professor and head of graduate programs in educational leadership at the University of Auckland, New Zealand. Her research focuses on practices that support leaders to solve complex leadership problems and on effective approaches to professional learning. She has published extensively on interpersonal effectiveness, leadership for educational improvement, organizational change, and effective professional learning. She brings knowledge and skills in understanding organizational change, the development of professional capability, and effective leadership to her research, teaching, and international consulting with leaders and organizations.

Cheryl LeMaster is the managing partner at TruEdge Consulting LLC. She is a change/agility consultant and certified leadership coach with 30 years of experience in adult education, organizational development, management, coaching, and consulting. Cheryl has a Bachelor's in Education and an M.A. in human and organization development from the George Washington University. She has a PhD in Leadership and Change from Antioch University where she did her research on leading change in complex systems.

Lindsay Lyons (she/her) is an educational justice coach who works with teachers and school leaders to inspire educational innovation for racial and gender justice, design curricula grounded in student voice, and build capacity for shared leadership. Lindsay taught in NYC public schools, holds a PhD in Leadership and Change, and is the founder of the educational blog and podcast, Time for Teachership.

Rita Michel, is a psychologist (PUC/RS Brazil) with an MBA focused on human resource management and a specialization in group dynamics through the Brazilian Society of Group Dynamics. She has international certification in Transformational Ontological Coaching by Leading Group, Argentina. She is an Executive Master Coach by the Integrated Coaching Institute. She is the founder of Parallax Institute and the creator of Be a Mentor methodology. She has more than 25 years in organizational consulting, executive coaching, and leadership development.

Cherie Bridges Patrick (she/her) is a leadership educator, coach, and consultant who works with equity-focused counseling and educational professionals. She is the founder of Paradox Cross-Cultural Consulting, Training & Empowerment LLC. She uses neuroscience-based coaching and facilitation to help professionals establish safety, repair disconnects, normalize generative, justice-centered dialogue, and heal relationships that have been harmed by racial and social trauma. Cherie is a licensed clinical social worker and holds a PhD in Leadership and Change.

Mohammed Raei is an independent leadership and organization development consultant based in Jordan. He has consulted on strategic planning and program evaluation. Additionally, he has facilitated workshops on trust, adaptive leadership, and immunity to change. Moreover, he has facilitated gatherings, meetings, and retreats for a variety of clients. He previously served as programming chair for the Pacific Northwest Organization Development Network. He completed a Ph.D. dissertation titled "Development and Validation of the Adaptive Leadership with Authority Scale."

Harriette Thurber Rasmussen, Assistant Clinical Professor at Drexel University's School of Education. She consults internationally, coaching educational leaders and their systems toward greater capacity with cutting edge research around adult learning, organizational effectiveness, and the socio-political aspects of executive leadership. A resident of Seattle, Washington, Harriette received her EdD from Fielding Graduate University. Her research interests and writing emphasize teacher efficacy, instructional coherence, organizational complexity, adult development and, of course, adaptive leadership.

Jonathan Reams, Associate Professor in the Department of Education and Lifelong Learning Faculty of Social and Educational Sciences at the Norwegian University of Science and Technology (NTNU). He practices the cultivation of leadership through awareness-based consulting, coaching, and action research on leadership development program design and delivery. He serves as editor-in-chief of Integral Review, and is a co-founder of the Center for Transformative Leadership and of the European Center for Leadership Practice. His work focuses on how developing our inner capacities can meet today's complex challenges.

Matthew Rich-Tolsma (www.complexityguys.com) is an executive coach, organizational consultant, and mediator based in the Netherlands. He has worked with a wide range of organizations across Europe, Africa, and Asia. He has a background in education and has expertise in developmental psychology, complexity, improvisation, and working with intersectionality and diversity. He is a certified trainer with the Centre for Nonviolent Communication and a Fellow of the Institute of Coaching.

Risako (Lisa) Watanabe, founder of Watanabe & Associates, is a researcher at Keio University Global Research Institute, and a developmental coach operating at the nexus of research and practice. She offers executive training focused on leadership development and organizational culture change using adult development psychology and adaptive leadership. She is a fellow of the Institute of Coaching at McLean, Harvard Medical School Affiliate, a certified Immunity-to-Change™ Coach, and a certified Reliable Subject-Object Interview Scorer. She has earned an Ed.M. at Harvard University and an MPA at the University of Pennsylvania.

Ryosuke (Reo) Watanabe, Ph.D. Candidate at the School of Leadership and Education Sciences, University of San Diego and a researcher at Keio University Global Research Institute. His research focuses on the intersection of adaptive leadership and adult development. He teaches adaptive leadership using the case-in-point method and offers executive training both in the USA and Japan. He is a certified Reliable Subject-Object Interview Scorer and a certified coach of Global Leadership Profile. He has earned an MPA at Harvard Kennedy School and an MBA at the Wharton School of the University of Pennsylvania.

Forward

It was the fall of 1996. My mind was in turmoil and nothing seemed to fit. The experience was intense and difficult. Still, I could sense that something important was happening and that the process was worth sustaining.

And so I did, not only during those four months of the adaptive leadership course I took with Ronald Heifetz in my Master of Public Policy studies at Harvard, but since then until now. It has been a 25-year journey of experimentation, disequilibrium, and a lot of learning through teaching, research, and consulting. I started on my own when I returned to my country, Chile, doing a first-course rehearsal of Heifetz' lessons in adaptive leadership. Today we are a community of more than 70 people in Chile, Peru, Colombia, and Australia who continue to learn about adaptive leadership practices as we teach in three universities and help organizations make progress in their toughest adaptive challenges through our consulting firm-CLA Consulting.

An important part of this adventure has been meeting and connecting to hundreds of academics and practitioners around the world who are advancing adaptive leadership, among whom are the editors of this book and the authors of its different chapters. Reading what they have written has been a wonderful exercise and has made me resonate with much of what I have lived and reflected, allowing me to make connections, delve into some ideas, and challenge myself in others.

When I started talking about adaptive leadership in Latin America, the first question that inevitably appeared was the cultural one: "And how applicable are these American ideas in our context?" Embedded in those words, as I came to understand over time, was an avoidance mechanism, generated by the disequilibrium I was introducing, initially without being even conscious that I was doing so. But it was also necessary to understand that this Latin American context was very determined by authoritarianism, which made it especially difficult for these adaptive concepts to be assimilated, something similar to what happens in Eastern Europe, as Tomas Hancil and Matthew Rich-Tolsma tell us in Chapter 16 of this volume.

For most people, entering that liminal space that Renee Charney and Lisa Gick talk about in Chapter 7 was an adaptive challenge too deep to face, representing significant losses of power, skills, and assurance that they were not willing to accept. Over time, however, the evidence of that complexity that Mohammed Raei and Cheryl LeMaster refer to in Chapter 1 has grown stronger and harder to avoid. If the expression "systemic" became famous with the financial crisis of 2009, it is precisely because since then we have witnessed a path without return toward ever greater degrees of complexity in the world, which require that systemic view and, at the same time, more and more adaptive capacity, at a social, organizational, and individual level.

It was in 2011, when the world was reeling with the multiple movements that began with the Arab Spring, that I started writing the book *Adaptive Capacity*, taking advantage of a sabbatical during which I settled on the east coast of the United States. Netflix was just starting with its streaming service and WhatsApp did not yet exist. The exponential development of new technologies has been a fundamental trigger of what we have experienced since then, connected with what we have seen as strong citizen empowerment, questioning of authorities everywhere, polarization—aided by the large-scale activism that Jeffery Hardesty, Michael Boyce and Harriette Thurber Rasmussen speak of in Chapter 9—and, of course, the emergence of those charismatic authorities (and how not to refer to Donald Trump in this regard) who seek to provide simple answers to complex problems.

What we are experiencing, and what we can anticipate for the future, is more complexity and deeper adaptive challenges, with or without pandemics, for which the commensurate need for adaptive leadership and adaptive capacity, two sides of the same coin, will become increasingly self-evident, as Jacinda Ardern has shown us in New Zealand and Deidre Le Fevre explains in Chapter 10. The contribution of this book in this regard is great and we must thank its authors, because these pages will help more people ask themselves difficult questions and evolve in their own ways of understanding and exercising leadership, even in cultures where the adaptive work that is required for that to happen is greater. Thank you for inviting us to this reflection... and to exercise leadership adaptively!

Juan Carlos Eichholz
Santiago de Chile, July 2021

Introduction

Harriette Thurber Rasmussen and
Mohammed Raei

We, the editors, come to the field of adaptive leadership (Heifetz et al., 2009) in very different ways—Mohammed through his own attempts to address adaptive challenges with technical solutions, stumbling upon adaptive leadership in a powerful reckoning on what he might have done differently. As a result, adaptive leadership and its conception of authority oriented his doctoral studies. Harriette was introduced to adaptive leadership through her work with the Bill and Melinda Gates Foundation and various projects at Harvard University, learning directly from Heifetz in their attempts to realign school systems across the United States. Eventually, she would go on to teach adaptive leadership in doctoral studies at Drexel University. We met over Mohammed's doctoral dissertation and soon discovered other mutual interests that you will see throughout this book, such as adult development theory and the increasingly volatile, uncertain, complex, and ambiguous (VUCA) world in which we live. Our experiences as academics and practitioners led us to conceive this volume.

Harriette has been known to tell her students that most collaborative leadership theories are incomplete and that adaptive leadership addresses the role of authority in ways that others do not. The current literature around collaborative leadership, for example, complexity leadership (Uhl-Bien et al., 2007), relational leadership (Uhl-Bien, 2006), leadership-as-practice (Raelin, 2016), and ensemble leadership (Rosile et al., 2016), leaves out the opportunities of positional leadership addressed by Heifetz and colleagues. This distinction, however, is not well called out in the literature and offers an opening for scholars and practitioners as an enhancer of understanding and application. Both of us have found that adaptive leadership encompasses the realities of deep change, with its focus on stakeholder engagement and loss, the proverbial holding environment, and the importance of the balcony view. At the same time, we have felt that there may be a next level of application to Heifetz and colleagues' written work and have wondered how it is applied across the globe, in non-Western cultures, and in our increasingly complex society.

DOI: 10.4324/9781003099109-101

Our quest coincided with the advent of the 2020 global pandemic where the need for crisis-oriented leadership became a familiar theme.

As is the case in all edited volumes, the themes we believe most relevant to adaptive leadership (and interesting to us) are most prevalent in this book. Certainly, being in the midst of a VUCA world leads much of our exploration of adaptive leadership. The idea that some problems can be solved using existing methods while others cannot is not entirely new and actually predates Heifetz's work by decades; almost 20 years before Heifetz published his first book, Rittel and Webber (1973) made the distinction between tame problems—problems that can be solved using existing knowledge, and wicked problems—problems that require new learning.

Wicked problems in their original conception are complex problems that lack social complexity. They are consistent with what Ackoff (1979) described as messes: "Managers are not confronted with problems that are independent of each other, but with dynamic situations that consist of complex systems of changing problems that interact with each other" (p. 99). If we include social complexity in wicked problems as other scholars have done, then wicked problems start to resemble adaptive challenges. Yet even as wicked, adaptive problems may not be new, the circumstances that led scholars to consider them decades ago bear little resemblance to today's environment of political divide, complicated by technology with its wonders and its foibles. A global economy on its own exceeds their assumptions; add artificial intelligence and social media and all bets are off. Regardless, as Conklin et al. (2007) point out, "There are no single stakeholder wicked problems" (p. 4). This combination makes today's wicked problems "wicked-er"—and pushes adaptive leadership beyond its roots. We are, we believe, in new territory. This book intends to aid that exploration.

At the same time, the basic premise of Heifetz's original framework is, we argue, still a solid set of practices to apply to wicked, adaptive challenges. Throughout this volume, you will see certain practices referenced again and again, so it makes sense to orient our readers to the ways in which we explain certain aspects of adaptive leadership. For those of you picking up this volume without prior knowledge of adaptive leadership, this volume will be instructive; each chapter's discussion of these practices includes some level of explanation of the practices themselves. At the same time, the included glossary will be a useful beginning.

The Adaptive Leadership Framework

Adaptive leadership practices begin by **identifying the adaptive challenge and diagnosing the system,** best known through its distinction between adaptive and technical problems. As you will read throughout this book, technical problems are those able to be addressed by an expert; they rely on existing solutions and matching the right practice, or expert, to the problem (Rittel and Webber's "tame problems"). Adaptive challenges, on the other hand, require new knowledge, typically falling into the category we discuss above as "wicked." Resolution of adaptive challenges frequently involves some level of loss, for some, if not all, involved and emerges through adaptation and experimentation, which is why **building a system's capacity for continuous learning** is a core concept of adaptive leadership.

Most leadership theories ignore the political reality of organizations. One of the main contributions of adaptive leadership is viewing leadership and change as inherently political. Successful political maneuvering involves navigating a multitude of relationships and few leaders would deny that **acting politically** is a significant part of leading. Adaptive leadership relies on **mobilizing the entire system and its stakeholders**–stakeholders who may need to be tapped on the shoulder and invited to join. Stakeholders and their inherent loyalties play a key role in adaptive work as adaptive challenges typically require those impacted (stakeholders) to rethink or re-prioritize values, ultimately accepting some level of loss in order to see progress. Importantly, adaptive leadership recognizes **resistance as loss**; people don't resist change, Heifetz et al. (2009) claim; they resist loss.

As noted above, the political framing of adaptive leadership includes the **strategic use of formal and informal authority**. Adaptive leaders do not necessarily rely on position to navigate adaptive challenges. Relationships and influence can be as, or more, effective as formal authority when asking stakeholders to accept what they may not immediately see as a worthwhile sacrifice. Formal authority, however, can be used strategically to, as an example, **create a holding environment**, a psychologically safe zone in which leaders can **orchestrate conflict, keeping distress within a tolerable zone** so that people are able to engage in ways that are productive (adaptive) but not beyond their limits of tolerance for ambiguity and the loss associated with adaptive change.

These premises served as our backdrop for constructing this book, but in the context of a VUCA crisis-oriented environment, other themes became evident as we reviewed the chapters by our wonderful contributing authors. Particular ways of thinking about adaptive leadership practices were unexpected to us, meaning that although they resonated, we did not name these themes in our call for chapters. Thus, we feel these important to call out here, even with the limited evidence this volume produces, as we were surprised to see these patterns of thought emerge. Let's just call them noteworthy.

Although this was not the first time we (the editors) have examined **constructive adult development theory** in relation to adaptive leadership (see Rasmussen & Raei, 2020), we were surprised, and excited, to see others associate higher mental complexity with the skills required for adaptive work (Chapters 2, 5, 12, and 16). **Single- and double-loop learning** with its distinction of espoused values versus values-in-use, along with the necessity of **improvisation and/or experimentation** in adaptive work was a recurring theme (Chapters 2, 7, and 9). The role of dialogue, or conversation, and ways to make that productive was addressed (Chapters 2, 8, 9, and 15)–and **crisis management, or leadership,** perhaps because of the era in which these chapters were written, came up again and again (Chapters 4, 7, 10, and 13). Finally, **diversity** was discussed by several contributors not only as a cornerstone of adaptive work (Chapters 4, 7, 9, and 14) but also as an adaptive challenge itself (Chapters 1, 8, and 15).

Beyond Flexibility

Yukl and Mahsud (2010) defined adaptive and flexible leadership as leadership that involves "changing behavior in appropriate ways as the situation changes" (p. 81). However, Heifetz's adaptive leadership goes beyond flexibility, to leaders themselves being adaptive. Our questions about possible limits of leader adaptability are one of the main reasons for constructing this volume. We wondered how this Western construct applies to the norms and cultures in other parts of the world. Moreover, we were curious as to how culture becomes an aspect of the "situation" and how these situations might be described by scholars and practitioners who have studied Heifetz's work and considered it in, perhaps, very different environments than those experienced by Heifetz and his colleagues. We intentionally sought chapters from a non-Western perspective, by authors who might introduce us, and our readers, to the ways in which adaptive leadership needs to be modified to fit other cultures. Over 4,000 invitations to write chapters for this volume were distributed and more than twice as many proposals for chapters were received than we were able to use. And we found, as is so often the case when we access the power of diversity, that these perspectives deepened our own understandings of adaptive leadership—its roots, its application, and its possibilities.

Overview of the Volume

This volume is organized into three parts: Foundations, Adaptive Leadership in Action, and Adaptive Leadership Across Cultures. Foundations explores the practices of adaptive leadership themselves, hoping to draw our readers into a deeper understanding of adaptive leadership through new perspectives. In Chapter 1 Raei and LeMaster compare adaptive leadership with complexity leadership theory, arguing that while complementary, the two are different in key areas (i.e., control, assumptions), and that in tandem they offer a stronger platform to address adaptive work than adaptive leadership on its own. Chapter 2 then examines key theoretical underpinnings of adaptive leadership, and "gives credit where it's due" as its authors argue that adaptive leadership is not a theory per se, but a framework of practices that represent deep theoretical constructs. Rasmussen and Boyce summarize these constructs to explain the reasoning behind adaptive leadership practices, why they are effective, and provide a jumping-off point for those who wish to delve more deeply into the scholarship associated with adaptive leadership.

In Chapter 3, Eggers adds the concept of resilience to adaptive leadership as she introduces the *LeadershipShift®* resilience framework. The way in which she explains the role of resilience in adaptive leadership illustrates how it can enhance the teaching of adaptive leadership while furthering adaptive work. Rasmussen, Hawkins, and Crow consider another additive construct to enhance adaptive leadership in Chapter 4 as they explain the components of improvement science. They illustrate its use as a complementary tool for adaptive leaders through a case example of a school district navigating equity goals amidst the twin crises of COVID-19 and highly politicized racial strife in a small rural community. Part 1 concludes with an insightful and provocative piece by Reams as he ponders who, really, is on the balcony. Taking a transpersonal perspective and drawing on neuroscience, neurocardiology, and neuroplasticity, Chapter 5 argues that the soul is on the balcony and the self is on the dance floor. It concludes by describing how the soul creates a field of awareness that opens spaces and creates holding environments.

Part 2 of this volume focuses on Adaptive Leadership in Action, discussing adaptive leadership practices in the context of current events. Beginning with Chapter 6, Bilal outlines the unique array of adaptive challenges faced by global virtual teams and how adaptive leadership practices can address barriers frequently experienced in a work environment that is increasingly virtual. This is followed by Charney and Gick's exploration in Chapter 7 of liminal folds, rhizomic spaces, and adaptive mindsets in the healthcare industry. Curious about what that means? So were we (!) and were not disappointed as we learned about the gray areas associated with complex systems and how adaptive leadership practices offer a guide through the murky territory that often produces wicked, and wicker-er, problems. Chapter 8 takes you directly into the folds of racism and explains how White supremacy culture has heretofore controlled the conversation around racial justice. Bridges Patrick and Lyons draw on work by Eichholz (who wrote the forward for this volume) and research in the field of social work, offering a framework for adaptive leaders to guide stakeholders out of entrenched patterns of the past to "modify the stories they tell." In Chapter 9 Hardesty, Boyce, and Rasmussen then challenge the efficacy of large-scale activism, advocating instead for small, micro-interactions to move beyond the polarization that characterizes the political climate. Curiously, both Chapters 8 and 9 challenge the reality of "safe space," replacing the illusion of comfort with action-oriented discourse that spurs dissonance, drawing on the practice of orchestrating conflict in a holding environment. Chapter 9 reviews single-, double-, and triple-loop learning as a strategy to uncover stakeholder values and assumptions, introducing disposition mapping as a strategic structure to promote progress on issues that might otherwise be polarizing.

This part concludes with a close look at the application of adaptive leadership in managing crises: Le Fevre profiles the leadership of The Rt Hon Jacinda Ardern, prime minister of Aotearoa New Zealand. Chapter 10 looks at Arden's leadership style, characterized by caring and compassion, in her response to that country's Christchurch terrorist attack and COVID-19, widely considered to be one of the most successful responses to the global pandemic in the world.

Part 3 moves us out of Western perspective into Adaptive Leadership Across Cultures, beginning with Raei's exploration of how adaptive leadership might be applied in China, where culture is steeped in Confucian values and conflict is generally avoided in the interest of saving face. Taking a Taoist orientation involving the interplay of Yin-Yang, Raei in Chapter 11 discusses the modifications needed to apply adaptive leadership in the Chinese context.

Watanabe and Watanabe then take us to Japan in Chapter 12 where they present their concept of Kabuki leadership. Kabuki is a form of improvisational theater in Japan and in this chapter it becomes a powerful metaphor for cultivating adaptive leadership in the hierarchical collectivist society that characterizes Japanese culture. We conclude our examination of adaptive leadership in Japan in Chapter 13 with Egitim's discussion of Japanese universities' response to the global pandemic crisis and how harnessing collective intelligence activated and accelerated adaptive and collaborative leadership practices.

Inspired by the oral tradition common in Indigenous cultures, Kenny and Four Arrows dialogue in Chapter 14, considering adaptive leadership in the Indigenous context. They present Democratic Indigenous Adaptive Leadership (DIAL), an American Indian women's leadership model, to examine the ways in which an Indigenous worldview addresses the many crises faced across the globe. Chapter 15 discusses how a mentoring stance can enhance the development of adaptive leadership in Brazil. Kaspary and Michel explain how awareness-of-self becomes a baseline for building collaborative, holistic, and systemic adaptive leadership capacity in Brazil's inherently hierarchical culture. And lastly, Hancil and Rich-Tolmsa take us to their consulting practice in Eastern and Central Europe where they reveal in Chapter 16 the idiosyncrasies they experienced that caused them to adapt adaptive leadership. They introduce the formal theory of organizational bullshit to this volume and the ways in which it intertwines with adaptive leadership practices, illustrating their practice through vignettes that highlight the ah-ha moments of corporate leaders in the Central and Eastern European context. They conclude the chapter by questioning some of the assumptions and applicability of adaptive leadership when applied outside the West.

In creating this volume, we wanted to provide something that would appeal to practitioners and scholars alike. We think this volume will leave the reader with a deeper and more nuanced understanding of adaptive leadership practices, applicable in VUCA environments, to crisis management, across cultures and sectors, and with insight into the complex journey of developing leaders capable of addressing the adaptive challenges of the 21st century. Leadership, we believe, is a decision to act, with or without authority, to listen, and to engage others in the multitude of ways this book describes. Most importantly, adaptive leadership is about curiosity and learning, which is ultimately what this volume intends to spark.

References

Ackoff, R. L. (1979). The future of operational research is past. *The Journal of the Operational Research Society, 30*(2), 93. 10.2307/3009290

Conklin, J., Basadur, M., & VanPatter, G. K. (2007). Rethinking wicked problems: Unpacking paradigms, bridging universes. *NextD Journal, 10*(1), 1–29.

Heifetz, R. A., Grashow, A., & Linsky, M. (2009). *The practice of adaptive leadership: Tools and tactics for changing your organization and the world.* Harvard Business Press.

Raelin, J. A. (2016). *Leadership-as-practice: Theory and application.* Routledge.

Rosile, G. A., Boje, D. M., Claw, C. M. (2016). Ensemble leadership theory: Collectivist, relational, and heterarchical roots from indigenous contexts. *Leadership, 14*(3), 308–328. 10.1177/1742715016652933

Rasmussen, H. T., & Raei, M. (2020). I'll only follow if I trust you: Using adult development to accelerate trust. In J. Reams (Ed.), *Maturing leadership: How adult development impacts leadership* (pp. 103–128). Emerald Publishing Limited.

Rittel, H. W., & Webber, M. M. (1973). Dilemmas in a general theory of planning. *Policy Science, 4*(2), 155–169. 10.1007/bf01405730

Uhl-Bien, M. (2006). Relational leadership theory: Exploring the social processes of leadership and organizing. *The Leadership Quarterly, 17*(6), 654–676.

Uhl-Bien, M., Marion, R., & McKelvey, B. (2007). Complexity leadership theory: Shifting leadership from the Industrial Age to the knowledge era. *The Leadership Quarterly, 18*(4), 298–318. 10.1016/j.leaqua.2007.04.002

Yukl, G., & Mahsud, R. (2010). Why flexible and adaptive leadership is essential. *Consulting Psychology Journal: Practice and Research, 62*(2), 81–93. 10.1037/a0019835

Part I

Foundations

1 Adaptive and Complexity Leadership: Stronger Together

Mohammed Raei and Cheryl LeMaster

The third decade of the 21st century has erupted in a multitude of momentous events: a worldwide pandemic exposing the ugly disparities that lurk just below society's surface; the Black Lives Matter movement highlighting the consequences of centuries of American inequality; the rise of insurrectionists shocking the world with a politically induced attack on the United States Capitol; pandemic-related economic instability disproportionately effecting the most vulnerable; and finally, weather-related effects of climate change, a threat likely to inflict irreversible damage to our planet. Equally fearsome, according to Freedom House's annual report, *Freedom in the World 2020*, world democracy has been in retreat for 14 consecutive years (Repucci, 2020). The politics of fear and rage gave rise to the election of "strong man" leaders in established democracies around the world: Putin in Russia, Erdogan in Turkey, Modi in India, Bolsonaro in Brazil, and of course, former President Trump in the United States.

The world feels precarious and the search for a better way bears intense urgency. To survive and thrive in this radically altered landscape demands the skill to adapt. It calls for innovative thinking and new mental models. It requires the capacity to shed the old and embrace the new. It makes essential the ability to harness the conflict and tension that fear, ambiguity, and difference can generate. We believe that the promise of a brighter tomorrow demands that we cast hate and zealotry aside, embrace opposition and criticism with truly open minds, listen closely to our perceived adversaries, reject the power of self-interest, and work together for the greater good. Above all, adapting to our volatile, uncertain, complex, and ambiguous (VUCA) world means that we must embrace new approaches to leadership and change.

Leadership scholars Uhl-Bien and Arena (2017) argue that we *must learn* to enable adaptive, rather than ordered, responses to complexity. In this chapter, we compare and contrast two leadership models with the capacity to help transform our thinking from mechanistic to adaptive and create the organizational agility necessary to survive and thrive in today's world.

DOI: 10.4324/9781003099109-1

The chapter is divided into four sections: first, we look at Heifetz's adaptive leadership (AL) framework; second, we review complexity leadership (CL) theory and one of its key models; third, we compare and contrast the two approaches. Finally, in closing, we posit how these approaches can be used synergistically in organizations to harness change and spark innovation.

Adaptive Leadership

Heifetz (1994) distinguishes between adaptive challenges and technical problems. Technical problems have an existing solution and do not require much learning to solve; frequently, one can hire an expert to resolve the problem. Adaptive challenges, on the other hand, require both the stakeholders and leaders to engage in learning as no clear solution exists for the problem. Adaptive problems are generally not clearly defined and a technical solution is insufficient. Consider that developing emotionally intelligent leaders in a large engineering firm is an adaptive challenge, but improving cyber security in the company is a technical challenge.

Heifetz et al. (2009b) explained that adaptive challenges are typically grounded in the complexities of beliefs, values, and loyalties rather than technical complications; they stir intense emotions rather than dispassionate analysis. For these reasons, organizations often avoid the value-laden facets of a problem and try to solve the issue through technical means (Heifetz et al., 2009b).

Adaptive leadership (AL) encourages learning by asking tough questions and by reframing expectations. This type of learning, which Heifetz (1994) calls adaptive learning, moves beyond learning new skills or knowledge; it involves learning new ways of acting and being, and learning to resolve "conflicts in the values people hold" (Heifetz, 1994, p. 22). Moreover, it is a learning that requires unlearning (Heifetz & Laurie, 2003).

Adaptive learning is difficult and can result in negative feelings, including psychological pain and a sense of loss (Heifetz, 1994), as well as feeling incompetent, irrelevant to others, and betrayed (Heifetz et al., 2009b). Because of these negative feelings, stakeholders resist change and engage in adaptive work avoidance. Work avoidance can be seen through a propensity to focus on technical issues instead of the adaptive challenge, blaming positional leadership, other stakeholders, or external enemies for the problem or absence of a solution, denying that problems exist, or jumping to conclusions. Thus, one of the main responsibilities for an adaptive leader is to overcome adaptive work avoidance and keep the focus on the adaptive issue.

In AL, the leader uses interventions—such as encouraging frank conversation about conflicting opinions or strategies—to create progress on adaptive challenges. However, adaptive challenges can lead to distress and if the stress is too high, stakeholders might "fight, flee, or freeze" (Heifetz et al., 2009a, p. 66). Therefore, a leader must maintain the pressure of adaptive work within a tolerable zone. Conversely, if the stress is too low, there is little action on the adaptive challenges. Heifetz (1994) has employed the metaphor of a pressure cooker to describe this dynamic: When pressure is too high, the leader decreases the heat; when inertia is detected, the leader increases the heat.

The psychological environment in which adaptive work takes place is called a holding environment (see Chapter 5 for a discussion of the interior condition required to create the holding environment). It is a place to hold the distress caused by adaptive work, where the conflicts between the various stakeholders are surfaced in a psychologically safe manner. The holding environment provides a structure to discuss specific perspectives, values, and ideas vis-à-vis adaptive challenges (Heifetz et al., 2009b). Leaders strengthen the holding environment by establishing lateral bonds of affection, trust, and camaraderie along with vertical bonds of trust with those in authority. The conflicts around adaptive challenges are not interpersonal conflicts, though they might initially present themselves as such. The goal, then, of AL is to allow for disagreement on issues, perspectives, or values (Heifetz et al., 2009b) instead of attacking personal character.

For Heifetz (1994), leadership was strictly defined in relationship to adaptive work and dealing with adaptive challenges. The strategies that leaders employ to create movement on an adaptive issue depend on whether they possess or lack authority (Heifetz, 1994). Leadership with authority comes with advantages and limitations. The advantages are an ability to create and control a holding environment, access to the systemic issues surrounding the challenge, and knowing the different issues facing an organization or community. Additionally, authority allows a leader to "(a) direct attention to the issues; (b) gather and test information—perform reality testing; (c) manage information and frame issues; (d) orchestrate conflicting perspectives; and (e) choose the decisionmaking [sic] process" (Heifetz, 1994, p. 113).

According to Heifetz (1994), a leader with authority also:

- identifies the adaptive challenge and diagnoses "the situation in light of the values at stake, and unbundles the issues that come with it" (p. 128);
- keeps the distress level within an endurable range;
- keeps attention on ripening issues and not distractions, and responds to work avoidance;
- gives the work back to the group at a level they can handle; and
- protects "voices of leadership without authority" (p. 128), providing cover to those who ask tough questions and create distress.

AL intervention strategies include asking questions regarding problem definition and possible solutions, showing the reality of external threats, disorienting people from their existing roles, allowing for conflict, and challenging norms.

Complexity Leadership

CL is a model that provides guidelines and tools for navigating a VUCA landscape. Derived from the physical realm and common to all life forms, complexity theory is an approach that suggests an organic process originating from interacting systems and the rich connectivity of a system's parts. It offers a fundamentally different perspective on leadership and the processes for how leaders can structure and manage adaptation and innovation in organizations. With a complexity systems perspective, leaders can channel the power of self-organization and emergence to produce adaptive responses.

Complexity theory is concerned with the emergence of order in dynamic nonlinear systems. Ralph Stacey was the first to apply the theory to organizations (Burnes, 2005). Burnes mapped the complexity course ahead when he shared others' convictions that leaders would need to "rethink the nature of hierarchy and control, learn the art of managing in changing contexts, promote self-organizing processes, and learn how to use small change to create large effects" (Burnes, 2005, p. 82). Derived from the study of complex dynamical systems known as complexity science, CL is a form of organizational "governance" that moves from top-down, command and control, heroic leadership to a more organic form of shared leadership practice.

To fully appreciate CL, it is helpful to understand the fundamental principles of the originating science. The following section describes basic complexity constructs that are evident in adaptive organizational practices, and provides a powerful metaphor for how leaders may increase organizational agility by enabling adaptive (versus ordered) responses to complexity.

Complexity Science

Complexity science is a theory about the interaction dynamics among multiple, networked agents (people, technology, information, resources), and how emergent events—such as creativity, learning, or adaptability—arise from these exchanges (Marion, 2008). We note that the term "complexity" does not mean complicated or intricate. The meaning is based on the Latin form of the word *complexus*, as in comprehension and wholeness. It refers to the dynamical interaction of agents in a complex adaptive system (CAS) and it speaks to the emergent properties at work in the (whole) system. Simply put, complexity is about rich interconnectivity.

The emergence of an organizational theory based on complexity has enabled new ways of examining and theorizing about organizational activities (Styhre, 2002; Tsoukas, 1998).

According to Olson and Eoyang (2001), "Rather than focus at the macro 'strategic' level of the organizational system, complexity theory suggests that the most powerful processes of adaptation occur at the micro level, where relationships, interactions, small experiments, and simple rules shape emerging patterns" (p. xxxiii).

According to Wheatley (2006), the growth of complexity science has seen the merging of natural sciences with business management to tell a story about the nature of how people interact. Through the use of metaphor and the lens of complexity, Wheatley sees systems rather than isolated players and parts that transform themselves from machines to dynamic, interconnected living systems, possessing the capacity to adapt and grow.

In 2021, Wheatley's interconnected and interdependent systemic challenges are on full display in the global pandemic. A powerful illustration of the author's message is offered by Tufekci (2020) as she considers complex systems thinking and its role in our response to global threats:

> We had time to prepare for this pandemic at the state, local, and household level, even if the government was terribly lagging, but we squandered it because of widespread asystemic thinking: the inability to think about complex systems and their dynamics. We faltered because of our failure to consider risk in its full context, especially when dealing with coupled risk—when multiple things can go wrong together. We were hampered by our inability to think about second- and third-order effects and by our susceptibility to scientism—the false comfort of assuming that numbers and percentages give us a solid empirical basis. We failed to understand that complex systems defy simplistic reductionism. (p. xx)

Complex Adaptive Systems

To grasp the importance of complexity theory to organizational practice, we begin by understanding complex adaptive systems (CAS) as units within complexity science that are found in every organization. Contrary to mechanical systems, CAS are like living organisms that have the ability to self-organize and adapt to one another and their environment, where the behavior of individual agents following simple rules can lead to patterns that can be identified and discerned.

DISSIPATIVE STRUCTURES

Fundamental to the notion of organizations as CAS is the work of Illya Prigogine on dissipative structures. Prigogine's contradictory term "dissipative structure" is meant to convey a paradoxical reality, that disorder can be the source of the new order (Prigogine & Stengers, 1984). From an organizational perspective, dissipative structures signify necessary loss and regeneration. In a dissipative structure, anything that disturbs the system plays a crucial role in helping the system self-organize into a new form of order (Wheatley, 2006). If an organization, as a living system, can absorb disruption and maintain its identity, it can self-organize to a higher level of complexity and achieve a new form of itself that is better able to deal with the present. Examples include: the horse-drawn buggy that gave way to the automobile, Blockbuster that succumbed to Netflix, and Amazon, the online bookstore that became the everything store.

ATTRACTORS

An important element essential to the change process in CAS is the concept of attractors. In essence, an attractor is a dynamic that influences behaviors, and can create behavioral trajectories. In organizations, vision and values are examples of attractors; attractors can be either positive or negative (Berger & Johnston, 2015).

EDGE OF CHAOS

A central construct in complexity theory—at the heart of an organizational adaptive process—is Stacey's (1995) notion of nonlinear dynamics yielding "bounded instability" located at the "edge of chaos" The phrase edge of chaos means a form of organizational function or agent inter- action found in the transition phase between order and disorder zones of operation for CAS (Stacey, 1995). It is in this transition phase that organizations can move to a higher level of complexity and fitness (ability to adapt to changes in the environment) and as a result, greater crea- tivity, innovation, and learning are produced.

EMERGENCE AND SELF-ORGANIZATION

Emergence and self-organization are considered by many academics and practitioners to be complexity theory's most important phenomena (Jennings & Dooley, 2007). Lichtenstein (2014) argues that emergence is one of the most ubiquitous processes in the world and yet one of the least understood. A protest group is an anthropological example of an emergent entity that represents a creation qualitatively different from its original elements. Simple rules dictate that individuals gather in one location and stand or march together to voice and act in dissent in a non-violent manner. The Black Lives Matter movement has converged around several powerful attractors, the most recent being the death of George Floyd. In an organization, the culture of a company, an attractor, may become an emergent property that serves a specific purpose, is guided by an organization's vision, values (simple rules), and is distinctive from its original elements.

Innovation, creativity, and learning occur when emergence forms a previously unknown solution (new pattern) to a problem or creates new, unanticipated outcomes, also known as adaptive change (Uhl-Bien et al., 2007). The authors assert that adaptive processes are the source of creativity, adaptability, and learning in a complex system.

In summary, the complexity constructs described here—CAS dissipative structures; attractors, edge of chaos; emergence; and self-organization, transform the way we perceive and act on leadership in complex systems, moving us from the single-hero leader to a model that leverages shared leadership, dispersed intelligence, interactive dynamics, and whole systems thinking. The following section introduces complexity leadership theory and explores the role of human interaction in organizational systems and complexity processes.

Complexity Leadership Model

CL represents a growing sentiment that traditional models of leadership are insufficient for understanding the dynamic, distributed, and contextual nature of leadership in organizations (Marion, 2008; Uhl-Bien & Arena, 2017). A principal complexity leadership model derived from complexity leadership theory comes from Uhl-Bien et al. (2007). The model was later modified (Arena & Uhl-Bien, 2016; Uhl-Bien & Arena, 2017, 2018) to clarify leadership functions and enhance the interplay within CAS. CL recognizes that leadership is not merely an act of one individual; rather, it is a complex interplay of many interacting forces (Lichtenstein et al., 2006; Uhl-Bien et al., 2007) designed to build an organization's adaptive capacity.

The authors define the three CL functions as follows:

> *Operational leadership* is the formal design and alignment of systems and processes for efficiently executing on ideas and converting them to productive outcomes. *Entrepreneurial leadership* is the source of new ideas, innovation, learning and growth for the organization. *Enabling leadership* is the enabling of conditions that effectively support and sustain adaptive space. (Uhl-Bien & Arena, 2017, p. 14)

The interaction of the three CL functions—the "operational" function is entangled with the "entrepreneurial" function and these are supported by the "enabling" function—represent an interplay of forces that create the adaptive process. The three functions operate within CAS and aid an organization's agility efforts in a VUCA environment.

In CL, formal leadership occurs primarily within the operational function, but this function operates differently than it might in more traditional approaches. Rather than leading change from the top-down, operational leaders design appropriate meso contexts in the form of systems, structures, and policies that allow for rich information (and resource) flows to create adaptive dynamics (Uhl-Bien & Marion, 2009). Operational leaders understand that innovation and adaptability are core to organizational survival and they work to balance the bureaucratic "pull to order" with an organization's vital entrepreneurial thinking (Uhl-Bien & Arena, 2017).

Echoing complexity principles, the three functions of CL are not exclusive to any one individual. Agile organizations are able to draw from leadership at all levels. However, Uhl-Bien and Arena (2017) argue that highly agile complexity leaders are able (but not required) to "transition between entrepreneurial, enabling, and operation thinking to introduce, adapt and advance novel ideas into the system in the form of new adaptive order" (p. 14).

Complexity leadership's enabling function creates the conditions that support the adaptive space needed to achieve an organization's adaptive capacity. In CL's adaptive framework, "Enabling adaptive space involves leveraging complexity dynamics and network structures to feed and fuel emergence for adaptive responses" (Uhl-Bien & Arena, 2017, p. 17). With an emphasis on adaptive organizational capacity, Uhl-Bien and Arena (2018) offer their model as an overarching framework for understanding and practicing leadership in a complex world.

Adaptive Space in Complexity Leadership

In organizations, adaptive space is a platform for the interconnectivity of organizational agents within CAS that facilitates the adaptive process. Arena et al. (2017) define adaptive space "as the network and organizational context that allows people, ideas, information, and resources to flow across an organization and spur successful emergent innovation" (p. 40). Bridging an organization's operational and entrepreneurial systems, adaptive space is a structure that operates similarly to the phase transition found at the edge of chaos. In other words, it operates between equilibrium and disequilibrium to create space for adaptive behaviors. Adaptive space represents the "contexts and conditions that enable networked interactions to foster the generation and linking up of novel ideas, innovation, and learning in a system" (Uhl-Bien & Arena, 2017).

In CL brokerage and group cohesion are key network structures within adaptive space that work to create adaptive capacity. They are complexity dynamics associated with an organization's idea generation and flow and refer to the way individuals are connected to others. Specifically, brokerage involves opening avenues of communication across the enterprise by making connections from one group to another. Brokers can be anyone or thing in an organization that "links up" to create conditions that facilitate discovery and the introduction of novel ideas that can be amplified (scaled-up) through the system. Group cohesion enables diverse agents to quickly share information under conditions of high trust. It is a dynamic that provides a safe environment for pressure testing and iterating ideas (Uhl-Bien & Arena, 2017).

Like brokerage and group cohesion, conflicting and linking up are dynamics associated with idea generation and flow that make complex systems adaptive:

> Conflicting is the tension created when agents bring diverse needs, worldviews, preferences, or values to interactions. It motivates or pressures a system to change. ...Linking up occurs when agents find commonality that allows them to bond in relationships and networks. Linkages are the connections that hold bonded agents and aggregates together. (Uhl-Bien & Arena, 2017, p. 13)

At the heart of adaptive space are the pressures found in dissipative structures that signify loss and regeneration, or the disorder that can be the source of new order (emergence). An organization's internal pressure may be represented by changing strategy, new organizational initiatives, budget reductions, and shifting employee demographics. External pressure might be new competitive situations (e.g., Netflix, Amazon), new regulatory policies, procedures, radical advancements in technology, and economic shifts. These pressures push the system away from equilibrium toward the edge of chaos where innovation and creativity thrive.

Dissipative structures are complexity dynamics at play in adaptive spaces that work with other dynamics (adaptive tension, linking up, and information flows) to create CAS. As construed by CL, adaptive space bridges the operational and entrepreneurial systems and enables emergent solutions. According to Uhl-Bien and Arena (2017), adaptive spaces are temporary structures that innovative organizations excel at creating. They are used to embrace rather than stifle the dynamic tension between administrative efficiency and entrepreneurial innovation.

Adaptive and Complexity Leadership Contrasted

Adaptive Leadership (AL) and Complexity Leadership (CL) share the same critical objective; that is, to develop adaptive capacity. Both AL and CL are methodologies designed to meet the demands of a VUCA world. The first is a leadership approach that, primarily, builds adaptive capacity using interpersonal and group level interventions. The latter is a model with a focus on developing an organization's adaptive capacity, primarily at the system and structural levels. By virtue of their respective focus (people and organizations), the two methodologies can support one another to strengthen leadership effectiveness and achieve positive results for individuals and organizations. Table 1.1 below outlines the key difference between AL and CL.

Both CL and AL use a definition of leadership that is not tied to position. In CL, leadership is defined as a function and "an emergent, interactive dynamic" (Uhl-Bien et al., 2007, p. 298) out of which collective change and action emerges. The three leadership functions (operational, entrepreneurial, enabling) represent a process that occurs in the interactions between any two individuals. It takes place through individual and group adaptive actions to local problems and conditions. Moreover, it is enabled through a process that allows for adaptive action to take place while at the same time managing the entanglement with the operational part of an organization. In AL, leadership is defined as an activity, creating movement on adaptive challenges. It is not tied to a position; although a leader with authority may have the tools to expedite movement on adaptive challenges, anyone who focuses attention on adaptive issues can be considered a leader, even if that person lacks authority.

Conflict plays a central part in AL; different stakeholders come together to resolve it and manage the subsequent losses. Similarly, in CL, leaders "might even create a disruption as a way of destabilizing the system and encouraging self-organizing" (Plowman & Duchon, 2008, p. 160). However, a disruption is not necessarily a conflict. Conflict in AL goes beyond opinions, ideas, or interpersonal tension to include deeply held beliefs and values. In the original CL model, conflicts were conceptualized to be about ideas, not necessarily including values. However, in Uhl-Bien and Arena's more recent scholarship, a key component of the model, conflicting, includes tension between the operational function and the entrepreneurial function. These conflicts could be considered values-based, an example being prioritizing the stability of operations over innovation (an entrepreneurial function).

Due to the different conceptualization of leadership, the nature of intervention between the two frameworks is also different. In CL, the goal is to increase interactions among interdependent, semi-autonomous agents and move a system closer to the edge of chaos or disequilibrium. In other words, its actions intend to pull the system away from its proclivity toward order (operational) and encourage its movement toward innovation (entrepreneurial). Interventions in CL include eliminating bureaucratic barriers and creating rules to apply pressure to coordinate with other agents. In AL, the goal is to keep attention on an adaptive challenge. AL interventions include making observations, asking questions, using silence to create tension, and quelling a diversion.

Table 1.1 Adaptive and Complexity Leadership Compared

Attribute	AL	CL
Leadership is Defined as	Activity (Heifetz, 1994).	Function and "an emergent, interactive dynamic" (Uhl-Bien et al., 2007, p. 298) out of which collective change and action emerges.
Role of Conflict	Generates conflict; sheds light on conflict or allows it to emerge (Heifetz, 1994).	Conflict and divergence as the initial step in change. Conflicting is a key emergent process in adaptive space (Uhl-Bien & Arena, 2017).
Interventions	Asking questions, taking action, making observations, and offering interpretations, (Heifetz & Linsky, 2017); using a word, gesture, action, or inaction (Parks, 2005); being less predictable to get attention, using silence, shining light on a difficult issue, quelling a diversion (Heifetz et al., 2009b).	Using storytelling (Velsor, 2008), structural interventions to loosen control; using simple rules; creating rules that apply pressure to coordinate (Uhl-Bien et al., 2007); eliminating bureaucratic barriers (Plowman & Duchon, 2008).
Relation of Change to Equilibrium	Change happens outside equilibrium. However, there is a tolerable zone of distress. Relationship to distress curvilinear.	Emergence takes place far from equilibrium (Goldstein, 2008), change happens near or at the edge of chaos (Quade & Holladay, 2010).
Trust	Vertical and lateral trust strengthens the holding environment (Heifetz et al., 2009b); relational trust can strengthen the holding environment (Rasmussen & Raei, 2020).	Trust within diverse, cohesive groups generates adaptive responses. Trust within human relationships produces a rich flow of information to enhance complexity processes (Uhl-Bien & Arena, 2017).
Assumptions about Leadership Ability to Control	In control of some aspects but not others. In control of the holding environment (leadership with authority), one's own actions, and designing	Not in control, use of influence instead (Uhl-Bien & Marion, 2009); control over structure, rules, interactions, interdependencies, tension, and culture (Goldstein,

(Continued)

Table 1.1 (Continued)

Attribute	AL	CL
	interventions to keep the conflict within a tolerable zone and make progress on adaptive issues. Also, in control of their personal life so that it does not become a distraction (Heifetz & Linsky, 2017). Not in control of other's actions, but influences through interventions; not in control of the outcome of adaptive work (Heifetz et al., 2009b).	2008); self-organization as the opposite of control (Kilduff et al., 2008).

Both AL and CL assume that equilibrium conditions prevent change. Thus, both recommend that a system be taken out of equilibrium. AL assumes the existence of an optimal zone of disequilibrium; if there is too much distress in a system change stops and the leader with authority might be removed from power. In fact, AL views adaptive work as dangerous to the leader; *Leadership on the Line,* one of the three key texts on AL, is devoted to the dangers inherent in leading adaptive change. In CL, change and innovation happen far-from-equilibrium. To achieve higher levels of organizational fitness in accordance with new environmental conditions, CL works to move a system close to the edge of chaos while avoiding chaos itself. However, CL does not articulate specific dangers to leaders who attempt to move the system closer to the edge of chaos, nor does it provide guidance on how to mitigate these dangers.

The role of trust is explicit in AL; trust between peers (lateral trust) and vertical trust (trust in the authority figure and organizational structure) strengthens the holding environment and allows for additional heat and pressure in the system. CL recognizes trust as a key component of cohesive groups. High levels of trust in groups with strong cohesion enables agents to quickly share information. When ideas are introduced in cohesive groups, they are more likely to be adopted and enhanced locally (Uhl-Bien & Arena, 2017). It is important to note that cohesion in this context does not mean homogeneity. It refers to the degree a diverse group of agents are connected to one another—in a psychologically safe space—via shared values, a shared need, or by familiarity.

Both AL and CL abandon assumptions of control and predictability. CL assumes no control over the individual interactions of the agents. In fact, when a system is at the edge of chaos, a spontaneous movement to an alternative attractor (dynamic force) is possible. However, through the application of simple rules and attractors, CL assumes some guidance over agent interaction and enabling conditions. AL does not operate with the same level of unpredictability. AL assumes that adaptive work comes without the ability to control individuals, groups, or the outcome of adaptive work. The locus of control is the leader and their interventions.

The Interplay of Adaptive and Complexity Leadership

Adaptive leadership (AL) and Complexity leadership (CL) are unique leadership models that seek to create organizational agility by building adaptive capacity. AL's focus is changing agent behavior at the dyad, group, and organizational levels. In contrast, CL assumes a whole-systems approach to create conditions for self-organization and emergence that involve the dynamic interplay of leadership functions at the micro, meso, and macro levels. Working together, the practice of AL and CL can merge their respective powers to significantly strengthen an organization's adaptive capacity.

AL deals with adaptive challenges by orchestrating conflict over values, distributing losses, and overcoming a tendency to avoid adaptive work. CL strives to create organizational systems and structures that increase interaction of interdependent, semi-autonomous individuals and create the conditions for adaptive response. Yet, at the interpersonal level of an organization, CL is insufficient to deal with conflict, loss, or work avoidance. In many cases, attempts to break silos and increase interaction can spark resistance and a sense of powerlessness and identity loss. In concert with CL's focus on adaptive conditions, AL can activate interpersonal dynamics by mitigating resistance through a holding environment and prompting stakeholders to discuss new realities, make sense of change, and find solutions to distribute their losses.

In order for agents to interact productively, both AL and CL require trust. CL is limited, however, in its capacity for trust-building at the interpersonal level. Its system and structural foci limit guidance to the micro-level interplay and trust development among agents, whereas AL outlines an explicit role for leaders in establishing vertical and lateral trust.

In addition to using both types of trust to strengthen the holding environment, lateral trust can be employed to improve agent interaction and productivity as it increases group cohesion.

While CL primarily operates at the macro and meso-levels through the provision of simple rules, AL assumes more intervention by the leader to ensure smooth application of these rules. As an example, AL recognizes that stakeholders are not likely to address and adjust simple rules (i.e., conflicting values) effectively at the first attempt. Through skillful intervention and management of the tension, leaders keep stakeholders focused on the rules that impede or address the challenge at hand. AL recognizes that engaging different factions around the status quo enhances ownership, essential to accepting loss. Conflicts that arise in the process of diagnosing a problem and proposing solutions (new simple rules) are possible through a strong holding environment, allowing conflicts to be resolved without personal attack.

A key tenet of CL is increasing the interaction of heterogeneous semi-autonomous agents in the CAS and creating diverse and cohesive groups. However, the theory and the model provide little explanation for how this can be accomplished. Diversity is a strength, while on certain occasions it presents as a challenge. In their study of diversity in groups, Mannix and Neale (2005) point to multiple differences in groups that can affect performance: social category (race, age, ethnicity), knowledge or skills, values and beliefs, personality, and community status. They concluded that surface-level social category differences are more likely to have negative effects on the ability of groups to function effectively. Deeper differences, such as functional background, are more often positively related to performance when, as an example, facilitating group problem solving and/or creativity. However, this occurred only when the group process was carefully controlled.

AL is helpful in embracing diversity and minimizing marginalization. Diversity demands leadership as adaptive work (Heifetz, 1994). DiTomaso and Hooijberg (1996) suggest that leaders of diverse environments will have to work with

> multiple frameworks of meaning that organizational members may presume, help them bridge their differences in this regard, and strive for creative solutions that rise above the morality as some see it without violating or ignoring the differences. It may mean accepting ambiguity, withholding judgment, and creating new "adaptive cultures" that tolerate, even embrace, the differences among groups despite their ethical presumptions. (p. 179)

We suggest that the adaptive aspects of integrating diversity in the workplace cannot be solved simply by engaging CL's enabling leadership function to build trust and enhance group cohesion (for an illustration of an adaptive approach to dealing with diversity and racism, see Chapter 8). AL can improve cohesion in diverse groups through an array of adaptive practices and interventions. For example, leaders can create and strengthen a holding environment, acknowledge the presence of different stakeholders and factions, and empathize that movement to a more diverse workplace can result in the loss of status and power. Moreover, AL can provide enough pressure to surface undiscussables.

CL suggests that brokerage can bridge the connection from one group to the next and that ideally these diverse groups have a high degree of group cohesion through trust. However, group cohesion can be both a positive and negative attractor. A negative outcome may occur if group cohesion leads to groupthink. AL interventions like the use of silence, asking tough questions, and protection of leadership voices without authority can neutralize negative attractors.

The concept of adaptive space is similar to a holding environment, with significant overlap between the two constructs. The crucial difference between the two is that a holding environment is created with the sole purpose of dealing with an adaptive challenge. The primary purpose of adaptive space is to create temporary structures that facilitate the movement of novel ideas across an organizational system. A holding environment can bring focus to adaptive space to ensure ideas and solutions are generated, manage tensions between the entrepreneurial and operational functions, and deal with any associated value-laden issues.

Another area of synergy between AL and CL is in managing the movement toward disequilibrium. CL does not explicitly account for the level of distress and resistance generated by disequilibrium. AL's strong holding environment allows the ramifications of these conditions to be considered, adjusting the heat to keep the distress within a tolerable zone. There may be instances where, in the interest of reducing pressure in the system, an adaptive leader temporarily stops the adaptive work and reverts to technical work. For example, when interactions among the agents are too disorganized or counter-productive, and leaders need to pull back from the far-from-equilibrium conditions to reduce the heat and restore tolerable normalcy.

Learning is a final area where AL and CL can play together. As agents interact and engage in adaptive action to solve organizational problems and produce novelty, there is ongoing learning from these interactions and experiments. AL provides an additional level of learning (adaptive learning) that examines assumptions and values (for a detailed discussion of learning in adaptive leadership, see Chapter 2). Moreover, AL provides the holding environment, the place, and structures for this type of learning to occur.

Concluding Thoughts

Without question, today's challenges are highly complex. While both AL and CL equip leaders to manage complex problems, we suggest that as complexity increases, no single framework is sufficient to deal with the myriad of challenges faced by organizations in the ever-increasing complexity of a VUCA world.

In this chapter, we have outlined how AL can enhance CL in several important areas; namely, managing loss, improving the application of simple rules, enhancing trust, providing a holding environment so that diversity can be approached as an adaptive challenge, keeping stress in a tolerable range when an organization is operating at the edge of chaos, and enhancing learning in adaptive space. Therefore, we have made the case that blending these two leadership models into a seamless approach can significantly strengthen an organization's adaptive response to evolving conditions.

References

Arena, M., Cross, R., Sims, J., & Uhl-Bien, M. (2017). How to catalyze innovation in your organization. *MIT Sloan Management Review*, *58*(4), 39–48.

Arena, M. J., & Uhl-Bien, M. (2016). Complexity leadership theory: Shifting from human capital to social capita. *People and Strategy*, *39*(2), 22–27.

Berger, J. G., & Johnston, K. (2015). *Simple habits for complex times: Powerful practices for leaders*. Stanford University Press.

Burnes, B. (2005). Complexity theories and organizational change. *International Journal of Management Reviews*, *7*(2), 73–90. 10.1111/j.1468-2370.2005.00107.x

DiTomaso, N., & Hooijberg, R. (1996). Diversity and the demands of leadership. *The Leadership Quarterly*, *7*(2), 163–187. 10.1016/s1048-9843(96)90039-9

Goldstein, J. (2008). Conceptual foundations of complexity science: Development and main constructs. In M. Uhl-Bien & R. Marion (Eds.). *Complexity leadership: Part 1: Conceptual foundations* (pp. 31–62). Information Age Publishing, Inc.

Heifetz, R. A., Grashow, A., & Linsky, M. (2009a). Leadership in a (permanent) crisis. *Harvard Business Review*, *87*(7), 62–69.

Heifetz, R. A., Grashow, A., & Linsky, M. (2009b). *The practice of adaptive leadership: Tools and tactics for changing your organization and the world*. Harvard Business Press.

Heifetz, R. A., & Linsky, M. (2017). *Leadership on the line: Staying alive through the dangers of change*. Harvard Business Press.

Heifetz, R. A. (1994). *Leadership without easy answers*. Harvard University Press.

Heifetz, R. A., & Laurie. (2003). The leader as teacher: Creating the learning organization. *Ivey Business Journal*, *67*(3), 1–9. https://iveybusinessjournal.com/

Jennings, P. L., & Dooley, K. J. (2007). An emerging complexity paradigm in leadership research. In J. K. Hazy, J. A. Goldstein, & B. B. Lichtenstein (Eds.), *Complex systems leadership theory: New perspectives from complexity science on social and organizational effectiveness* (pp. 17–34). ISCE Publishing.

Kilduff, M., Crossland, C., & Tsai, W. (2008). Pathways of opportunity in dynamic organizational networks. In M. Uhl-Bien & R. Marion (Eds.), *Complexity leadership: Part 1: Conceptual foundations* (pp. 97–114). Information Age Publishing, Inc.

Lichtenstein, B. B. (2014). *Generative emergence: A new discipline of organizational, entrepreneurial, and social innovation*. Oxford University Press.

Lichtenstein, B. B., Uhl-Bien, M., Marion, R., Seers, A., Orton, J. D., & Schreibe, C. (2006). Complexity leadership theory: An interactive perspective on leading in complex adaptive systems. *Emergence: Complexity and Organization*, *8*(4), 2–12.

Mannix, E., & Neale, M. A. (2005). What differences make a difference? The promise and reality of diverse teams in organizations. *Psychological Science in the Public Interest*, *6*(2), 31–55. 10.1111/j.1529-1006.2005.00022.x

Marion, R. (2008). Complexity theory for organizations and organizational leadership. In M. Uhl-Bien & R. Marion (Eds.). *Complexity leadership: Part 1: Conceptual foundations* (pp. 15–30). Information Age Publishing, Inc.

Olson, E. E., & Eoyang, G. H. (2001). *Facilitating organization change: Lessons from complexity science*. Pfeiffer.

Parks, S. D. (2005). *Leadership can be taught: A bold approach for a complex world*. Harvard Business School Press.

Plowman, D. A., & Duchon, D. (2008). Dispelling the myths about leadership. In M. Uhl-Bien & R. Marion (Eds.). *Complexity leadership: Part 1: Conceptual foundations* (pp. 143–168). Information Age Publishing, Inc.

Prigogine, I., & Stengers, I. (1984). *Order out of chaos: Man's new dialogue with nature*. Bantam.

Quade, K., & Holladay, R. (2010). *Dynamical leadership: Building adaptive capacity for uncertain times*. Gold Canyon Press.

Rasmussen, H. T., & Raei, M. S. (2020). I'll only follow if I trust you: Using adult development to accelerate trust. In J. Reams (Ed.), *Maturing leadership: How adult development impacts leadership* (pp. 103–128). Emerald Publishing.

Repucci, S. (2020). *Freedom in the world 2020: A leaderless struggle for democracy*. Freedom House. https://freedomhouse.org/report/freedom-world/2020/leaderless-struggle-democracy

Stacey, R. D. (1995). The science of complexity: An alternative perspective for strategic change processes. *Strategic Management Journal*, *16*(6), 477–495. 10.1002/smj.4250160606

Styhre, A. (2002). Non-linear change in organizations: Organization change management informed by complexity theory. *Leadership & Organization Development Journal*, *23*(6), 343–351.

Tsoukas, H. (1998). Introduction to chaos, complexity and organizational theory. *Organizations*, *5*(3), 291–312.

Tufekci, Z. (2020, March 24). It wasn't just Trump who got it wrong: America's coronavirus response failed because we didn't understand the complexity of the problem. *The Atlantic*. https://www.theatlantic.com/world/

Uhl-Bien, M., & Arena, M. (2017). Complexity leadership: Enabling people and organizations for adaptability. *Organizational Dynamics*, *46*(1), 9–20. 10.1016/j.orgdyn.2016.12.001

Uhl-Bien, M., & Arena, M. (2018). Leadership for organizational adaptability: A theoretical synthesis and integrative framework. *The Leadership Quarterly*, *29*(1), 89–104. 10.1016/j.leaqua.2017.12.009

Uhl-Bien, M., Marion, R., & McKelvey, B. (2007). Complexity leadership theory: Shifting leadership from the industrial age to the knowledge era. *The Leadership Quarterly*, *18*(4), 298–318. 10.1016/j.leaqua.2007.04.002

Uhl-Bien, M., & Marion, R. (2009). Complexity leadership in bureaucratic forms of organizing: A meso model. *The Leadership Quarterly*, *20*(4), 631–650.

Velsor, E. V. (2008). A complexity perspective on leadership development. In M. Uhl-Bien & R. Marion (Eds.), *Complexity leadership: Part I: Conceptual foundations* (pp. 393–430). Information Age Publishing.

Wheatley, M. J. (2006). *Leadership and the new science: Discovering order in a chaotic world*. Berrett-Koehler Publishers.

2 Giving Credit Where It's Due: The Theories That Support Adaptive Leadership

Harriette Thurber Rasmussen and
Michael Christopher Boyce

We, the authors, argue that adaptive leadership is not a theory per se, but instead a set of practices that together constitute a framework to make progress on complex, or adaptive, challenges. The theoretical roots of these practices come from scholarship in such areas as resistance to change, organizational learning, psychological safety, conflict mediation, and systems thinking. This chapter delves into the theoretical depths of these practices and how they inform adaptive leadership practices. The theories explored here occupy a parallel adjacent space and can synergize with adaptive leadership. Although we provide only a snapshot of each theory, our goal is that this chapter is a route to more extensive study. Our final section, "A System of Theories," explains their convergence into what we claim to be a solid theoretical base for adaptive leadership.

We begin with the thorniest of issues, resistance to change.

Recrafting Resistance: Leading the Inevitable Losses of Change

Heifetz' assertion that resistance to change is really resistance to loss becomes increasingly explicit with each of his published works on adaptive leadership (Heifetz, 1994; Heifetz et al., 2009; Heifetz & Linsky, 2017). By 2009, Heifetz et al. (2009) had outlined processes to formally assess potential losses of each stakeholder as an essential route to managing change. They maintained that addressing stakeholder losses is key to acting politically—an essential consideration in mobilizing a system (Heifetz et al., 2009) and, we add, successful change.

Heifetz's ideas run parallel to German psychologist Kurt Lewin's model of episodic change, relevant for organizations pressured to adjust in response to environmental conditions (Weick & Quinn, 1999). While we argue that adaptive leadership occupies a middle ground between planned and unplanned change, Lewin's description of episodic change incorporates numerous aspects of adaptive leadership. For example, Lewin ascribes the motivation to change to disequilibrium, a central component to addressing adaptive challenges. In the first phase of

DOI: 10.4324/9781003099109-2

change, explained as "unfreezing," episodic change is equated with such terms as "disconfirmation of expectations, learning anxiety, provision of psychological safety" (Weick & Quinn, 1999, p. 366). Heifetz et al. (2009) would describe this phase as "giving the work back" and adjusting the level of disequilibrium by turning the heat up and down. The next phase, which Lewin refers to as "transition" involves repositioning of norms and values, again, mirroring the type of cognitive and internal adjustments Heifetz et al. (2009) argue are essential to adaptive change. Lewin's final phase, "refreezing" may be less aligned to adaptive leadership practices, where ongoing organizational learning is needed to address the continuous nature of complex, adaptive work. However, some aspects of adaptive work become more technical over time, as stakeholders successfully let go of longstanding habits and values. In these cases, Lewin's third phase of refreezing could align with adaptive leadership.

Around the time Heifetz began to write about adaptive leadership, another change theorist was also repositioning change, focusing more on the process of change than the episode itself, somewhat in line with Lewin's conception of continuous change. Bridges (2001) described change as "a situational shift," focusing on the internal transitions stakeholders experience during change as "the process of letting go of the way things used to be" (p. 2). He equates letting go as the recognition and acceptance of loss, mirroring Heifetz et al.'s view of change. Regardless of who first positioned change as loss, and it is very possible that both scholars arrived at these ideas independently, it is worth exploring Bridges' theory of transition to inform ways leaders can support stakeholders through the inevitable losses associated with adaptive work.

Bridges describes the transitions that accompany change as occurring in three stages: endings; the neutral zone; and new beginnings. We explain these below.

Letting Go of the Familiar

Bridges (2001) proposes that change "involves relinquishing the old habits and expectations and developing new ones that fit the new situation" (p. 33). He also maintains that change processes often fail because of a failure to acknowledge what has actually occurred–the losses that are inherent in what is being left behind, adopting instead a stalwart attitude of "moving on." Rites of passage, on the other hand, allow for recognition of loss and a symbolic, if not physical, letting go. Bridges terms this phase one of "endings". He is clear that pointing toward the future without acknowledging the past is tantamount to a failed change effort. Instead, as do Heifetz et al. (2009), Bridges encourages leaders to validate losses that may appear insignificant, to display compassion, and to look for signs of grief among stakeholders. One of us had the experience of working with a divisive staff, barely able to speak to one another following the departure of a beloved CEO. She instinctively decided to hold a "wake," asking what had been so loved about this individual. The outpouring of stories was accompanied by relief and surprise that talking about the former CEO need not be disloyal to his replacement. Instead, that "ending" event allowed the staff to move into the next phase of transition, also known as the neutral zone.

The Neutral Zone

Seasoned tennis players are familiar with a space on the court known as "no man's land"—an area in which players are disadvantaged because they are not able to play in ways that lead to a successful outcome; they are neither at the net nor at the baseline. Bridges' neutral zone, characterized as a time when "all the old clarities break down and everything is in flux" (2003, p. 40) is similar. Nothing seems to work. The old is gone, but the new has not yet arrived; emotionally it can feel like one is groping in the dark for clarity, for something stable, yet without a sense of direction. Tensions are high, tempers flare. Anyone who has gone through the pain of losing someone close can relate to the confusion that can permeate one's brain—often leading to the impatience of others who may admonish someone to "buck up and move on." Bridges, who frequently uses the terms "emptiness" to describe the neutral zone explains that

> in the neutral zone, people are overloaded, they frequently get mixed signals, ... priorities get confused, ... people lose their confidence in the organization's future.... It is easy for people to become polarized, ...consensus easily breaks down and the level of discord rises. (2003, p. 41)

As unpleasant as the neutral zone may be, Bridges maintains it as a necessary element of moving through the process of change and ultimately into productivity. Bridges notes this zone as one of opportunity, a time in which there is space for creativity and innovation as vanished norms make way for new ways of thinking. It is a time for stakeholders to glean insight through reflection, making the most of cognitive dissonance and the insight that such can cause. This is the zone in which a system is most ripe for adaptive work and we argue that it is the work of adaptive leaders to find and maintain productivity in the neutral zone. In Heifetz et al.'s (2009) terms, this is the "productive zone of disequilibrium" where "the stress level is high enough that people can be mobilized to focus on and engage with the problem they would rather avoid" (p. 30).

How the Neutral Zone Supports Adaptive Work

Key to finding opportunity in the neutral zone is maintaining that sweet spot of disequilibrium, where stakeholders are uncomfortable enough to engage, but not so shaken by uncertainty that attention fragments and the worst-case scenarios of the neutral zone surface. Bridges' suggestions to advance adaptive work, what he terms as creativity, in the neutral zone align with practices of adaptive leadership. Heifetz et al. (2009) discuss the need to orchestrate conflict to advance adaptive work; Bridges (2003) speaks of exposing the "gap between the old and the new" to bypass a return to "pre-transition … ways of doing things" (p. 50). While we discuss conflict in the next section, what is important to consider here is the role of conflict in establishing a productive neutral zone, or in adaptive leadership terminology, the productive zone of disequilibrium. Bridges (2003) offers suggestions to leverage the neutral zone, shifting through conflict toward the type of creativity needed to address adaptive challenges. We've called out just a few to illustrate our point:

- Emphasize discovery and innovation and teach stakeholders how to think creatively. As Bridges (2003) says, "Some people simply don't know how to get out of their rut. Help them" (p. 51).
- Promote what Berger and Johnston (2015) term "safe-to-fail experiments," small pilots of new ideas that are low risk, but can yield big results and, more importantly, bring out creative instincts that can emerge when the stakes are low.
- Celebrate failure as opportunities to learn—and educate stake-holders on the "implementation dip" (Fullan, 2011), a reality that things often get worse before they get better.
- And speaking of new beginnings, don't rush it; "restrain the natural impulse in times of ambiguity and disorganization to push prematurely for certainty and closure" (Bridges, 2003, p. 51).

Just as Heifetz et al. (2009) have confidence in the ability of stakeholders to tackle adaptive challenge in a holding environment, Bridges (2003) asserts that "people can work out much of the necessary business of the neutral zone if you protect them, encourage them, and give them the structure and opportunities they need to do it" (p. 54).

And with that, we arrive at new beginnings.

New Beginnings

Bridges refers to new beginnings as action, the making of a beginning, and the final phase in the transition cycle. Importantly, Bridges' theory of transition "involves an inner realignment and a renewal of energy, both of which depend on immersion in the chaos of the neutral zone" (1980, p. 136). As such, new beginnings also represent internal work, a "psychological phenomena... marked by a release of new energy in a new direction ... a new identity" (2003, p. 57). In adaptive work, new beginnings may represent acceptance of one's choices in service of larger goals, a letting go or prioritization of deep-seated values. At an organizational level, it may represent the establishment of an adaptive culture, a capacity to bring forward certain elements of the neutral zone into an institutionalized zone of continuous learning. And, as we have seen happen over time, it may mean the adjustment of what was once an adaptive challenge into an element of technical work, representing a new normal and perhaps perpetual comfort with Lewin's notion of "unfreezing" toward continuous change and adaptive learning (Weick & Quinn, 1999).

The Nature of Adaptive Learning

Heifetz et al. (2009) argue that adaptive challenges, above all else, require learning, a need for new thinking, "going beyond any authoritative expertise to mobilize discovery" (p. 19). As Lewin emphasized the importance of continuous learning, Heifetz et al. (2009) also claim the need for learning that is continuous. Organizational capacity for continuous learning, however, depends on getting the learning part right.

Heifetz et al.'s (2009) admonition that "organizations get trapped by their current ways of doing things, simply because these ways worked in the past" (p. 51), or, as one might say, stuck in a technical way of thinking, takes us to Argyris and Schön (1978; 1996) and their framing of single- and double-loop learning. In Agyris' (1991) classic work, "Teaching Smart People how to Learn," he describes the very challenge that Heifetz et al. (2009) address with leaders who "have risen in the ranks ... because of an ability to ... solve people's problems and provide answers" (p. 287). Argyris and Schön's view of organizational learning addresses this challenge as they distinguish between single- and double-loop learning, the latter of which involves examination of operating values and beliefs, characteristic of adaptive work, and a precursor to rethinking what might otherwise remain technical solutions. Thus, we present Argyris and Schön's model of single- and double-loop learning as the most applicable learning theory related to adaptive leadership.

Our Theories of Action

Key to understanding Argyris and Schön's theories around adult learning is their presentation of the schema that governs how we understand and act in the world. They argue that these "rules" not only inform our own behavior but are also how we "understand the behavior of others"

(Argyris, 1991, p. 7). Argyris (1991) claims these "theories of action" to be "so taken for granted that people don't even realize they are using them" (p. 4). Yet often the theories of action we espouse—what we claim governs our ethics and behavior—do not always align with our actions. Most of us do not operate with "espoused theories of action" but instead with what Argyris and Schön (1978) term, "theories in use." Again, most of us are unaware of the discrepancy…until we are. This is where single- and double-loop learning come in.

Single-Loop Learning

Argyris (1991) argues that organizational learning should begin with individual reflection, consideration as to how one contributes, as an individual, to an organizational reality they wish to change. Particularly in situations in which we are invested, most of us prefer to remain in control and, as noted earlier, use our expertise to solve problems. This is precisely the cycle that Argyris and Schön term single-loop learning. A particular result suggests whether or not a strategy or approach to a problem was successful. When unsuccessful, we change our tactics to get a different result: action–result–action–result, and so on. Shifting strategies when results aren't where we want them to be can work very well with technical problems, those that have been well researched and can be solved by expert knowledge, even if one needs to choose between several options. Single-loop learning makes sense for technical challenges. Moreover, it preserves the control of those in charge, maintaining position, reducing vulnerability, and effectively masking any signs of incompetence. There may be some learning taking place, but that learning remains within the same set of "rules" that subconsciously guide us, what Argyris terms our "theories-in-use" and may well be adequate for technical work.

But how well does single-loop learning work with adaptive challenges, those that require new learning and that, as Heifetz et al. (2009) stress, "can only be addressed through changes in people's priorities, beliefs, habits, and loyalties?" (p. 19). Addressing challenges that require us to rethink the rules that have typically governed success suggests a need to revisit those rules and, at a minimum, understand any contradictions in our theories-in-use and those we espouse. Thus, addressing adaptive challenges effectively requires double-loop learning.

Double-Loop Learning

Whereas single-loop learning may focus on appropriate strategies from a bank of experts, or technical solutions, double-loop learning gets beneath the surface of the challenge itself. This may mean surfacing the assumptions stakeholders make about the challenge itself. Double-loop learning may require an examination of the beliefs that govern a system's current reality and how those beliefs hold the existing reality in place. Double-loop learning reveals an individual's schema that must be addressed in order to fully understand and address an adaptive challenge. As Heifetz et al. (2009) assert, adaptive work takes place through dissonance, rethinking old patterns, exposing values, and surfacing contradictions. As we hope has been made clear in our earlier discussion of the neutral zone, cognitive dissonance is an essential component of change. Double-loop learning, which stems from scaffolded cognitive dissonance "is not simply a function of how people feel. It is a re-election of how they think–that is, the cognitive rules or reasoning they use to design and implement their actions" (Argyris, 1991, pp. 4–5). Significantly, double-loop learning may mean a discovery of action-inconsistency between an individual's espoused values and theory-in-use, triggering a defensive response or outright rejection to relieve associated dissonance. This type of dissonance can be a root cause of work avoidance and we assert, as do others (Nicolaides & McCallum, 2013; Norris, 2018), the alignment of single- and double-loop learning to technical and adaptive work, thus making this the most applicable learning theory to consider for adaptive leaders. (see Chapters 8 and 9 for further discussion on single- and double-loop learning).

We conclude this section on the nature of adaptive learning with a note about the role of authority in double-loop learning. Argyris (1991) warns that "change has to start at the top because…if professionals or middle managers begin to change the way they reason and act, such changes are likely to appear strange—if not actually dangerous—to those at the top" (p. 11). His warning acknowledges that those in positions of authority have the power to establish what type of learning is and is not psychologically safe. Adaptive work pivots on the quality of learning among a system's stakeholders, reinforcing the need for Heifetz et al.'s (2009) holding environment and the psychological safety that holding environment intends to create. We turn, then, to psychological safety as a key element to adaptive learning.

Psychological Safety and the Holding Environment

Heifetz et al. (2009) advise adaptive leaders to "display your own in-competence" (p. 287), a curious way of thinking about leadership until one considers the need for psychological safety in a learning relationship and the role of leaders in creating that safety. The concept of psychological safety grew out of the change literature in the 1960s, when Schein and Bennis (1965) examined the interpersonal risks associated with change, declaring the need for those managing change to feel secure. In the ensuing half-century, psychological safety became a backbone of successful teaming as Edmonson and others (Edmonson, 2019, 2008;

Edmonson & Lei, 2014) studied the ways in which interpersonal relationships promoted, or detracted, from effectiveness. Central to psychological safety is that its presence "facilitates the willing contribution of ideas and actions to a shared enterprise" (Edmonson & Lei, 2014, p. 24). In other words, without psychological safety, learning is compromised in a culture where to be wrong is to be ridiculed, to not know is unacceptable, and to experience dissonance—especially in the presence of others—may be to one's detriment. Risk-taking, inherent in double-loop learning, is unwise if one wants to retain one's standing in a collective (Edmonson, 2019). The research is convincing: The presence of psychological safety positively impacts organizational performance, organizational learning, interpersonal trust, team effectiveness, and the ability to learn from failure (Edmonson & Lei, 2014). Edmonson and Lei (2014) assert that

> psychological safety is particularly relevant for understanding organizational learning … and that a climate of psychological safety can mitigate the interpersonal risks inherent in learning in hierarchies. People are more likely to offer ideas, admit mistakes, ask for help, or provide feedback if they believe it is safe to do so. (p. 36)

Absent psychological safety, adaptive work retreats to a technical space or, what Heifetz et al. (2009) refer to as work avoidance.

The Holding Environment

This is why Heifetz has continually admonished adaptive leaders to create a holding environment as they orchestrate the type of conflict one might experience in adaptive work when "things can get nasty" (Heifetz et al., 2009, p. 155). Titled in reference to the need for an infant to "be held" in order to thrive, Heifetz et al. (2009) assert holding environments to be spaces "for people to surface and discuss the particular values, perspectives, and creative ideas they have on the challenging situations they all face" (p. 155). Here we draw you back to several key theories discussed in this chapter, most recently **double-loop learning,** in which one may come to grips with the ways in which their actions do not align with their values or be asked to surface and set aside previously held assumptions, and Bridges' **neutral zone,** one we equated to Heifetz et al.'s productive zone of disequilibrium. In each of the ways Heifetz explains how leaders establish holding environments, psychological safety is present.

Authority and Psychological Safety

We return now to the role of authority, something Heifetz (1994) suggests is a "resource for leadership" (p. 103) as it relates to psychological safety. In their chapter titled "Applying Power," Heifetz et al. (2009) suggest that holding environments, and by extension, psychological safety, are advantaged through positional authority. Edmonson (2008) takes this further as she asserts that "the most important influence on psychological safety is the nearest boss" (p. 6).

Edmonson's (2019) extensive research on psychological safety suggests deliberate action by leaders to establish psychological safety while detailing what she terms "avoidable failure" from "leaders who welcome only good news" and thus "create fear that blocks them from hearing the truth" (p. 71). A lack of psychological safety, she found, leads to "dangerous silence" where "people fail to speak up with their concerns or questions" (p. 97). This is in contrast to an environment in which "people are willing to fail" because "when they do, they learn" (2008, p. 5).

Edmonson's advice to leaders, built around decades of research, mirrors Heifetz et al.'s positioning of the role of authority in an adaptive challenge. First, she recommends framing the work as a learning challenge, or, as Heifetz and Linsky (2017) would say, giving the work back to those who will have to live with the solution. Edmonson (2008) found that when leaders "admit that they don't know something or made a mistaken, their genuine display of humility encourages other to do the same" (p. 6). Secondly, she claims that leaders should model curiosity, asking authentic questions in ways that acknowledge one's own fallibility, making it safe for others to do the same.

Psychological safety, where speaking up is expected, failure becomes an opportunity, and leaders are fallible, is a critical backdrop to orchestrating conflict, which takes us now to conflict and how it becomes productive

Conflict and Productive Orchestration

As we have identified, conflict is an integral part of the adaptive leadership repertoire. Any discussion of conflict in the realm of theory must recognize the work of Deutsch (1973), Fisher et al. (2011), and perhaps most relevant to this discussion of foundational theory, Johnson and Johnson (2009, 2014). The constructive controversy work of David Johnson and Roger Johnson spans back to the late sixties when David Johnson (1967) first began proposing the idea of role reversal in conflict environments. Combined with Deutsch's (1973) deeper examination of the destructive and constructive elements of conflict, Smith et al. (1981) established the transformative and educative role of carefully cultivated conflict. As mentioned earlier in this chapter and throughout this volume adaptive leadership relies heavily upon the potential energy of disequilibrium to productively engage in adaptive work. Johnson (2015) terms this constructive controversy.

A basic tenet of constructive controversy (Johnson & Johnson, 2009) is the skillful orchestration of controversy/conflict to elicit the dissonance necessary to unfreeze thinking, promoting an epistemic curiosity to advance through the neutral zone (Bridges, 2001) into a level of greater motivation, achievement, and creativity, ultimately producing an adaptive environment (Heifetz et al., 2009). Using role reversal in constructive controversy and a focus on a shared positive outcome, Johnson and Johnson (2009) short-circuit the need to be beholden to any individual or group's particular result and in doing so create a zone of psychological safety for adaptive evolution.

When presenting constructive controversy, Smith et al. (1981) establish that the process of seeking concurrence—a natural response to conflict—is actually an anathema to constructive work. Recall earlier in this chapter when we noted Bridges' (2003) admonition not to rush out of the neutral zone. Seeking concurrence, the active process of enforcing consensus prematurely, before the disequilibrium and cognitive conflict needed to generate alternate thinking has been allowed to develop squanders the benefit of conflict, producing a result not unlike that of Heifetz et al.'s (2009) work avoidance. To address Smith et al.'s thoughts on concurrence, Chapter 9 proposes a productive use of concurrence and disposition mapping to further the adaptive agenda of an activist leader.

Role Reversal

Role reversal as a deliberate process lies at the heart of constructive controversy (Johnson, 1967). Simply put, it involves the production of empathy through perspective-taking. By taking one's opponent's view, judgment of the "other" is mitigated, resulting in a shift of perspective toward the individual arguing against their viewpoint. Role reversal enables stakeholders to recognize the importance of a systematic view to best capitalize on the constructive capacity of conflict. As a practice, role reversal is reliant upon the deep understanding of all aspects of the controversy. Weisbord and Janoff (2007) offer specific tactics for role reversal through artful subgrouping to interrupt polarization—having like-minded people dialogue with each other in the presence of the opposition, followed by intra-group and inter-group reflection. By first adopting and defending one's side of a controversy and then reversing roles, using all of the other side's information and resources, then finally working together to select the best of all sides for the best possible outcome, stakeholders gain a deep systemic view of the controversy, enabling productive conflict on the dance floor and informing the balcony.

Up on the Balcony

When Heifetz and Linsky (2017) encourage leaders to jump to the balcony, they argue the need to see an entire system, to understand the ways in which that system's parts impact each other, and to see patterns and trends, as opposed to isolated events. The roots of this advice come from the field of systems science. Systems theory dates back to the work of Ludwig von Bertalanffy (1968), later popularized by Senge's (1990) discussion of learning organizations. It has since become somewhat commonplace in leadership practices, with numerous tools to help "see" what a system is up to. Systems science helps to inform leadership interventions through an understanding of systems principles and functioning. As examples, systems science understands that systems seek stability and concurrence (i.e., resist change), and that a system's structure drives its behavior (i.e., structures that advance single-loop learning lead to technical solutions). Systems comprise multiple cause and effect relationships that, when illuminated (e.g., causal loop diagramming), explain the results that the system yields. To be on the balcony is to practice systems thinking: to see the patterns of the dance floor, the dynamics of the stakeholders, and to understand the interactivity of a system's components while orchestrating intentional conflict to create disequilibrium and the associated epistemic unfreezing and advancement.

But Heifetz et al. (2009) go a step further in their balcony metaphor when they ask leaders to consider the relationship of self to system and a leader's contribution to the system in which an adaptive challenge resides (see also Chapter 5). They are not the only ones to suggest that leaders can be unaware of their own role in perpetuating an adaptive challenge. Scharmer (2016), as an example, calls this phenomenon a leader's blind spot. Heifetz and Linsky (2017) note that it is easier to navigate the balcony metaphor in its simplest construct, maintaining one's distance, than to confront the personal nature of one's leadership. We have intentionally left this section to last as it draws on the theories discussed throughout this chapter: double-loop learning, orchestrated intentional conflict, psychological safety, and the losses that accompany a recognition of fallibility. Each of these constructs converge in this final discussion of leader as self.

Heifetz et al. (2009) write extensively on seeing oneself as a system and this chapter does not pretend, nor intend, to replicate Heifetz et al.'s earlier writings. It *is* our intention, however, and as noted earlier, to point to the deeper theoretical constructs we find especially relevant to adaptive leadership practices that, when explored, can deepen one's understanding of how and when to apply such practices. And while we cannot know which theories are, as an example, embedded in Heifetz and Linsky's (2002) assertion to distinguish one's role from self, we argue here that its origins lie in the study of subject-object relations and find Kegan's (1982) early writing about self and other as a reasonable and important base of understanding (see also Chapter 12 for more discussion of adult development stages).

In his writing on constructive adult development, Kegan (1982), and later Kegan and Lahey (2002; 2009), bring to the forefront the concept of subject-object relations. In its simplest terms, they explain that throughout one's lifetime we increasingly see the world–including ourselves within that world–as something that can be examined (an object) rather than as self-defining (in ways to which we are subject). By the time adults assume positions of leadership, many have developed a defined internal framework, or schema, of self—with ideological and moral framing, or set of governing rules. Kegan and Lahey point out that typically we are not aware of our internal schema—until we are, as per Scharmer's (2016) conception of one's blind spot. Subject-object relations theory claims that we are "subject to" these schemas; we see the world through the lens of our own authority, but without any awareness that we do so. But, when Heifetz et al. (2009) ask leaders to see themselves as systems, separating their identities from the choices they make as leaders, we argue that they are asking for a higher level of cognitive development, one in which leaders hold their schema "as object." Kegan and Lahey (2009) explain,

> If one is not to be forever captive of one's own theory, systems, script, framework, or ideology, one needs to develop an even more complex way of knowing that permits one to *look at*, rather than *choicelessly* through, one's own framework. (p. 53, emphasis in original)

In other words, in order to see one's role in and contributions to a system, one must be able to hold one's cognitive, emotional, and physical positioning in that system as object. As Kegan famously says, you want to hold "it," (e.g., schema, ideology, assumptions) rather than having "it" hold you.

Let's stop for a minute and consider subject-object perspective alongside the nature of adaptive work and what we have argued in this chapter about the theoretical underpinnings of adaptive leadership. We maintain that the convergence of these theories themselves, a view from the balcony, suggests a system of theories and practices best able to tackle the persistent and complex challenges of the 21st century. Here then, and in conclusion, we describe the relationships among them that constitute a system of theories through the lens of subject-object perspective and the ability of leaders to see themselves as systems.

Adaptive Leadership: A System of Theories

Perhaps most importantly, adaptive work requires rethinking old patterns and behaviors to address challenges to which there are no known answers. This is a central connection to the importance of holding oneself as object; adaptive challenges require a release from the mental schemas to which we have been subject. Seeing oneself as a system may, in fact, be the most critical component of adaptive leadership. In our experience, it is a last consideration when confronting an adaptive challenge.

Consider, too, our discussion of organizational learning—Argyris and Schön's model of single- and double-loop learning. Single-loop learning, while often appropriate for technical problem-solving, does nothing to address the mental schemas that may be preventing progress in adaptive work. Double-loop learning requires one to surface and rethink one's own constructs, perhaps triggering capacity to not only see oneself in and as a system, but to begin a sometimes painful separation from the certainty of a world view to which we are subject, to a view that is more accepting of the nature of adaptive work. The mental disruption and cognitive conflict involved in double-loop learning require a psychologically safe holding environment, one that exposes the ways in which a leader may act out values that may be, in fact, in conflict with those they espouse (Argyris & Schön, 1996, 1978).

And finally, the perhaps painful and dissonant separation from one's comfort zone of certainty into a mindset that is ambiguous and without structure reminds us of Bridges' transition theory and Heifetz et al.'s (2009) suggestion that the epistemic freeze of resistance to change is, in fact resistance to loss. What greater loss might we experience than the disruption of a world that has heretofore been shaped by our authority and certainty of self?

We conclude this chapter by stressing the critical nature of this work, acknowledging the courage of adaptive leaders while encouraging a path of continued development. Progress will only begin with recognition of what we don't know and don't see. This chapter's glimpse of the theories that parallel the practices of adaptive leadership intended to expose what might have been unseen with the hope that a deeper look will fortify the audacity and daring of leaders to venture into the unknowns so inherent to adaptive work.

References

Argyris, C. (1991). Teaching smart people how to learn, *Harvard Business Review. 69*(3), 99–109.

Argyris, C. & Schön, D. A. (1978). *Organizational learning: A theory of action perspective*. Addison-Wesley.

Argyris, C. & Schön, D. A. (1996). *Organizational learning II: Theory, method and practice*. Addison-Wesley.

Berger, J. G. & Johnston, K. (2015). *Simple habits for complex times: Powerful practices for leaders*. Stanford Business Books.

Bertalanffy, L. (1968). *General System Theory: Foundations, Development, Applications*.George Braziller.

Bridges, W. (1980). *Transitions: Making sense of life's changes.* Addison-Wesley.

Bridges, W. (2001). *The way of transition: Embracing life's most difficult moments.* Da Capo Press.

Bridges, W. (2003). *Managing transitions: Making the most of change* (2nd ed.). Da Capo Press.

Deutsch, M. (1973). *The resolution of conflict: Constructive and destructive processes.* Yale University Press.

Edmonson, A. C. (2008). The competitive imperative of learning. *Harvard Business Review, 86*(7/8), 60–67.

Edmonson, A. C. (2019). *The fearless organization: Creating psychological safety in the workplace for learning, innovation, and growth.* Wiley.

Edmonson, A. & Lei, Z. (2014). Psychological safety: The history, renaissance, and future of an interpersonal construct. *Annual Review of Organizational Psychology and Organizational Behavior, 1*(1), 23–43.

Fisher, R., Ury, W. L., & Patton, B. (2011). *Getting to yes: Negotiating agreement without giving in.* Penguin.

Fullan, M. (2011). *Change leader: Learning to do what matters most.* Jossey-Bass.

Heifetz, R. A. (1994). *Leadership without easy answers.* Harvard University Press.

Heifetz, R., Grashow, A., & Linsky, M. (2009). *The practice of adaptive leadership: Tools and tactics for changing your organization and the world.* Harvard Business Press.

Heifetz, R. A., & Linsky, M. (2017). *Leadership on the line, with a new preface: Staying alive through the dangers of change.* Harvard Business Press.

Johnson, D. W. (1967). Use of role reversal in intergroup competition. *Journal of Personality and Social Psychology, 7*(2p1), 135.

Johnson, D. W. (2015). *Constructive controversy: Theory, research, practice.* Cambridge University Press.

Johnson, D. W., & Johnson, R. T. (2009). Energizing learning: The instructional power of conflict. *Educational Researcher, 38*(1), 37–51.

Johnson, D. W., & Johnson, R. T. (2014). Constructive controversy as a means of teaching citizens how to engage in political discourse. *Policy Futures in Education, 12*(3), 417–430.

Kegan, R. (1982). *The evolving self: Problem and process in human development.* Harvard University Press.

Kegan, R. & Lahey, L. L. (2002). *How the way we talk can change the way we work: Seven languages for transformation.* Jossey-Bass.

Kegan, R. & Lahey, L. L. (2009). *Immunity to change: How to overcome it and unlock the potential in yourself and your organization.* Harvard Business Press.

Nicolaides, A. & McCallum, D. C. (2013). Inquiry in action for leadership in turbulent times: Exploring the connections between transformative learning and adaptive leadership. *Journal of Transformative Education, 11*(4), 246–260.

Norris, S. D. (2018). *An adaptive leadership approach to adult learning and organizational research.* IGI Global.

Scharmer, C. O. (2016). *Theory U: Leading from the future as it emerges.* Berrett-Kohler Publishers.

Schein, E. H., & Bennis W. (1965). *Personal and organizational change through group methods.* Wiley.

Senge, P. J. (1990). *The fifth discipline: The art & practice of the learning organization.* Currency Doubleday.

Smith, K., Johnson, D. W., & Johnson, R. T. (1981). Can conflict be constructive? Controversy versus concurrence seeking in learning groups. *Journal of Educational Psychology, 73*(5), 651–663.

Weick, K. E. & Quinn, R. E. (1999). Organizational change and development. *Annual Review of Psychology, 50,* 361–386.

Weisbord, M., & Janoff, S. (2007). *Don't just do something, stand there!* Berrett-Koehler Publishers, Inc.

3 How Teaching Resilience Can Enable Adaptive Leadership

Jennifer Eggers

The universal dilemma facing those teaching adaptive leadership is how to influence leaders to make critical trade-offs between traditional hierarchical leadership styles and the more inclusive, collaborative adaptive leadership required to mobilize people to solve adaptive challenges. In many cases, effectiveness demands leaders to be more open, vulnerable, and less "leader-like" than they have ever envisioned a good leader to be. The irony is that in order to make progress on the more complex challenges and disruption facing organizations today, traditional leadership is becoming increasingly less effective. Adaptive leadership invites leaders to think and act differently. It invites leaders to ask difficult questions, mobilize stakeholders to find answers, and create open dialog to expose root causes, hidden agendas, and unspoken issues that could make people uncomfortable. An adaptive leader does not hide from reality. They invite dissent, expose conflict, and allow disorientation instead of restoring order and maintaining norms. Choosing adaptive leadership is frequently not the safe or easy path, but in the face of adaptive challenges, it may represent the only path to progress. The question becomes how to prepare leaders for the trade-offs between, as examples, certainty and ambiguity, or between harmony and dissent—and then equip them for a new way of leading.

Based on the author's work teaching adaptive leadership and resilience, and leading organizational restructuring using adaptive leadership practices in global corporations, this chapter presents an approach that has helped shorten the time it takes for leaders to learn to lead adaptively. It seeks to help leaders bridge the gap between traditional and adaptive leadership by articulating how to equip leaders and organizations to increase adaptive capacity, specifically by increasing resilience.

This chapter explains the linkage between adaptive leadership and resilience. It refers to several bodies of work in and around adaptive leadership that have not been explicitly linked. Specifically, definitions of resilience are presented followed by a discussion of how each component of the LeaderShift® resilience framework (Eggers & Barlow, 2019) supports adaptive leadership. This novel approach to accelerating adaptive

DOI: 10.4324/9781003099109-3

capacity has proven successful in the corporate sector as well as in non-government organizations and academic institutions. Building resilience as a way to equip leaders to be adaptive is an approach that increases self-awareness and accelerates leaders' ability to lead adaptively. It has proven successful in over 20 years of practical application.

While working with several corporate leadership teams to improve their ability to adapt to significant complex adaptive challenges brought on by disruption from 2017–2018, the author uncovered a strong and replicable link between resilience and adaptive leadership. The link was discovered when two organizations (both in the financial services sector) running leadership development cohorts opted to switch the standard order of content delivery (recommended by the author) and put their team through a workshop designed to build individual and organizational resilience before a workshop designed to increase adaptive capacity. This simple switch in the delivery order of workshops involving two executive teams was noteworthy. In both cases, the teams that did the work to build resilience first seemed to be able to understand and execute the distinctions on which the adaptive leadership framework is based faster than those that did not. These teams also seemed more equipped and less resistant to demonstrate the different kinds of thinking required to effectively mobilize stakeholders to make progress on adaptive challenges in their organizations. This improvement, however anecdotal, was significant enough to warrant further investigation into whether the work of intentionally building resilience increases adaptive leadership capacity. It is also notable that the improvement first occurred with senior finance executives, a group that is not known for demonstrating the behaviors generally linked to adaptive leadership success (inclusive, open, vulnerable, willing to be wrong, agile).

Applying the LeaderShift Resilience Framework in a Corporation

One of the leadership development cohorts mentioned above was a group of high potential leaders from a global middle-market payments company that had acquired seven small companies with related product adjacencies. The acquisitions shared a similar focus, but little had been done to integrate them or capitalize on their synergies. The CEO's intent was to increase the group's skills in adaptive leadership and to build the company's adaptive capacity while working to address three complex challenges. Many individuals in the group experienced significant personal breakthroughs during the six-month period as they learned to let go of their own desired outcomes, be more vulnerable and inclusive in mobilizing people, and be open to new possibilities. Perhaps the greatest impact, however, was organizational. The group aligned around intentional preparation to strengthen their organization's ability to emerge stronger, faster, more united, and more energized from disruption (its organizational resilience). This work clarified what and who they wanted to become as an integrated organization, solidified the company's purpose as something much larger than profit, and identified areas where additional work was needed to improve organizational resilience. The group invited the CEO to a conversation where they highlighted areas where the organization was not acting in accordance with stated values and where they felt organizational resilience was being derailed. Together they built a critical two-way dialog with a broad group of stakeholders and the factions they represented, a critical component of adaptive leadership. This dialog, while controversial, deepened their understanding of stakeholders' needs and provided new and useful information that previous assumptions had missed. Several months after the program concluded, the CEO stated that, "the entire company had more courage because 12 people had come together and made the effort to build resilience." Today, that team is more connected, more aligned, and more equipped to deal with adaptive challenges—especially, as the COVID-19 pandemic impacted many of their customers' profitability. Yet, this organization continues to thrive.

Linking Resilience to Adaptive Leadership

Figure 3.1 links the work of several luminaries (Ronald Heifetz, Marty Linsky, and Chris Agyris) to resilience, including its relationship to adaptive leadership. This linkage challenges individuals to go deep into the heart of who they are as people as they strive to lead in the face of complex challenges (Johnathan Reams describes this as the soul in Chapter 5). The premise of the link between resilience and adaptive leadership is that who a leader is, as a person, shapes the way they lead and that they can, if they are aware of it, chose to be who they are, intentionally.

The kind of leadership required to mobilize people to solve complex challenges is distinctively different than a more traditional, hierarchical approach (Heifetz, 1994). Adaptive leadership is more reliant on stakeholders and requires leaders to be open and

- **inclusive** of others because answers are more likely to derive from collaboration,
- **vulnerable** because they may not have the answer or even know how to define the problem,
- willing to be **wrong** or usurped by a different point of view as more perspectives are considered,
- **different** from what is expected from a leader as they create a holding environment for others to build understanding and wrestle with trade-offs, and

RESILIENCE IS A
FUNCTION OF:

CHOICES

CORE
BELIEFS

MINDSET

ADAPTIVE
LEADERSHIP
REQUIRES OPENNESS TO BE:

- Inclusive   • Different
- Vulnerable   • Agile
- Wrong

BUT

UNDER
STRESS,
HUMANS FALL INTO TRAPS:

- Win/don't lose   • Negative emotion ↑
- Need to be right   • Maintain control ↓
- Comfort ↓

This shows up as politics, hidden agendas & "every man for himself" at work

Which makes it very difficult to be

RESILIENT LEADERS
ARE LESS STRESSED AND...

- More aware of how they show up as leaders

PAUSE   **AND**

- Make more INTENTIONAL CHOICES Aligned to their purpose
- Are open to the collaboration required to mobilize people to solve ADAPTIVE CHALLENGES

intentionally
We must equip leaders to replace human nature in the face of adaptive challenges

Figure 3.1 The Case for Resilience in Organizations.

Note: The graphics in the right-hand corner is from Eggers and Barlow (2019, p. 34). Reprinted with permission.

- **agile** or flexible enough to shift as issues become ripe or new information is made available (Heifetz et al., 2009).

When facing an adaptive challenge, lacking openness to be inclusive, vulnerable, wrong, different, or agile will threaten a leader's ability to mobilize people. For example, a leader who lacks a willingness or ability to be vulnerable or who is not open to being wrong may have difficulty accepting an idea or solution from elsewhere in the organization that is counter to their own. They may struggle to accept other original ideas or include those who think differently because it may expose a weakness in them in some way. In the author's experience, when a leader cannot (or is not willing to) be vulnerable they are not likely to lead effectively in an adaptive situation and struggle to mobilize a broad enough group of stakeholders required to solve adaptive challenges. Adaptive leadership requires a willingness to be wrong, coupled with an openness to answers that might come from where it is least expected. This type of vulnerability also produces psychological safety, a key element in a holding environment (Heifetz et al., 2009). In a corporate environment, the need for innovation caused by market disruption frequently presents the most adaptive of challenges. If the leader is reluctant to be wrong, those critical solutions to adaptive challenges (in many cases the most revolutionary innovative ideas) may never be revealed.

Also true is that vulnerability can be stressful and under stress all human beings, including great leaders, fall into the similar well-researched traps (Argyris, 2000) that can derail the best of intentions. As examples:

- Highly stressed people do not collaborate well; instead, they typically focus on being right or on winning versus losing in a conversation (Argyris, 2000). It is human nature to avoid being wrong, to a point where one can shut down an open exchange of ideas.
- When faced with difficult conversations, a typical response is to maximize comfort and minimize negative emotions (Argyris, 2000). This can lead to skirting a truth that might hurt someone's feelings, or that might raise the tension in the room.
- An inherent need to maintain control (Argyris, 2000) can diminish the ability to hear others or to understand alternate perspectives.

According to Eggers and Barlow (2019, p. 31), "In corporations, these traps show up as politics, hidden agendas, and every [person] for themselves at work. They make it extremely difficult for leaders to mobilize people effectively enough to advance solutions to adaptive challenges."

Adaptive leadership requires not only inclusivity and vulnerability, it also demands that leaders invite other points of view to diagnose and solve complex ambiguous problems with solutions that may not have been tried before. It requires pivoting when a solution comes from a place they might least expect. When stress causes a leader to cling to control or to be right, it is difficult to be inclusive; instead, stress can cause one to default to hierarchical leadership.

In the face of adaptive challenges, a leader cannot change human nature, but they can intentionally equip themselves to transform default behaviors through intentional and alternate approaches when called for. Learning and applying a resilience framework is one way to do this. The LeaderShift® resilience framework (presented below) is an example of a framework that can be leveraged to build both individual and organizational resilience. It provides a step-by-step method to build resilience intentionally *before* it is needed *and* a means of creating an inventory of work required to increase resilience. Individuals and organizations can use this framework as a guide to create their specific resilience framework as they clarify core beliefs, mindset, and the basis on which they will make choices. Resilient leaders experience less stress and are more aware of how their actions are perceived by others. When disruption occurs, resilient leaders pause and think. They tend to make more intentional choices aligned to their purpose and are open to the kind of inclusive collaboration required to solve adaptive challenges (Eggers & Barlow, 2019).

A resilient mindset (one component of which is authenticity) is, in fact, a system for making more intentional choices; these choices include core beliefs which are critical components of resilience (Eggers & Barlow, 2019). Therefore, it is not surprising that resilience better equips leaders and their organizations to be more adaptive; resilience and adaptive leadership are tightly coupled. Building resilience may not be a requirement for adaptive leadership, but the author submits that the intentional work required to support building a resilient mindset can increase a leader's ability to demonstrate adaptive leadership when needed.

Resilience Defined

Eggers and Barlow define resilience as "the power to be energized and elevated by disruption. It is the internal fortitude to emerge stronger and more effective from tough situations" (Eggers & Barlow, 2019, p. 15). Figure 3.2 illustrates a framework depicting the components that increase resilience.

The main premise of the framework is:

- Resilience is a direct result of our **mindset** and the **choices** we make.
- Our **mindset** is a function of our **authenticity** and **attitude**.

Resilience IS A RESULT OF:

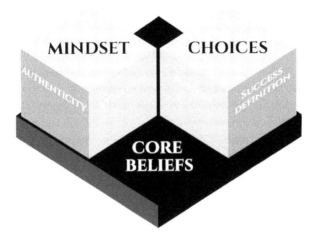

Figure 3.2 LeaderShift® Resilience Framework.

Note: Eggers and Barlow (2019, p. 34). Reprinted with permission.

- Our **choices** are a function of our **purpose** and how we **define success**, either in life or a situation.
- Underlying our mindset and choices are a set of **core beliefs** that form the bedrock that support them.

Eggers and Barlow assert that in the face of complex challenges, "it is difficult to stand up, when you have nothing to stand on" (Eggers & Barlow, 2019, p. 161). The framework is equally applicable to individuals and organizations. In organizations, the vernacular may be a bit different; purpose, for example, may be replaced with mission. The core concepts of the framework, however, are the same. Establishing these components equips leaders, stakeholders, and organizations to be more adaptive.

Box 3.1   One Resilient Team's Focus on Adaptive Leadership

The cohort at the payments company described earlier was coached on both resilience and adaptive leadership. Teams were formed, each with a significant adaptive challenge to address. To prevent reverting to a hierarchical leadership dynamic, the group was challenged to spend its first two months creating a holding environment focused solely on diagnosing the challenges. This was followed by a solution-building phase. The requirement to spend an entire two months creating a holding environment was painfully slow for a team used to running fast toward an undefined goal. But because they had done the resilience work to clearly align around their mindset, core beliefs, purpose, and definition of success, including the fact that success might not be a resolution of the challenge in the way they would have normally expected, they were able to consciously maintain focus on the diagnosis. When it was tempting to jump to action, they frequently referred back to the components of the resilience work to center themselves. Importantly, the CEO was instrumental in maintaining the holding environment, even when doing so appeared to slow things down.

During this time, the team that focused on improving sales dug deep into stakeholder analysis. They used their diagnosis time to gather input from a broader group of stakeholders than was typical. During interviews with the stakeholders, they sought to understand the "factions" each stakeholder represented, along with those factions' history, and motivations. This enabled the team to diagnose the sales problem more accurately. This diagnosis took longer, but it led the team to mobilize the sales system differently, shifting from geographic product sales to more holistic solutions targeting clients with higher need and more resources to buy. Ultimately the team's diligence resulted in an increase in sales of over 25% and enormous time savings gained from streamlining their client base, a solution that had never been considered.

Using the Leader*Shift*® Resilience Framework to Drive Adaptive Leadership

Intentional development of individual and organizational resilience is best leveraged through structure and focus; a framework can provide the elements required for building resilience and guidance on how to build them. At the same time, the actual work must be highly customized to an organization and starts with administering an inventory to identify gaps and critical areas of focus (see Appendix 3.1: Getting Started Building Resilience). The author has found that it is easier to build organizational resilience when the individuals within an organization have done personal resilience-building work as they are then more apt to understand the depth and rigor required. They are also more likely to embrace an open adaptive environment. Building resilience in organizations requires focus on two factors: (1) customizing a clear resilience framework for every individual and for the organization, and (2) laser-like alignment to a clearly articulated strategy. As Eggers and Barlow (2019) argue, if leaders are going to mobilize teams or organizations through the rapid changes that are rampant in today's marketplace—dotted with shifts in ways of working and market disruptors—they need to not only talk about resilience, they had better get good in order to build teams that are energized and elevated by disruption too. Because notably, most of that disruption is either caused by or causes an adaptive challenge.

As shown in Figure 3.2, the Leader*Shift*® resilience framework consists of three core elements, mindset, choices, and core beliefs. Explained below, these elements create a system of factors that create intentional focus on resilience and enable leaders to leverage disruption to address adaptive challenges.

Mindset: Authenticity and Attitude

Mindset is most critical when diagnosing a system, acting politically, creating a holding environment, and orchestrating conflict, each of which are key adaptive leadership practices (Heifetz et al., 2009). Preparation to build a resilient mindset begins with an awareness of authenticity. Leaders and organizations are authentic when the image they project to the world reflects who they are at their core, as opposed to, for example, hiding a personality trait. Understanding one's core and recognizing when the actions of others are authentic builds trust and equips leaders and organizations to be transparent. Transparency and trust are then tightly coupled with the ability to be vulnerable and invite dissent. Awareness of the origins of dissent and disparate views among stakeholders is critical to accurately diagnosing a system and mobilizing its people.

When leading adaptive work, it is only a matter of time before a leader needs to act politically and orchestrate conflict, which represent risk for the leader. Adaptive challenges are often wrought with emotion as stakeholders struggle to make trade-offs in values and resist loss. A leader's ability to stay the course, manage tension, and create a holding environment is largely dependent on managing their mindset, including their ability to be authentic. Managing (and choosing) one's mindset is easier when a leader is able to pause, see the big picture, understand where they fit into it and manage their own and others' emotions. Viewing a challenge "from the balcony" plays a significant role in a leader's ability to make conscious choices about mindset. The choices leaders make in these critical moments related to mindset enable a leader to be adaptive.

Box 3.2   Changing Leadership Mindsets

A North American retailer worked with its distribution center managers to deepen their understanding of how who they were as people shaped how they were behaving as leaders. The managers acquired skills related to authenticity, transparency, and trust. In the workshop, this gruff group of men took a step back from their egos and focused on the mindset required to mobilize people. At the end of the program, when asked what they would do differently, one particularly ornery leader stood up and announced, "I've been riding on a high horse. That horse's name is judgment. It's time that I come down." In the months that followed, his willingness to be vulnerable, inclusive, and authentic drove clear changes across his team and their willingness to openly surface critical issues improved. As a result, his organization increased speed and accuracy metrics by 40%, an adaptive breakthrough that required extreme cross-functional collaboration and stakeholder involvement.

Choices: Purpose and Definition of Success

The mechanisms used to make choices are critical to the adaptive leadership practices of mobilizing a system, responding to resistance as loss, modulating the provocation, and increasing a systems capacity for continuous learning. Clarifying a leader's purpose in a given situation and defining success provide criteria that can be used to guide their (and the organization's) choices. When such criteria are engrained in the mind of the leader and across an organization, decisions made under stress are more likely to be purposeful and aligned with established criteria. The consistency that ensues builds trust in both the leader and the system, critical for adaptive leadership.

Clarifying purpose in a given situation and defining success in advance provide a mechanism for measuring progress. In the face of adaptive work, few measures exist to ground an organization. A means to identify progress goes a long way towards maintaining a holding environment and staying the course when things are ambiguous.

Box 3.3   Choices Drive Results

A New York finance/technology company was under tremendous pressure to grow exponentially. The leadership team was not collaborative, and the internal competition and infighting were getting in the way of their ability to provide the kinds of new, cross-functional solutions their customers required. They were stuck in the way they had always operated and their inability to keep up with market disruption was impeding their growth. After missing several opportunities that relied on collaboration, the CEO brought the team together. They worked together to apply the LeaderShift® resilience framework–checking their mindset and how they worked together, aligning around a 3-year mission, a new way to define success, and their purpose. Once they became clear and united, they accelerated delivery of their strategy by solving a previously "impossible" cross-functional adaptive challenge that delivered their financial targets 3 years earlier than projected. They did this by pausing, creating a holding environment to get "on the balcony," and clearly defining the challenge before going to market. They also let go of their expectations and mobilized a cross-functional group of employees that had not previously collaborated to contribute to this particular challenge. This increased both the innovation and speed to execute it. The clarity the leadership team created while focusing on resilience factors enabled the adaptive leadership that drove their success.

Core Beliefs

Core beliefs are critical to supporting a leader and an organization in managing the stress of adaptive leadership. A commitment to core beliefs can be the impetus to tackle and continue adaptive work. A deep understanding of core beliefs is the foundation of individual resilience; it allows others to recognize our authenticity, and allows us to be intentional about our attitude, to chose a purpose that aligns with who we are, and define success. The same holds true for organizations. The critical addition required for building organizational resilience is that the people within an organization must align around the beliefs that are core to the organization. Organizational alignment around espoused beliefs may show up in values, mission, purpose, or principles. These are the elements of organizational life that stakeholders *know* to be true and *not* the things they *wish* were true. This is a critical component, that an organization's codified beliefs are actualized through everyday actions and decisions. This "lived" alignment around a set of core beliefs creates the freedom for individuals to act independently, in accordance with beliefs, whether or not they have authority. This is an expression of trust that breeds commitment. When an organization is aligned at every level around a common purpose and values (components of resilience), adaptive leadership practices like mobilizing the system and its stakeholders, leveraging informal authority, and giving back the work to the people suddenly become more enabled and expected. Alignment enables release of responsibility from the individual (leader) to the collective (stakeholders) as these criteria for decisions become common, beyond any single individual.

Box 3.4   Core Beliefs Shape Decisions

In 2009, a new CEO took over a large and struggling manufacturing company. When one of their factories had a fatal accident, this CEO referred to a set of principles the organization had posted in every office; one of them was safety. The accident investigation revealed that there was a device that could have prevented the accident had it been installed, the high cost of the device had deterred its installation and, even though faced with a troubled bottom line, the new CEO risked his career and invested in the costly device. "If safety is a principle here, there is only one option," he said as he put a team together to proactively look for other safety issues. Today that CEO is able to engage stakeholders and mobilize quickly for action because of his willingness to transparently live that company's espoused beliefs.

The three components of resilience link to nearly every adaptive leadership practice. The section above demonstrated how the elements of the Leader*Shift*® resilience framework have furthered the practices of adaptive leadership in corporations. Table 3.1 below outlines how the components of resilience enable adaptive leadership practices.

Characteristics of Resilient People and Organizations

Coutu (2002) outlined characteristics of resilient people and organizations, noting that a leader or an organization needs *all* the following characteristics to become truly resilient.

1   A firm grasp of **reality**, termed by Coutu (2002) as "staunch acceptance" (p. 4).
     Coutu challenges a common belief that resilience stems from optimism. While it seems unpopular to deny that optimism is helpful, optimism *only* contributes to resilience when it does not distort reality. Truly resilient people share an ability to do the grueling work of "staring down" reality. This allows them to sort through what they *can* and *cannot* change and is critical to making trade-offs in an adaptive challenge.

Table 3.1 How Resilience Enables Adaptive Leadership Practices

Adaptive Leadership Practice	Components of Resilience (Eggers & Barlow, 2019)		Core Beliefs
	Mindset (Authenticity & Attitude)	Choices (Purpose & Success Definition)	
Diagnosing the system and the adaptive challenge	An authentic, open, and inclusive mindset encourages collaboration and invites alternative points of view. This increases the likelihood of effective diagnosis.	A clear understanding of the purpose and diagnosing the challenge prior to action increases the leader's ability to prevent a premature diagnosis.	A clear understanding of core beliefs ensures that all parties are aligned around the goal and can recognize progress. Core beliefs form a platform to guide choices and mindset.
Mobilizing the system and its stakeholders	Authenticity and transparency are critical to building the trust required to create a holding environment. An attitude with a firm grasp of reality deepens trust and creates an understanding of the challenge.	A clear purpose and a shared definition of success is critical to rallying stakeholders around the challenge.	
Acting politically, including the strategic use of formal and informal authority	Determining where and when to act, leverage formal authority, or use informal authority are important strategic decisions. A leader's mindset is critical to seeing the big picture and selecting which moves to make	Making political choices in accordance with an intentional purpose and definition of success ensures that choices are aligned to end goal.	Core beliefs provide something to stand on or lean into when adaptive work becomes difficult.
Creating a holding environment	The holding environment is a spaces to modulate the tension and discomfort of adaptive work. Authenticity is critical to working	The ability to make choices to adjust the tension in the holding environment to keep it within a productive range	

Orchestrating conflict and keeping distress within a tolerable zone	through discomfort with others. An open mindset creates sensitivity to the disorienting and productive aspects of distress.	(holding versus exploding) is critical to enabling stakeholders to make progress on an adaptive challenge. A clear purpose and definition of success are critical to guiding those choices.
Responding to resistance as loss	An attitude of openness and genuine recognition of loss equips adaptive leaders to help stakeholders understand and make the trade-offs necessary to advance progress on adaptive challenges.	Responding to resistance as loss demands that we make trade-offs. When guided by purpose and definition of success, these trade-offs become transparent and easier to accept. These elements of resilience provide support and reduce the chance of making an emotional decision in the moment.	Core beliefs form the basis for making trade-offs between loyalties and values that emerge as stakeholders manage losses and work through provocation.
Modulating the provocation	Trust is critical to modulating provocation with disparate stakeholders. A resilient mindset, including authenticity, and vulnerability ensures that the leader is "in the game" with stakeholders and builds the trust required to allow provocation without causing stakeholders to shut down.	Intentional choices around when and how to provoke the system within a holding environment are critical to progress. They are more likely to be well thought out when guided by a clear purpose and definition of success.
Increasing a system's		

(Continued)

Table 3.1 (Continued)

Adaptive Leadership Practice	Components of Resilience (Eggers & Barlow, 2019)		
	Mindset (Authenticity & Attitude)	*Choices (Purpose & Success Definition)*	*Core Beliefs*
overall capacity for continuous learning	Resilience enables those navigating adaptive challenges to emerge stronger *as a result of* disruption. One of the characteristics of resilient people and organizations is the ability to find meaning in situations that ensure continuous learning. • Mindset supports this learning by creating the space to find it. • Choices support this learning by providing a basis to evaluate decisions and progress. • Core beliefs support this learning by providing a foundation to evaluate whether decisions or progress were indeed authentic, true to stakeholders' principles.		

2   A deep belief that life is **meaningful**.

Coutu (2002) states that "meaning can be elusive and just because you found it once doesn't necessarily mean you'll keep finding it again" (p. 6). This directs us to the importance of values, which are the glue that holds resilient companies together during down-turns. Coutu continues, "strong values infuse an environment with meaning because they offer ways to interpret and shape events" (p.6). "Making meaning is how resilient people build bridges from present-day hardships to a fuller, better constructed future" (p. 5).

Resilient people and organizations seek meaning, even in terrible times. This is critical to creating trust and engaging stakeholders facing an adaptive challenge.

3   An uncanny ability to **improvise**.

Resilient people improvise. They think fast on their feet. It is one of their most powerful assets and defines their ability to succeed no matter what the situation. They can improvise because they have a framework or set of tools at their disposal that they practice and know how to use.

The ability to improvise requires small, in-the-moment decisions to solve problems without usual or obvious tools. Improvisation requires creative, solution-focused thinking. It means making do with what you have and doing more than you thought you could with the resources available to you. It is the ability, determination, and grit to solve a situation using whatever means necessary and it also is a trait that enables leadership to come from anywhere, with or without authority in an adaptive challenge.

Each of these characteristics equips leaders and organizations to be adaptive. Resilience not only equips them to be elevated and energized by disruption so they can emerge stronger and more effective faster, it *also* prepares them to respond more adaptively. The adaptive leader must:

- Strategize on who to engage and how to best mobilize them to make progress. This requires a firm grasp on reality to clearly see the whole picture with unvarnished truth.
- Be able to translate meaning effectively to stakeholders to help them make the trade-offs necessary to move forward, determine if progress has been made and how much, and understand what they are doing in the context of the broader situation. This requires the ability to find meaning in situations.
- Be able to leverage available resources creatively to surface issues, build alliances, adapt to change, and make progress from anywhere in the organization. This requires the ability to improvise and change as new information is revealed.

Box 3.5   Example of A Resilient Organization

Large retail companies rely on new store openings to increase sales. Several years ago, a major auto parts retailer had an aggressive goal to open over 300 new stores, but by the middle of that year, when only 250 stores were opened, it became apparent that the company was not going to meet the goal. An increasingly competitive market combined with the rapid growth of a major competitor predicted a disastrous outcome. The leadership team reviewed the facts and accepted their reality. There was no blame or pointing fingers at the vice president of new store openings for failing to meet targets. Their grasp of reality drove them to quickly collaborate. Solutions to bridge the revenue gap were solicited from every corner of the company. Every idea was considered, no matter where it came from. The company overcome this obstacle, with minimal drama, astounding speed, and no debate.

They had put mechanisms in place ahead of time including a well-aligned bonus structure that drove this degree of collaboration. Because of that, not meeting the company's sales goal would impact every single employee's income. With clear information about the reality they faced, employees at every level improvised to find a way to meet the sales goal without the need to open new stores. Brainstorming sessions were held in every department. Sales offered incentives, marketing ran promotions, and supply chain delivered products to stores faster. Even human resources found creative ways to bring on better talent and accelerate training that drove sales.

The company met its goals that year in the face of an adaptive challenge that disrupted them because its leaders had a firm grasp on reality and quickly mobilized people across the entire organization to think creatively, improvise, and pick up the slack in support of a clear purpose and definition of success. Functions traded the plans they had made and made sacrifices for the broader goal. Decisions regarding which ideas to implement were made based on the company's core values, which come to life every day. Every employee received a bonus of 100%. The company did an after-action review to ensure that critical learnings were captured. This resilient organization not only met Couto's criteria but also had every component of the Leader*Shift*® resilience framework in place

Coutu's three characteristics of resilient people and organizations tell us much about *what* resilience looks like so we can recognize it when we see it. Eggers and Barlow (2019) define resilience as "the power to emerge energized and elevated from disruption. The internal fortitude to emerge stronger and more effective from tough situations" (p. 15). This is more of an end goal, where Coutu provides a look into what we might see along the way. The Leader*Shift*® resilience framework provides a structure, process, and methodology for *how* to build it. Together, this body of work provides a complete look at what effective resilience *is*, *what* it looks like in action, and *how* it can be intentionally built at the individual and organizational levels.

Conclusion

One of the great dilemmas facing those trying to influence leaders to be adaptive hinges on the critical trade-offs between traditional leadership and adaptive leadership. Asking leaders to be more open, vulnerable, and adaptive is difficult and less effective without tools and a process to increase self-awareness and change engrained behaviors. One such tool is the Leader*Shift*® resilience framework. The core components of the Leader*Shift*® resilience framework enable the behaviors required to build both individual and organizational resilience. Throughout this chapter, I presented a case that building resilience and the components of the Leader*Shift*® resilience framework enable and reinforces the practices of adaptive leadership, leading to an increase in adaptive capacity. When leaders have applied the Leader*Shift*® resilience framework to themselves and their organizations, both have exhibited an increased ability to firmly grasp reality, find meaning in situations, and improvise. This increase in resilience has also enabled leaders to exhibit more inclusive, vulnerable, and open behaviors in the face of disruption. It mitigates the traps frequently caused by the stress of disruption (maintaining unilateral control, minimizing negative emotions, and wanting to be right), and helps them to focus more effectively on the adaptive leadership practices of diagnosing the system, mobilizing stakeholders, leveraging formal and informal authority, creating a holding environment, orchestrating conflict, responding to resistance as loss, modulating provocation, and continuous learning. Leaders in organizations that have used the framework indicate that they are more collaborative, inclusive, and courageous in raising tough issues with stakeholders. All of this points to the probability that building resilience can increase both leaders and organizations' adaptive capacity.

References

Argyris, C. (2000). *Flawed advice and the management trap*. Oxford University Press.

Coutu, D. L. (2002). How resilience works. *Harvard Business Review*, 80(5), 46–56.

Eggers, J. & Barlow, C. (2019). *Resilience: It's not about bouncing back: How leaders and their organizations can build resilience before disruption hits*. Best Seller Publishing.

Heifetz, R. A. (1994). *Leadership without easy answers*. Harvard University Press.

Heifetz, R., & Linsky, M. (2017). *Leadership on the line, with a new preface: Staying alive through the dangers of change*. Harvard Business Press.

Heifetz, R. A., Grashow, A., & Linsky, M. (2009). *The practice of adaptive leadership: Tools and tactics for changing your organization and the world*. Harvard Business Press.

Appendix 3.1. How to Get Started Building Resilience

When helping organizations increase their resilience, two factors are equally important: applying a **clear resilience framework** for every individual and the organization and (2) aligning that framework to a clearly articulated organizational (business) strategy. Organizationally, every person, every priority, and every investment must be aligned. There can be no question about what is most critical or who is onboard. This preparation is best completed before disruption hits to be most effective, although as we have seen in the midst of the COVID-19 pandemic, it is possible, with intense focus, to build the framework and create alignment around it in the heat of a crisis.

The Leader*Shift*® Resilience Framework can be used as a checklist or assessment to identify the gaps that must be closed to increase individual and organizational resilience. Closing these gaps strengthens the ability to both lead and participate in adaptive challenges and to be energized and elevated instead of fatigued when disruption gets difficult.

To get started, fill out the sample checklist in Table 3.2 to identify areas of focus for your organization. For better results, invite multiple leaders or team members to complete the assessment, aggregate, and discuss responses as a group to create alignment around key areas of focus in building organizational resilience. It is recommended that this be used to spark discussion, surface differences in perception, and create alignment around next steps rather than as a quantifiable survey or benchmarking tool. In this case, benchmarking is not nearly as helpful as figuring out where to make even an incremental shift in resilience. Progress on any one of these factors has proven to go a long way for an organization and making progress on all of them may require a longer-term commitment and plan.

If there are items on this list that cannot be checked off or there is disagreement on the part of the team, they should be discussed for further follow-up work and prioritized for where to focus as when organizations increase their resilience, they are better suited to be adaptive. They may not know the adaptive leadership framework, but when exposed to it, they will likely be able to execute it faster for having built resilience.

Table 3.2 LeaderShift® Resilience Framework Checklist (LeaderShift
    Insights®, 2020)

Mindset
□ I have confidence that my team has the frame of mind to jump in and take appropriate action in a crisis

Authenticity

□ My team has a shared set of values we live by every day
□ We do what we say we will do and are who we say we are. Written statements of who we are pass the 'snicker' test

Attitude

□ There is minimal internal competition, drama, and in-fighting on my team
□ My team is clear on our filters. We challenge each other when there is a more effective filter and/or recognize when we are at the edge of our comfort zone

Choices
□ I trust my team to make choices in alignment with our shared agenda when I am not available

Purpose

□ My team is clear on what we need to accomplish in our interactions with each other and those outside the team
□ My team is intentional about understanding the 'big picture' and knowing our purpose

Definition of Success

□ My team is clear and aligned on what success looks like in terms of both business results and 'how we got them'
□ My team lives by our definition of success even when people are not 'looking'

Core Beliefs
□ My team is clear on our purpose, mission, and who we serve
□ We have set aside time to align around shared values

4 Adaptive Leadership and Improvement Science: Natural Bedfellows

Harriette Thurber Rasmussen,
Jacqueline Hawkins, and Robert Crow

Although there are many uncertainties in life, one thing remains persistent; all things, in time, will change. The *rate* at which change takes place, however, will vary, along with its circumstances and, importantly, the context, or environment in which change occurs. Stable environments tend to be predictable, with change occurring slowly over time. Turbulent environments are less so. They call for a unique set of approaches by leaders who must react to rapidly changing circumstances while maintaining progress toward organizational goals. For example, educational leaders were particularly challenged by the turbulent environment that characterized 2020. With a mandate to educate all students, they were also charged with protecting students and the adults that served them during the COVID-19 pandemic while responding in politically astute ways to the varied demands of their stakeholders. One seasoned school superintendent described her work during 2020 as "emotionally exhausting among public health guidelines that constantly change" and predicted a plethora of retirements (R. Miner, personal communication, October 23, 2020).

While at some point the pandemic will subside, it is but one of many crisis points that Laszlo (2020) describes as leading to global "bifurcation" wherein a system, "instead of continuing to unfold smoothly and continuously," in other words, in a stable manner, "exhibits a sudden break" (p. 2). Laszlo (2020) maintains that instability affords the opportunity to "influence, perhaps critically influence, the way the system evolves" (pp. 2–3). We argue that this influence can and should come from leaders and that adaptive leadership practices are particularly well suited to find opportunities among the challenges inherent in a turbulent environment. In other words, environmental turbulence and the bifurcation that Laszlo asserts is upon us need not be seen as a crisis, but instead become pivot points to propel progress. Leaders can advantage turbulence toward adaptation with the right tools to support continuous learning.

This chapter focuses on one such tool, improvement science (IS), with which adaptive leaders can make progress, particularly in times of

DOI: 10.4324/9781003099109-4

environmental turbulence. We begin with a brief overview of environmental turbulence and its relationship to adaptive work, followed by a description of IS and its fit with adaptive leadership practices. We then illustrate adaptive work and IS in action, using the context of the environmental turbulence brought on by the pandemic and racial crises of 2020.

Environmental Turbulence and Adaptive Work

Environmental turbulence was first defined by Milliken (1987) in relation to the management of businesses and their responses to change. Specifically, he focused his efforts on the inability of a business to identify and determine the impact that certain external environmental influences could have on their current or future operations. Ansoff and McDonnell (1990) further explain that stable environments experience limited, often imperceptible, change, enabling leaders to respond in ways that are relatively predictable. For example, educational leaders have learned to plan for the rhythms of technological change in classrooms, periodically replacing equipment and software while supporting their staff. Essentially, managing change is within a leader's sphere of influence and control. Leaders tasked with implementing change in a stable environment have an action plan and solid management skills. Their oft-repeated refrain is, "It's all under control." Importantly, at the point of implementation, much of a leader's work might be considered largely technical–with solid expertise in place and the key learning behind them (Heifetz et al., 2009).

Conversely, the rate of change in turbulent environments pressures leaders to act swiftly in response to unforeseen challenges. Unpredictable events are often outside the control of a leader to manage; they may require rapid responses that engage the expertise of many team members and are often designed on the fly. Leaders must be decisive but ready to adapt when things do not go as planned. Consider, as examples, Hurricane Katrina in New Orleans, Louisiana in 2005, the water crisis in Flint, Michigan in 2014, and the global COVID-19 pandemic of 2020. (Chapter 7 brings crisis management to life with examples from the health care industry.) These disasters, outside the environmental sphere of influence of educational leaders, still required them to manage the impact these various disasters wrought upon their schools and communities. Management skills that emphasize planning and predictable implementation transitioned to rapid-response crisis management, adapting to swiftly changing circumstances. Responses to turbulent environments typically are quickly designed and implemented while engaging others toward community-appropriate outcomes. In times of environmental turbulence, the urgent mantra becomes, "Let's find a way to get it under control."

Getting things "under control" might be an important first step in turbulence, responding in ways that Heifetz et al. (2009) would term as technical: using formal authority to command order and draw from an existing set of appropriate solutions. At the same time, it is unlikely that the aftermath of "under control" moves the challenges wrought by environmental turbulence to the stable environment leaders might desire. Uncertainty across a community tends to expose deep-seated and previously undisclosed values and beliefs, often contradictory, and not easily managed through a directive. Although leadership, per se, will not rid an environment of its turbulence, leveraging the challenges that *arise* from environmental turbulence opens the opportunity to launch adaptive work and act in ways that, as Laszlo (2020) suggests, address the critical challenges of our time. To do so requires an understanding of the nature of adaptive work and practices of adaptive leadership.

Adaptive Work and Its Leadership

Heifetz has long claimed that the most common failure of leaders is to treat adaptive challenges as technical, meaning that as complicated as technical challenges may be, the knowledge exists to solve them (Heifetz et al., 2009; Heifetz & Linsky, 2017). Where there is access to the right expertise, a technical problem can be solved, often by leveraging authority. Adaptive challenges, on the other hand, rely on the engagement and learning of those who have the most at stake in the challenge itself, its stakeholders, as typically its resolution requires a shifting of priorities, a letting go of deeply held beliefs or loyalties, and an acceptance of the losses that accompany change and transition. The work of leaders in adaptive work, then, is to help "individuals, organizations, and communities deal with … tough questions, distinguishing [what] … is essential to conserve from [what] … must be discarded, and then innovating to create the … adaptability to thrive in changing environments" (Heifetz et al., 2009, p. 23). Said differently, adaptive leaders help their stakeholders navigate environmental turbulence in ways that illuminate opportunities for progress.

Heifetz and Linsky (2017) outline seminal practices of adaptive leaders to address adaptive challenges. These include **getting on the balcony**—viewing the contributors to the challenge within the context of the system itself—and the environment (turbulent or otherwise) in which the system resides. Once on the balcony, adaptive leaders **think politically** to understand those lives most impacted by the challenge, what is at stake, and for whom. They must determine which values, whose beliefs, and what loyalties must be surfaced to accurately understand the impact of the challenge itself. In doing so, adaptive leaders inevitably **orchestrate conflict**, recognizing that what matters to stakeholders must be reviewed *and* that the resulting dissonance from that conflict leads to deep learning by those whose lives are most impacted. Heifetz and Linsky term the latter as **giving the work back**, ensuring that resolutions to adaptive challenges are truly owned by those who must live with those outcomes. Heifetz et al. (2009) recognize the dissonance that accompanies deep and soul-shifting learning, arguing that adaptive leaders are responsible for maintaining a **productive zone of disequilibrium** to facilitate such learning. The balance is tricky, they assert; learning around an adaptive challenge is anything but linear, with outcomes that may not be clear, requiring "flexibility and openness even in defining success," warning leaders that "the resolution might be quite different from what [was] first imagined" (Heifetz et al., 2009, p. 31).

The characteristics of an adaptive challenge (ambiguous and personal), coupled with the practices of adaptive leadership (where certainty takes a back seat to learning), in the context of environmental turbulence (out of one's control), may seem insurmountable and yet these are the conditions confronting leaders several decades into the 21st century. But it was through these types of challenges–those without easy answers, that the development and use of a system of practices for new learning came to light. Enter IS.

Improvement Science

The components of IS have guided organizations for decades–albeit with a variety of different names, formats, and content focus. IS incorporates aspects of general systems theory (Von Bertalanffy, 1969), communities of practice (Wenger et al., 2002), total quality management (Deming, 1993), disciplined inquiry (Cronbach & Suppes, 1969), the improvement guide (Langley et al., 2009), and use of disaggregated metrics to focus on variations in outcomes (e.g., race/ethnicity, language, disability status, poverty). More recently these time-honored concepts have been brought together as a set of principles to enable consistent and authentic progress on persistent challenges, most of which could be categorized as adaptive–hence the connection to adaptive leadership. Built around six specific principles, IS was defined and tested through the work of the Carnegie Foundation for the Advancement of Teaching (Bryk et al., 2015). The six principles are:

> **Make the work problem-specific and user-centered.** Critical to any challenge is specificity around the problem itself: "What is the problem we are trying to solve?"
> **Focus on variation in performance.** This principle asks for specificity and disaggregation of the data that suggests a problem to begin with: "What works, for whom, and under what set of conditions?"
> **See the system that produces the current outcomes.** Understanding the contributors to a problem is critical to addressing the correct

elements, including teasing out which aspects are adaptive and which may be technical. Pertinent to this chapter are contextual elements, such as the degree of environmental turbulence, or factors out of one's locus of control. Bryk et al. (2015) suggest using this analysis to develop a theory of improvement while Hinnant-Crawford (2020) pivots the use of IS to guidance and tools that operationalize IS principles in practice while ensuring that equity is paramount.

We cannot improve at scale what we cannot measure. We pay attention to what we measure. Solid metrics allow theory testing and make progress, or lack thereof, visible.

Use disciplined inquiry to drive improvement. Disciplined inquiry represents the heart of systematic learning–trying things out to see what works, but with solid structures in place to address root causes, predict evidence of success, and study results before shifting or scaling strategies (Hawkins et al., 2019). Many systems use a Plan-Do-Study-Act (PDSA) cycle, one we will feature in our illustration below, along with additional tools to ensure that the causes, as opposed to symptoms, are being addressed.

Accelerate learning through networked communities. At the heart of this principle is the value of collaboration and the power drawn from diverse experience and perspective. Sharing results, pooling evidence, and building collective intelligence that can accelerate learning–and thus progress–allows one system to impact others.

As we have stressed above, making progress in adaptive challenges comes from continuous learning; IS describes a learning system of six principles that allow focus and study. Table 4.1 below shows how the principles of IS support the practices of adaptive leadership.

The tenets of adaptive leadership can be actualized through IS. As an example, IS offers consistent language with which adaptive leaders can begin to diagnose a problem. "What is the problem we are trying to solve" keeps a tight focus on the problem itself, pushing toward the root cause through tools associated with IS [e.g., fishbone diagram (Crow, 2019)]. Sharing key metrics of progress across systems through networked communities highlights the need for learning in order to resolve adaptive challenges and ensures adherence to measuring what matters. And careful disaggregation of data with a tight focus on the specific problem allows a spark for conflict when the data tells a story that may reveal long-held prejudices or hidden assumptions—both of which must be addressed before progress can be realized. Data can act as both spark and focusing agent for adaptive leaders to keep the rate of change and tension at a level their stakeholders can handle. The similarities noted between adaptive leadership and IS make these processes compatible;

Table 4.1 Intersections of Adaptive Leadership and Improvement Science

Adaptive Leadership Practices	IS Principles
Adaptive leaders begin by **diagnosing the problem and the system** to determine which aspects of the problem are adaptive.	IS is **problem-centered and user-specific.** It begins with a single question: "What specifically is the problem we are trying to solve?" It is heavily reliant on context, where users **see the system** that produces the current outcomes and focuses their efforts on root cause analysis.
Adaptive leaders **orchestrate conflict** in ways that enable progress on significant issues that often involve losses for the stakeholders. Through data and dialogue around what matters, stakeholders encounter dissonance that leads to deep learning.	IS is **problem-specific** and addresses **variations in performance** to assess progress. Disaggregated **measures** (both process and outcome) assess progress on important issues, orient learning, spark conflict, and illuminate potential loss. IS is essentially a set of tools to enable organizational learning about complex problems of practice.
By their very nature, adaptive challenges require learning.Because there is no direct path to their resolution, adaptive leaders are tasked with **increasing a system's capacity for continuous learning** in order to address adaptive challenges. Heifetz et al. (2009) provide a cyclical process of learning that involves observation, interpretation, and intervention.	IS emphasizes **disciplined inquiry** as a deliberate cycle of learning and accelerates that learning through **networked communities** that share results in **key outcomes and progress.** A cornerstone of disciplined inquiry is the PDSA cycle.

their differences allow one to propel the other to greater advantage and results, *especially* during times of environmental turbulence.

Adaptive Leadership and IS in Action

We, the authors, have worked with the tools of IS for decades, longer than the composite practice of IS has been around, in both stable and turbulent environments. Our experiences bear out Bryk et al.'s (2015) research that IS can, as they claim, "break the cycle of failed school reform." As well, we are struck by the compatibility of these practices with adaptive leadership and how attention to each can further accelerate progress. To illustrate the natural partnership of adaptive leadership and IS, we present a narrative of adaptive leadership in the turbulent events of 2020 to explain how IS becomes an essential tool to navigate environmental turbulence while making real gains toward organizational goals. The case presented in the next section employs pseudonyms.

The Context: Seeing the System

The Socroft School District is situated in the heart of a rich agricultural valley. Although predominantly White, one-third of its students are Hispanic, mostly children of agricultural workers. Half of its 3,600 students come from families categorized as low-income. Whereas student achievement data for this small district generally mirrors the state average, the Hispanic students typically score about 20 points below their White counterparts; those from low-income households are even further behind.

Now in his ninth year as Socroft's superintendent, Zane Laurel leads a team of 20 district and school leaders. IS has become a cornerstone of their work, a process Laurel maintains "has totally changed the way we think and lead." This has been critical in a district committed to closing a persistent achievement gap in a community where "the vocal majority do not see that we have a racial equity problem and not many are interested in talking about it." (See Chapter 8 for a discussion of the reluctance to talk about race.)

This is a classic adaptive challenge from many angles. The Socroft team's task was to articulate the existence of the district's systemic racist barriers that prevented their most marginalized students from succeeding. The team had strong data behind them, operating on the IS principle of being problem-centered and user-specific, even though creating awareness of their reality was certain to result in some level of conflict. Disproportionate outcomes for certain groups of students were considered normal variations in this community; repositioning the district's resources to shift those outcomes would most certainly result in losses for those who were advantaged by current practices. Adaptive leaders recognize the necessity of disrupting previously assumed norms and that conflict is inherent in sustainable change, but for those leading political institutions, such as school systems, surfacing conflict comes with significant risk; they must create enough dissonance to authentically address the challenge while not discrediting the institution they lead.

As well, the Socroft team resided in this community. The conflict they saw ahead could very well impact longstanding relationships and loyalties. Laurel realized that he might see conflict within the team if unrest in the community as a result of their actions started to impact personal relationships. Laurel was mindful of Heifetz and Linsky's (2017) guidance on the importance of working "with differences, passions, and conflicts in a way that diminishes their destructive potential and constructively harnesses their energy" (p. 102). Adaptive leadership practices include pacing the adaptive work to manage disequilibrium—or conflict—and preparation for the work itself not only serves this purpose but allows for the depth of planning required in IS. In fact, IS requires a significant amount of time to thoroughly investigate a problem, which, while difficult for educators who tend to want to "jump into a solution," allowed Laurel to balance the disruption, something he knew was critical to get right.

Digging Deeper into the System

IS often begins with a root cause analysis and this is where Laurel took the administrative team. They had already articulated what they believed to be a significant contributor to disproportionate student outcomes—systemic racial barriers—in response to the question of why these outcomes exist for these students. They had not yet, however, engaged in the rigorous and iterative process of mapping their system of barriers. Using available data and the experience among them, the team illuminated a system of contributors using a fishbone diagram (Figure 4.1). This systematic process asks why a particular barrier exists, lists the contributors to the problem, and reveals details that suggest varied pathways to intervention.

Bryk et al. (2015) are clear that both quantitative and qualitative data are necessary to thoroughly understand a problem and the context in which it resides. Laurel's team conducted empathy interviews (Portigal, 2013) with staff and students to gain a more comprehensive understanding of the problem. The results confirmed their initial model (fishbone), but also included surprises, for instance, the hardship placed on families required to purchase school supplies when they struggled to pay rent. Some of the data began to get uncomfortable for the team as they learned that some of their best intentions had generated unintended consequences. They learned that an absence of explicit phonics (reading) instruction left students without decoding skills, an omission that, coupled with limited academic vocabulary, became a critical contributor to low literacy rates. They discovered that their emphasis on a guaranteed viable curriculum for each student caused teachers to shorten or remove activities that fostered a sense of belonging and or enhanced vocabulary through, as examples, community meetings or reading out loud to students.

Anticipating the challenging nature of these conversations, Laurel tended to what Heifetz et al. (2009) term the team's holding environment with interpersonal commitments spelled out in advance, such as "assume positive intent" and "be okay with failure." He notes that the team relied heavily on these "norms" to stay focused on the work. The Socroft team also examined the technical and adaptive aspects of each of the fishbone's causal factors to help determine the scope required for successful intervention. Recall that technical challenges are those for which known responses exist and can often be realized through authority. Adaptive challenges address deeper, more nebulous barriers, such as values, beliefs, and loyalties. The team's fishbone model uncovered both technical and adaptive causes to their challenge of chronic underachievement and systemic racial barriers. They also experienced a taste of how the adaptive aspects of this challenge might be received in the broader

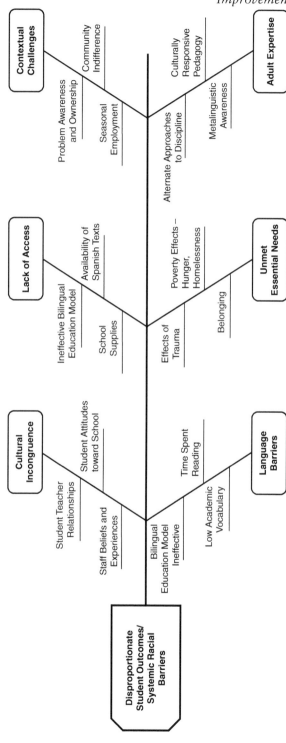

Figure 4.1 Fishbone Diagram Illustrating Causal Factors.

community through their own experiences as a team. They were acutely aware of the holding environment that made these conversations relatively safe and wondered how they could replicate this type of safety in the broader community.

The PDSA disciplined inquiry cycle begins by planning small-scale interventions to then study and act upon with appropriate refinement or scale, depending on the results of the intervention. Socroft's team chose what seemed to be a technical, non-controversial barrier: assuming the responsibility for school supplies, thereby relieving families of this financial burden. Even with this fairly simple adjustment, Laurel's team received pushback, but because of the preliminary root cause work, the plan prevailed and they moved to the "Study" phase of that initiative. "It was a small beginning," Laurel admits, "but *how* we approached this first step set us up for the bigger work ahead."

Continuous Change for Turbulent Times

Laurel's approach to begin with a small and somewhat technical change while surrounded by more complex, adaptive challenges—such as cultural incongruence, community indifference, and lack of student belonging—was deliberate as he gauged the level of disequilibrium within the team. Even though the administrators had each publicly committed to addressing racial barriers in order to eliminate the district's achievement gap, Laurel knew that each individual would likely experience divided loyalties as they confronted their own past behavior, well-intended or not, and that of their colleagues. He considered the team to be a microcosm of the Socroft community and knew that their experiences previewed what he might expect from Socroft's staff and broader community. Laurel was employing a continuous change strategy, especially useful in a turbulent environment and in line with research that suggests continuous change to be more appropriate in complex environments (Berger & Johnston, 2015; Weick & Quinn, 1999). These small shifts allow stakeholders to consider the impact of a relatively minor, but potentially impactful adjustment in behavior, resource allocation, and, over time, mental models.

Disciplined Inquiry through PDSA

During implementation, the "Do" element of their PDSA, the Socroft team carefully monitored implementation and collected the data they had agreed would measure the impact of these changes. As they moved into the "Study" phase, they analyzed their data, assessed what worked and what needed refinement before entering the "Act" and final phase of the PDSA cycle—determining what to continue, where to adjust, and what to stop, and then planning for a next cycle. PDSA cycles increase a system's capacity for learning. They provide a structure for learning and a discipline that routinely expands and revisits data, questions what has and has not been successful, and adjusts where needed. Simply put, PDSA cycles help a system to learn from itself, to adapt, allowing for adjustments in the midst of environmental turbulence. Entering the "Study" phase of PDSA, the Socroft team found that reallocating district resources in ways that allowed students to have access to school supplies had its intended effect (e.g., an increase in student preparedness and lower absentee rates). Thus, they moved to the "Act" phase, establishing a permanent budget line item, and sharing their actions and results broadly throughout the region. As noted above, membership in networked communities is a core principle of IS where sharing successes and failures are ways that build greater capacity within and across systems.

Heifetz et al. (2009) call out a similar cycle, Observe–Interpret–Intervene, in which their discussion of interpretation considers essential perspective when navigating an adaptive challenge (one might consider the "Interpret" in adaptive leadership practices to mirror the "Study" portion of the PDSA cycle). Heifetz et al. (2009) discuss the act of interpreting as "listening for the 'song beneath the words'," scanning the data for "the widest possible array of sensory information" (p. 34) to determine more accurately what is truly at stake for those with the most to lose. Laurel, in fact, was gathering data beyond that of the intervention itself; he was as much interested in the dynamics of the team as they grappled with the adaptive aspects of empathy interview data. He wanted to be certain they were ready to address significant adaptive challenges that stood as barriers for so many of their students. Satisfied that they had weathered this first PDSA cycle, Laurel readied the team to address an adaptive aspect of their problem of practice. They chose to focus on cultural incongruence as a key racial barrier, easing into the dialogue in ways that were challenging but productive.

Refocusing around Environmental Turbulence

Laurel's attempts to keep the rate of change within a tolerable level came to a head with the twin challenges of COVID-19 and racial equity protests in this conservative community. Laurel and his team's world went from one that was relatively stable to full-fledged environmental turbulence, with a mandated shift to distance learning amidst polarized stakeholders, most of whom did not believe COVID-19 to be a serious threat to public health. They had a distinct choice in front of them: to retreat from their commitment to address cultural incongruence or to use this juncture of bifurcation to launch a "small but potent 'initial kick'" (Laszlo, 2020, p. 3) and seize the opportunity to accelerate progress. They chose the latter.

Laurel reasoned that improving the environment inside their schools should occur before stepping into a highly politicized community approach and the team had already narrowed their next focus to teacher-student relationships as a key contributor to cultural incongruence. Forced into a virtual environment, where the classroom relationships they were trying to adjust become exponentially more challenging, Laurel and the team used another IS tool, a driver diagram, to map out their thinking (Figure 4.2). Bryk et al. (2015) explain that a driver diagram "focuses on a small set of hypotheses about key levers for improvement, specific changes that might be attempted for each, and the interconnections that may exist among them" (p. 73). Socroft's driver diagram illustrated the added complexity of a virtual learning environment to student-teacher relationships and helped them to craft a theory of action, making the rationale for their decisions explicit, and laying the groundwork for the "Study" portion of this PDSA.

Socroft's driver diagram spelled out their theory of action: *If we utilize data gathered through observation and monitoring, we will increase our knowledge about the realities of student-teacher relationships in virtual classrooms, so that we are able to better educate staff through structured collaboration and coaching support, increasing exposure to examples of successful practice to enhance student–teacher relationships in virtual environments.* The next stage of the PDSA cycle called for creating a plan to implement the strategy outlined in their theory of action (P) that they would then implement (D) and study (S), before going to scale (A). What is noticeably absent in Socroft's driver diagram, however, are aspects of this intervention directed at the adaptive elements of student-teacher relationships, such as staff beliefs and experiences, critical to address if they are to confront the racial barriers that, in this system, have as many human as institutional elements. Laurel was still treading softly, knowing that the team and their direct reports were embroiled in their own personal challenges brought on through environmental turbulence, beyond the confines of the school system.

A Hard Reset

What Laurel discovered, however, was that the structured tools of IS became an important component of his carefully moderated holding environment. Heifetz and Linsky (2017) point out that one strategy to reduce the level of dissonance around adaptive work is to "establish a structure for … problem-solving … by breaking the problem into parts and creating time frames, decision rules, and clear role assignments" (p. 111). Perhaps due to the structures of IS, Socroft's team began to rethink what didn't work particularly well before, ultimately resetting the work in ways that might leverage the disruptive nature of the environment. As teachers began to struggle with the level of engagement in their virtual classrooms, the team shifted the conversation to the broader question of how significantly students were engaged before distance

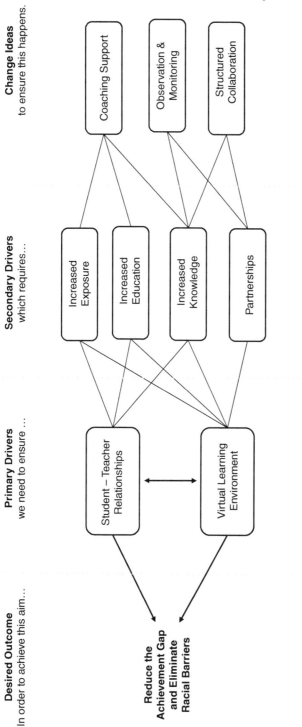

Figure 4.2 Driver Diagram.

learning, turning up the heat, so to speak, while providing ample support to teachers where needed. Laurel notes that some teachers naturally build and maintain strong relationships in a virtual setting; others really struggle. Their PDSA around teacher-student relationships moved to differentiated support for teachers, addressing the problem in ways that were more problem-centered and user-specific–a principle of IS. Differentiation allowed Laurel and the team to raise the temperature for some teachers by "draw[ing] attention to the tough questions;" for others, they chose to "slow down the process, [and to] pace and sequence the issues and [determine] who [comes] to the table" (Heifetz & Linsky, 2017, p. 111). In this way, Laurel and his team kept adaptive work in a range that was tolerable. The sequence of events in Socroft mirrors Heifetz and Linsky's (2017) advice to maintain pressure without moving beyond the limits of tolerance:

> To reduce heat you can start on the technical problems, deferring adaptive challenges until people are "warmed up." A little progress on a partial, relatively easy problem may reduce anxiety enough that the tougher issues can then be tackled. Negotiators commonly use this tactic: Strengthen the relationships–the holding environment–by creating shared successes. You can provide structure to the problem-solving process by breaking down the problem into its parts…. (p. 109).

This is exactly what Laurel and the team orchestrated in Socroft, using IS as a problem-solving structure, with the fishbone and driver diagrams to guide them through disciplined inquiry in a PDSA sequence. Their initial change efforts were primarily technical—reallocating resources to make sure their lower-income students were not further disadvantaged by not having school supplies, relying on that shift to build capacity for the more adaptive work ahead.

The New Normal: Disciplined Inquiry around Adaptive Work

As Socroft's administrative team and their staff grew adept with IS tools and more comfortable addressing adaptive challenges, Laurel found himself pushing the team toward the opportunities presented by the environmental turbulence of the 2020–2021 school year, in line with Laszlo's (2020) admonition to seize the moment of bifurcation. His message to the team was direct:

> It's on us. If we don't make changes to the structures now, when the slate is wide open, then people will step back naturally into what they were used to. If we do that, we have failed to seize the opportunity brought on by something completely out of our control.

As they made inroads in the challenges of virtual learning, they looked ahead to new opportunities afforded through the turbulence. Laurel's keynote address to returning staff in the Fall of 2020 laid the groundwork for continued progress: "We have an exciting opportunity through this crisis to change how we educate and we would be remiss if we went back to how we did things before." He keeps the team asking the important questions: "Why would we want to go back to a six-period day?" "How do we give students multiple opportunities to learn?" "How do we base our grades on the actual standard of learning?" And perhaps most importantly, "If environmental turbulence is our new normal, how do we use that to our advantage?"

The opportunities illuminated through IS have been invaluable in this time of crisis. Says Laurel,

> We consistently come back to the key question, "What is the problem we are trying to solve?" Just that one question has transformed how we lead and how our Board thinks about our, and their, work. In a way, it has given us permission to slow down–which is a challenge! We see a problem and the kids are hurting and we want to fix it. But by doing that, we may be making it worse.

The Socroft team is convinced that starting small and then building from success has made them feel that they are accomplishing something and credit IS for this perspective. "It's sort of a paradox–trying to come up with the perfect thing versus coming up with some place to start."

Laurel and the team acknowledge that this is a long journey. They are aware that the real systemic problems of equity won't be solved in a day, or maybe even in a generation. There are emotional aspects of these conversations that uncover wounds that date back generations. Creating that dialogue—hearing those difficult stories about how these problems have directly affected each side is uncomfortable, yet necessary. By rushing to a solution, they risk a tendency to simplify complex, layered issues that must be continuously monitored and addressed to make true progress. The question will always be, how hard to push, when to slow down, and what is, really, the rate of tolerance in a community? Adaptive leadership is about pacing the work, keeping it relatively safe but productive so that stakeholders are ready to address the adaptive challenges, in this case, the systemic and racial barriers that result in the achievement gap. IS has enabled the Socroft community to make a plausible and strong beginning to both the technical and adaptive aspects of that work.

The Long View

The complex challenges of the past decades seem to have come to a head in these increasingly turbulent times. Adaptive leaders have their work cut out for them, leading systems of protective and divided stakeholders to address problems that cannot be resolved without inciting conflict. We argue that the way forward is through the long view, an abundance of courage, and a plethora of tools. The tools of IS serve to strengthen an adaptive leader's holding environment. They illuminate systems in ways that suggest interventions to persistent problems, increase tolerance for adaptive work, and, indeed, shift belief systems over time. The old adage of "two heads are better than one" may ring true for leaders who feel buoyed by IS's process of networked improvement communities that organize around problem-solving.

As educators who have spent decades observing and guiding school systems through multiple iterations of change without much improvement to show for it, we echo Laszlo's (2020) urgent call to seize the opportunities brought on by disruption, to find the small cracks in certainties that come to light in an environment of turbulence. As the Socroft School District demonstrates in this vignette, IS can help a system to learn from itself through disciplined inquiry and in ways that allow adaptive leaders to maintain productive pressure toward real and sustainable improvement. Indeed, IS and adaptive leadership became natural bedfellows as one school district grappled with the extraordinary environmental turbulence at the start of the third decade of the 21st century.

References

Ansoff, H. I., & McDonnell, E. (1990). *Implanting strategic management.* Prentice Hall.

Berger J. G., & Johnston, K. (2015). *Simple habits for complex times: Powerful practices for leaders.* Stanford Business Books.

Bryk, A., Gomez, L., Grunow, A., & LeMahieu, P. (2015). *Learning to improve: How America's schools can get better at getting better.* Harvard Educational Press.

Cronbach, L. J., & Suppes, P. (Eds.) (1969). *Research for tomorrow's schools: Disciplined inquiry for education.* MacMillan.

Crow, R. (2019). Considering improvement science in educational leadership. In R. Crow, B. N. Hinnant-Crawford & D. T. Spaulding (Eds.), *The educational leader's guide to improvement science: Data, design, and cases for reflection* (pp. 3–12). Myers Education Press.

Deming, W. E. (1993). "4". *The new economics for industry, government, and education.* MIT Press.

Hawkins, J., Henry, G.A., Jones, S.J., Santi, K.L., & Butcher, K.A. (2019). Implementing professional learning communities: Improvement required. In Crow, R, Hinnant-Crawford, B., & Spaulding, D. (Eds.), *The educational leader's guide to improvement science: Data, design, and cases for reflection* (pp. 295–318). Myers Education Press.

Heifetz, R. A., Grashow, A., & Linsky, M. (2009). *The practice of adaptive leadership: Tools and tactics for changing your organization and the world.* Harvard Business Press.

Heifetz, R. A., & Linsky, M. (2017). *Leadership on the line, with a new preface: Staying alive through the dangers of change.* Harvard Business Press.

Hinnant-Crawford, B. N. (2020). *Improvement Science in Education: A Primer.* Myers Education Press.

Langley, G., Moen, R., Nolan, K., Nolan, T., Norman, C., & Provost, L. (2009). *The improvement guide: A practical approach to enhancing organizational performance* (2nd ed.). Jossey-Bass.

Laszlo, E. (2020). *How we can build a better world.* Waterside Productions.

Milliken, F. J. (1987). Three types of perceived uncertainty about the environment: State, effect, and response uncertainty. *Academy of Management Review, 12*(1), 133–143.

Portigal (2013). *Interviewing users: How to uncover compelling insights.* Rosenfeld.

Von Bertalanffy, L. (1969). *General systems theory: Foundations, development applications.* George Braziller, Inc.

Wenger, E., McDermott, R., Snyder, W. M. (2002). *Cultivating communities of practice: A guide to managing knowledge.* Harvard Business Press.

Weick, K. E. & Quinn, R. E. (1999). Organizational change and development. *Annual Review of Psychology, 50*(1), 361–386.

5 Soul Space for Adaptive Work

Jonathan Reams

A number of years ago, I attended a dialogue between two prominent figures of new paradigm thinking with a couple friends who knew very little about the speakers. We listened as each speaker took turns offering their thoughts on the topic and each other's remarks. After the event, my friends commented how much they were put off by one speaker, feeling he had been pontificating, talking down to them, and almost demanding his views be accepted, not only by the audience but by implication, all those who thought differently on the subject. They then commented on how they felt invited into an inquiry with the other speaker, encouraged to think for themselves and with a sense of a heartfelt connection.

The "work" this audience was invited to engage in was to consider new paradigm views on self and reality. It was certainly adaptive work, requiring a questioning of traditional views, values, and loyalties to deeply held assumptions and had implications for making changes in everyday habits. Yet it was clear that the holding environment for making progress on this work was not ideal. The lack of congruence between the message and the messenger from the one speaker generated an unhealthy tension in the holding environment, making it less supportive for adaptive work.

I open with this vignette as a simple case of the key theme of this chapter: What is the role and function of *self* in opening and holding space for adaptive work? Beyond this, what can soul bring to how leaders do this? In Heifetz's (1994) *Leadership Without Easy Answers*, he addresses the personal challenge facing leaders, "those who lead take responsibility for the holding environment of the enterprise" (p. 250). The concept of the holding environment can be understood as the spaces leaders create to enable adaptive work (see Chapter 2 for a rich discussion of how psychological safety plays a role in this). Heifetz lists three key principles involved: regulating distress, directing disciplined attention to the issues, and giving the work back to the people at a rate they can handle. The key process for leaders here is learning to get up on the balcony, which is essentially enabling perspective-taking and reflection.

In *The Practice of Adaptive Leadership* (Heifetz et al., 2009), this component of leading adaptive work is expanded. Part four invites the

DOI: 10.4324/9781003099109-5

reader to see themselves as a system and offers insightful points and examples. Yet there is much left between the lines, implicit in the advice and examples given. I believe there is room to reframe how self is understood and contextualized. This chapter will explore new perspectives on the conception of being, how it relates to self and its development to enrich our understanding and practice of adaptive leadership.

The Blind Spot of the Self

Heifetz et al. (2009) point to how we often use our intuitions to lead adaptive change, while also pointing out that this can lead us astray at times. They note that intuition "is likely to constrain you from seeing certain data, being open to certain interpretations, and making certain interventions outside your comfort zone" (p. 181). Human consciousness is inherently subject to a variety of biases (Kahneman, 2011); the self is prone to blind spots that limit the spaces we create.

Kahneman (2011) has shown that we are not the rational decision-makers we like to believe. What we often consider as intuition is primarily fast, or implicit thinking, internalized, automatically operating patterns of thought and emotion. In most instances, this implicit thinking serves us well. However, it also has limitations. Implicit thinking is limited to prior experience; it does not work well in novel situations. It can be suboptimal, made up of maladaptive habituated responses to difficult situations. Finally, it can be difficult to share with others in collaborative contexts. We cannot help but live and act within the world as we see and understand it. Yet despite knowing this, we act as if we know better.

It is this blindness to the deepest layers of our own fallibility that creates a major challenge to making interventions beyond our comfort zone. To increase the effectiveness of our interventions, we can start by recognizing limits to the ways we habitually deploy our intuitions in the contexts we encounter. Scharmer (2002) framed this by saying the ultimate blind spot of leadership is the self or the source from which leaders act. In *Theory U,* Scharmer (2007) quoted Bill O'Brien's observation, that the "success of an intervention depends on the *interior condition* of the intervener" (p. 7, emphasis in the original). Leading is an intervention and the space, or holding environment, leaders create is essential to the ability of stakeholders to engage in adaptive work. This interior condition is often seen as a vague and fuzzy place to explore, let alone understand. Scharmer's colleague Jaworski's (2012) journey, described in *Source*, further unpacks the kind of new paradigm thinking described in this chapter's opening story and illuminates subtler aspects of the self and how it intervenes in the world. I will explore this blind spot by sharing my own view, in the hope that it can bring some rigor and depth to conceptions of self and soul in the work of adaptive leadership.

Who Is on the Balcony?

Getting off the dance floor and up on the balcony to see oneself as a system is essential to leading adaptive work (Heifetz, 1994; Heifetz et al., 2009) (more on this can be found in Chapter 2). Yet this metaphor implies a subject from which to observe this self-system, which can be seen as an integrated set of conceptions, emotions, and physiology. If the self-system is the object to look at, *who is looking?* This is considered a perennial question, asked by inquiring minds and the generally curious of every age throughout history. How it is answered varies and often presents paradoxes and conundrums, leaving it only partially answered (see Chapter 16 for another perspective on this subject). Yet this question has significant consequences for how we lead adaptive work, as well as approach life in general.

In the spirit of this perennial inquiry and to get up on the balcony, it is important to direct attention upstream, to the implicit assumptions underlying one's worldview. An influential example of this kind of upstream inquiry is found in Bohm's (1992) work *Thought as a System*. His life was a deep inquiry into fundamental questions through both physics and philosophy. At the heart of this was seeing the universe as an undivided wholeness (Bohm & Hiley, 1993). Both self and the world are aspects of unlimited wholeness. His work described how we live within images of self and the world that are inherently limited constructions of a system of thought (seen as an integration of thought, feeling, and physiology). This also implies that the system cannot see itself in its entirety. Bohm saw it as critical to consider the existence of something beyond this system of thought.

When we take our perception (i.e., how the system of thought filters sensory data and adds layers of implicit meaning) to be real, we essentially fragment reality. This leads to the reification of our perception into a conception that we see things as they are. Bohm describes this as the fundamental incoherence in the system of thought. In relation to the perception and experience of a self, this also leads to identification with the self and aspects like thoughts, feelings, actions, and even roles. From exploring the limitations and implications of this, Bohm's (1992) main insight was that "the point is to have the notion of a creative being rather than of an identified being" (p. 169). Self is not a thing, but a process.

Building on this and many other related perspectives, I began my academic journey (Reams, 1999) by summarizing Bohm's inquiry, saying that *who we think we are* is an "image of self created by thought" (p. 320) that encompasses thoughts, emotions, and the body as well as things like career and role identities. Yet thinking cannot encompass the wholeness or essence of who we are. We can have moments in which we experience this essence, often simply as there being *something more*. There are many ways in which people have described this essential wholeness at the heart of our being. Aiming for simplicity, I choose the term soul.

The next steps on my journey involved attempting to bring a more rigorous description to the term soul (as opposed to a definition, which tends to become more reified than dynamic). For this, I characterized soul as "a creative unit of pure awareness" (Reams, 2012, p. 104). The next step was to investigate what was implied in the term awareness, as it has not only a general vernacular usage but a wide range of connotations across many fields of study. A later investigation of a number of relevant threads (Reams, 2016), led to describing awareness as "the experiential realization of the virtuality of self" (p. 81). This formulation allowed me to contextualize the everyday experience of self in relation to beingness as soul, or as a spiritual being having human experiences.

Thus, soul is on the balcony, and the self on the dance floor. In Kegan's (1994) terms, soul becomes a different modality of subject. The self as a system, as Bohm and Heifetz describe it, becomes the object. Kegan's idea is that we can notice, make conscious choices about and change what is object for us. Whereas we experience our *selves* as real, being subject to self has limitations. This is where the concept of the virtuality of self can help.

The Wisdom of the Virtuality of Self

To better understand what is meant by the virtuality of self, I will present two common examples in everyday life, both of which mediate forms of experience for us. First, we can conceive of the self like an avatar in a video game. We project personal qualities and characteristics onto the avatar. We undertake tasks to gain experience that builds skills or other resources to use in the game. We experience vicarious feelings from the encounters we have through our avatar. We can even come to identify with the avatar, internalizing its qualities and characteristics to contribute to our own sense of personhood.

A second common experience is how a well-conceived and well-played character in a movie can provide insight into our own lives, through a character's challenges, flaws, foibles, joys, sorrows, and overall journey. As we allow ourselves to feel along with a given character on screen, some aspect of human nature we can identify with is writ large for us, dramatized in order to externalize and make visible a facet of our character. This externalization is only possible because of the internal recognition of the particular aspect of human nature being portrayed. Yet as we enjoy falling into living out these vicarious experiences, the line between the on-screen externalization and internalized connection to the experience can easily blur, making us lose track of the witnessing quality of watching and giving us a false sense of identification with the externalized character.

The concept of the virtuality of self is not new. Transpersonal concepts found in Eastern thought can help us understand more about this conceptualization:

> The idea, in essence, is the traditional Buddhist claim that selfhood is a powerful and functional illusion, but is ultimately groundless, and that in becoming aware of the ways in which our sense of self is constructed and maintained we free ourselves from some of the limiting assumptions that hinder the development of wisdom (Rowson, 2008, p. 4).

When thinking about how our interior condition affects how we create a holding environment, we want to minimize limiting assumptions and maximize wisdom. Limiting assumptions narrows the space leaders create. They filter out options, steer conversations in directions that justify and reinforce existing beliefs, making adaptive work more difficult. A significant part of the work of leader development involves "cleaning up" (Reams et al., 2020, p. 45), or bringing into awareness limiting beliefs so we can do the adaptive self-leadership work of changing behaviors. As well, these limiting beliefs drive self-defeating behaviors (Kegan & Lahey, 2009) and invite others to collude with our justifications (The Arbinger Institute, 2006). The deepest limiting assumptions are tied to identity (Reams, 2016), making them very difficult to change. They also have a high leverage impact on the holding environments we create.

Wisdom can be conceived as wise acting (Rowson, 2008), in contrast to a sage accumulation of knowledge only possible with age. It can be simple acts of engaging a situation in a manner that makes things better. In terms of adaptive leadership, wise acting leaders will continually and dynamically regulate the holding environment. Rather than closing the space (through limiting assumptions affecting the leader's interior condition), such wise acting will open the space and enable stakeholders to better engage in adaptive work.

Being able to perceive the virtual nature of self appears to be the epitome of wisdom. This perceptive capacity arises from soul. Having a conception of self like a game avatar or a movie character allows us to take the self-system as an object of reflection. We can then consider a wider range of options and better regulate thoughts, emotions, and behaviors, all leading to greater possibilities for wise actions that enable adaptive work.

The Virtuality of Our Interior Condition

If the success of an intervention depends on our interior condition, then the work of leadership starts with our own adaptive work. Kegan (1994) describes the self-transforming mind as having a more fluid capacity to dynamically reinvent a self-authored mind. The roots of resistance to this developmental work lay in our sense of a fixed identity (Bohm, 1992; Reams, 2016). The conception of soul as a creative sense of being, combined with the virtuality of self, allows for exploring our interior condition in new ways.

The next step is to describe the relationship between soul and self. To the point, it is consciousness. While consciousness also has a wide range of common usage connotations as well as being a subject of study in many fields, my own formulation was to see consciousness as "soul's relationship with embodiment" (Reams, 1999, p. 318). Embodiment represents Bohm's notion of the self-image created by the system of thought. The more consciousness we have, the fuller a relationship soul has with thinking, feeling, and embodiment.

Soul, as a spiritual being having human experiences, and described above as a creative unit of pure awareness (i.e., the experiential realization of the virtuality of self), is constantly differentiating spirit. Spirit is conceived as unbroken wholeness always becoming more than itself. Soul's differentiation of spirit is shaped by consciousness, this relationship with the self of our interior condition—our particular thoughts, emotions, and ultimately actions. When these components of our interior condition are static and we are subject to them, this differentiation reifies into fixed forms with which we identify. Whereas this can be predicable and useful in many aspects of life, it is less useful when faced with adaptive challenges. Static forms of an identified interior condition easily become triggers that constrict the flow of life and weaken the holding environment.

Soul has a more dynamic, flexible relationship to the elements of this interior condition. This allows us to evolve the self, to sense our context, and adapt our interior condition in order to create the ideal holding environment for a given adaptive challenge (see Chapter 7 for another perspective on this related to rhizomic liminality). As soul, we can get outside of ourselves.

As a philosophical premise this can be supported by various types of argumentation and framing of evidence (see Reams, 2016 for a more extensive inquiry). There are also plenty of everyday experiences that give us moments of getting outside of ourselves. Losing a sense of self-consciousness or ego in play, having psychological time fly by as we are deeply engrossed in the moment, the state of flow (Csikszentmihalyi & Csikszentmihalyi, 1992), or a variety of meditative or mindful states (Davidson & Kaszniak, 2015), can all be seen as moments where we are not "ourselves" per se. Self is not the source, but the vehicle of experience. It is not about a cold detachment from experience, but rather a profound immersion in the moment of experience, yet also being able to zoom out and realize the dynamic, transitory nature of the self's experience.

The above outline of my view will serve as the basis for exploring a few implications for adaptive leadership. This will begin with examining self-leadership, then leading as learning and related to this, development, seen in relation to context and complexity. This will be followed by an exploration of neuroscience, including neuroplasticity and neuro-cardiology, also related to field theory and its implications for creating space for adaptive work.

Self-Leadership

Self-leadership, grounded in self-awareness, is considered a critical foundation for leading (Axelrod, 2012). This involves managing, or regulating, the various aspects of our interior condition (Scharmer, 2002). Such regulation can be a challenge due to two factors noted already; the static sense of identification with thoughts, feelings, habits of action, and so forth, and second, the challenge of trying to regulate these components of our interior condition from within the system itself.

Regarding the latter, as soul, we can step outside the constructed sense of self and witness the dance floor where the various aspects of our interior condition play out both intrapersonal and interpersonal aspects in the various contexts we find ourselves in. This can be described as nonattachment, the ability to be in an experience but not lose perspective. Seeing the self as a virtual entity can provide a bridge and give us a powerful tool, a mental model as a holding environment for self-leadership, to enable the work of adapting our interior condition to the needs of the context.

A key component of this is emotion regulation. There is research showing that the direction of our attention is largely governed by emotion. Barrett (2017) dispels many myths related to emotions as pre-existing states we all experience the same way. Instead, she shows how emotions are constructed through conceptual distinctions and associations we make over time. These become habituated, giving them the impression of being independently real states that people experience in common. Thus meanings, including feeling states, are not given but can be regulated through attention to the underlying processes of the system of thought.

To the first challenge mentioned above, the identification with the various aspects of our personal qualities, characteristics, and values, not to mention more external aspects like professional roles, job titles, and positions (see Senge, 1990), is noted by Bohm (1992) as the central impediment to coherence. These aspects of self are real enough and important, however, incoherence creeps in when we identify them as the essence or ground of being. As limited, temporal, and transient components of life, they do not offer a sufficient balcony space from which to work on ourselves. When the self itself becomes the balcony, bias is inevitable, and change is difficult.

This framing of self-leadership as the regulation and cultivation of self by soul can expand our understanding of areas relevant to how we create space for adaptive work. This work is essentially about learning. Heifetz (1994) ends *Leadership Without Easy Answers* by saying: "Leadership, seen in this light, requires a learning strategy" (p. 276). This takes us next into an examination of learning, context, and development.

Leadership as Learning and Development

Learning is central to leadership. Numerous researchers have identified learning as the core function or capacity of leadership (e.g., Coad & Berry, 1998; Robertson & Timperley, 2011). Learning in the context of technical problems is single-loop while learning for adaptive challenges is double (Argyris, 1982), or even triple-loop (Hawkins, 1991) (see Chapters 2 and 9 for more detailed descriptions of this topic). Learning can be understood as an ongoing, dynamic process of building more robust neural connections. Robustness means that we built multiple connections between different neurons. Another way of saying this is that the more perspectives we connect in relation to a given situation, the more agile we can be. This kind of "agile leadership" is becoming a popular way of talking about having an adaptive approach to leading situations. In simple terms, to lead is to go first and learn about a given adaptive challenge.

There are several aspects of learning relevant for adaptive leadership. How does a leader develop a capacity to read the situation? How do they enable learning and development for stakeholders through the challenge as well as support in the holding environment? In the lens being used here, how does soul, holding the self as virtual, enable learning and development of the self?

Complexity of Context

The capacity to read a situation is a first step for leading. Diagnosing a situation to determine the type of context involved in Heifetz's model has been presented as a distinction between technical problems and adaptive challenges, with most situations a mix of the two. Similar frameworks can be found in Grint's (2005) approach to types of leadership situations as well as in Snowden's (Snowden & Boone, 2007) cynefin framework. (For an in-depth discussion of complexity theory and complexity leadership, see Chapter 1). What all of these require is sufficient perceptual and conceptual distinctions being present for leaders to make good use of such frameworks.

Adaptive challenges have characteristics like being unpredictable, full of emergence, and focused more on networks of relationships than static parts. They require anticipation, probing, and experimentation. Rather than an application of expertise and authority, adaptive challenges require careful observation, listening, and learning.

What is less often discussed in relation to leading in adaptive challenges is the concept of requisite cognitive complexity in leaders (Rasmussen and Raei [2020] being an exception). Complex contexts have several features that parallel the development of cognitive complexity. There is a need to construct meaning beyond linear causality and make links between multiple considerations. There is a need to take layered causality into account, for example, considering nested relationships between dyadic relationships, group dynamics, organizational goals, and organizational, as well as societal, culture, and historical and contextual factors into account. All of this requires adequately complex thinking tools, or cognitive processes that are fit for the challenge.

Cognitive Development

There is more than 100 years of work in developmental psychology, from Baldwin's (1895) seminal ideas and how they influenced major figures like Piaget (1954) and Vygotsky (1978), carried on through Kohlberg's (1984) work on stages of moral development and into a broad range of domain-specific theorists (e.g., Perry, Selman, King and Kitchener). Domain-general theories are rooted in the work of Fischer's (1980) dynamic skill theory and are complimented by assessment models developed by Commons et al. (1998) and Dawson (2002).

A central idea relevant here involves the hierarchical integration of cognitive processes, enabling the cognitive load of processes at a given complexity of structure to be "chunked," freeing up bandwidth for making more connections between complex considerations. It is also important to understand that the concept of cognition used here is not merely intellectual activity, but implicitly includes emotions and action at all levels in a holistic and integrative manner (similar to how Bohm conceived the system of thought). From this, it is possible to develop the thinking tools necessary to perceive and work with the kinds of complex considerations noted above. This is fueled by learning that develops robust neural networks (more on this related to neuroscience later).

Self or Ego Development

However, cognitive complexity in and of itself is not sufficient for adaptive leadership. There is a need for a maturity of the self, not only in terms of socioemotional aspects (Goleman et al., 2004) but also in terms of ethical considerations (Boaks & Levine, 2015). How a leader relates to these aspects is a central consideration of the field of ego development.

Ego development has roots in the work of Loevinger (1976), which has been built upon by Cook-Greuter (1999) and Torbert & Associates

(2004), among others. Kegan (1982, 1994) also built a related model of how the self develops. Basic to these models is that as the self-sense evolves, it increases the breadth and depth of its relationship to the world. There are a variety of descriptions marking characteristics of this growth, mostly pointing to how these increases affect capacities.

Applying these ideas to leadership was pioneered by researchers like Torbert & Associates (2004) and Kuhnert and Lewis (1987) and further developed by scholars like Joiner and Josephs (2007), Day et al. (2009), and Kegan and Lahey (2016). Findings center around the increases in effectiveness that arise from greater cognitive complexity and emotional maturity (see Reams [2017] for a more detailed account). One example of this is from Rooke and Torbert (1998), who found that successful organizational transformation efforts were highly correlated with leaders' ego development. These organizational processes require sustained adaptive leadership, which is aided by a more mature sense of self (see Chapter 2 for more perspectives on how this field informs adaptive leadership).

Learning, in this context, is synonymous with development and becomes a central driver for increasing our capacity for leadership. It develops the requisite interior condition of the intervenor for meeting complex adaptive challenges. While these facets are central to understanding leading adaptively, I would be remiss if I did not also touch upon the growing body of research in the field of neuroscience.

Neuroscience

Neuroscience has become an important component in understanding the self as the vehicle for creating the holding environment that enables adaptive work. The brain is obviously a critical tool, with for example mental acuity and cognitive complexity correlated with performance, especially related to complex, adaptive challenges that require leaders to hold complex relationships between perspectives, stakeholders, as well as contextual influences, all in dynamic consideration. I want to address two elements related to this: neuroplasticity and neurocardiology.

Neuroplasticity

Neuroplasticity (Begley, 2008) is one way of looking at the adaptive capacity we gain by working from the notion of the virtuality of self. It refers to the brain's ability to change and adapt both structure and function in response to new situations. Neural networks are not fixed in adulthood as was thought in the past but can form and disappear dynamically throughout life.

But how is this process directed? Self-directed neuroplasticity is a concept that specifically addresses the capacity to proactively modify cerebral function through volitional control and the intentional practice of focusing attention. In other words, the mind can consciously change the brain (Klein et al., 2019). As a number of researchers find the concept of mind problematic, (e.g., Mascolo & Kallio, 2019; Koplowitz, 2007), it is also possible to conceive of soul directing at least some of these processes.

The ongoing process of making robust neural connections, as noted above in relation to learning, is critical to the development of the requisite cognitive capacity for adaptive leadership. However, the importance of cleaning up has been noted as well. This means that part of what makes neural networks robust is the pruning of incoherent neural connections. Thus, neuroplasticity fits well with the conception of soul dynamically adapting the interior condition, including the brain. Yet the brain is not the only focus of neuroscience relevant here. An even more interesting branch of neuroscience is neurocardiology.

Neurocardiology

Leading from the heart is a phrase often used to imply a kind of caring, emotionally sensitive leadership. As well, we know that things like psychological safety and empathy are important to adaptive leadership (Heifetz et al., 2009). But there is more science behind this than we might have thought.

The discovery of a "little brain" of about 40,000 neurons in the heart has led to research on its nature, functioning, and potential. McCraty et al. (2009) note that the heart does far more than pump blood—it conducts a flow of information throughout the body. They found four distinct psychophysiological modes of the heart: mental focus, psychophysiological incoherence, relaxation, and psychophysiological coherence. The coherent state, understood as "a harmonious state of sustained, self-modulated positive emotion" (p. 15), is shown to have a significantly positive effect on functioning in numerous areas of health and well-being. They establish a direct link between coherent psychophysiological states as the source of emotional well-being and also show evidence for positive effects on cognitive functioning. The coherent state has significant implications for adaptive leadership.

The impact of the heart also goes into the realm of electromagnetic fields. The patterns of information with the most influence will be those with the strongest field, and "the heart generates by far the most powerful and most extensive rhythmic electromagnetic field produced in the body" (McCraty et al., 2009, p. 55). McCraty et al.'s research show that the heart has 60 times greater electrical voltage amplitude and 5,000 times stronger magnetic field than those produced by the brain. This electromagnetic field "can be measured several feet away from the body," (p. 55) thus providing "a plausible mechanism for how we can 'feel' or sense another person's presence and even their emotional state, independent of body language and other signals" (p. 55). The state of our heart not only has a significant impact on the body and brain but also generates a field that can be detected by other people. This has significant implications for how leaders create holding environments.

The interior condition of the self, cognitively, emotionally, and neurologically, is constantly creating spaces which impact how others are able to respond in a given context. Conceiving of this self as a virtual entity, with soul on the balcony dynamically adapting the self's interior condition, enables self-leadership that best supports adaptive work for all.

Soul Leading through Opening Space

It is now time to weave together the strands discussed in this chapter. Chatterjee (1998) states that "leadership is not a science or an art, it is a state of consciousness" (p. xix) and that "we can now begin to grasp the phenomenon of leadership as the field of awareness rather than a personality trait or mental attribute" (p. 24). These quotes align with the view outlined above; soul creates a field of awareness that is at the heart of a holding environment.

The type of field and holding environment our presence as soul generates has, in relation to the self, two possible directions; self-embeddedness or self-transcendence (Carey, 1992). The former reifies the self, closing space and restricting the flow of life. The latter, aided by conceiving the self as virtual, opens space and increases the flow of life. Which of the two directions we choose in our lives has a profound impact on the holding environments we create.

Quoting Gandhi, Chatterjee (1998) describes the power of lessening the resistance to this flow of life by getting out of its way; "there comes a time when an individual becomes irresistible and his action becomes all-pervasive in its effect. This comes when he reduces himself to zero" (p. 51). This does not mean we cease to exist. Rather, as soul, we realize the virtuality of self and allow the full flow of life, as spirit always becoming more than itself, to infuse the contexts in which we lead.

Circling back to the interior condition of the self, Chatterjee's assertions, applied to the virtuality of self, mean that the more coherent we can make our "virtual self," the more powerful the space we create will be. The various thoughts, feelings, and actions of this self will differentiate the flow of life with a greater perception of and sensitivity to the adaptive work faced by stakeholders we are leading.

References

Argyris, C. (1982). The executive mind and double-loop learning. *Organizational Dynamics*, 11(2), 5–22.

Axelrod, S. (2012). "Self-awareness": At the interface of executive development and psychoanalytic therapy. *Psychoanalytic Inquiry, 32*(4), 340–357. 10.1080/07351690.2011.609364

Baldwin, J. M. (1895). *Mental development of the child and the race: Methods and process*. McMillan.

Barrett, L. F. (2017). *How emotions are made: The secret life of the brain*. Houghton Mifflin Harcourt.

Begley, S. (2008). *Train your mind, change your brain: How a new science reveals our extraordinary potential to transform ourselves*. Ballantine Books.

Boaks, J., & Levine, M. P. (2015). *Leadership and ethics*. Bloomsbury Publishing.

Bohm, D. (1992). *Thought as a system*. Routledge.

Bohm, D., & Hiley, B. (1993). *The undivided universe: An ontological interpretation of quantum theory*. Routledge.

Carey, M. (1992). Transformational leadership and the fundamental option for self-transcendence. *Leadership Quarterly, 3*(3), 217–236.

Chatterjee, D. (1998). *Leading consciously: A pilgrimage toward self-mastery*. Butterworth-Heinemann.

Coad, A. F., & Berry, A. J. (1998). Transformational leadership and learning orientation. *Leadership & Organization Development Journal, 19*(3), 164–172. 10.1108/01437739810210211

Commons, M. L., Trudeau, E. J., Stein, S. A., Richards, F. A., & Krause, S. R. (1998). Hierarchical complexity of tasks shows the existence of developmental stages. *Developmental Review, 18*(3), 237–278. 10.1006/drev.1998.0467

Cook-Greuter, S. (1999). *Postautonomous ego development: A study of its nature and measurement*. [Doctoral dissertation, ProQuest Information & Learning].

Csikszentmihalyi, M., & Csikszentmihalyi, I. S. (1992). *Optimal experience: Psychological studies of flow in consciousness*. Cambridge University Press.

Davidson, R. J., & Kaszniak, A. W. (2015). Conceptual and methodological issues in research on mindfulness and meditation. *American Psychologist, 70*(7), 581–592. 10.1037/a0039512

Dawson, T. L. (2002). A comparison of three developmental stage scoring systems. *Journal of Applied Measurement, 3*(2), 146–189.

Day, D., Harrison, M., & Halpin, S. (2009). *An integrative approach to leader development: Connecting adult development, identity and expertise*. Routledge.

Fischer, K. (1980). A theory of cognitive development. The control and construction of hierarchies of skills. *Psychological Review, 87*(6), 477–531.

Goleman, D., Boyatzis, R., & McKee, A. (2004). *Primal leadership: Learning to lead with emotional intelligence*. Harvard Business Review Press.

Grint, K. (2005). *Leadership: Limits and possibilities*. Macmillan International Higher Education.

Hawkins, P. (1991). The spiritual dimension of the learning organization. *Management Education and Development, 22*(3), 172–187.

Heifetz, R. (1994). *Leadership without easy answers*. Harvard University Press.

Heifetz, R., Grashow, A., & Linsky, M. (2009). *The practice of adaptive leadership: Tools and tactics for changing your organization and the world*. Harvard Business School Press.

Jaworski, J. (2012). *Source: The inner path of knowledge creation.* Berrett-Koehler.

Joiner, B., & Josephs, S. (2007). *Leadership agility. Mastering core competencies for handling change.* Jossey-Bass.

Kahneman, D. (2011). *Thinking, fast and slow.* Penguin Books.

Kegan, R. (1982). *The evolving self: Problem and process in human development.* Harvard University Press.

Kegan, R. (1994). *In over our heads: The mental demands of modern life.* Harvard University Press.

Kegan, R., & Lahey, L. (2009). *Immunity to change: How to overcome it and unlock the potential in yourself and your organization.* Harvard Business Press.

Kegan, R., & Lahey, L. (2016). *An everyone culture: Becoming a deliberately developmental organization.* Harvard Business Review Press.

Klein, T., Kendall, B., & Tougas, T. (2019). Changing brains, changing lives: Researching the lived experience of individuals practicing self-directed neuroplasticity. [Master's thesis, St. Catherine University].

Kohlberg, L. (1984). *The psychology of moral development: The nature and validity of moral stages.* Harper & Row.

Koplowitz, H. (2007). How I lost my mind and found the meaning of "life". *Integral Review,* (4), 59–72.

Kuhnert, K. W., & Lewis, P. (1987). Transactional and transformational leadership: A constructive/developmental analysis. *Academy of Management Review, 12*(4), 648–657.

Loevinger, J. (1976). *Ego development: Concepts and theories.* Jossey-Bass.

Mascolo, M. F., & Kallio, E. (2019). Beyond free will: The embodied emergence of conscious agency. *Philosophical Psychology, 32*(4), 437–462. https://doi.org/10.1080/09515089.2019.1587910

McCraty, R., Atkinson, M., Tomasino, B., & Bradley, R. (2009). The coherent heart: Heart-brain interactions, psychophysiological coherence, and the emergence of system-wide order. *Integral Review, 5*(2), 4–107.

Piaget, J. (1954). *The construction of reality in the child.* Basic Books.

Rasmussen, H. T., & Raei, M. (2020). I'll only follow if I trust you: Using adult development to accelerate trust. In J. Reams (Ed.), *Maturing leadership: How adult development impacts leadership.* Emerald Publishing Limited.

Reams, J. (1999). Consciousness and identity: Who do we think we are? *New Ideas in Psychology, 17*(3), 309–320. 10.1016/S0732-118X(99)00030-6

Reams, J. (2012). Integral leadership. Opening space by leading through the heart. In C. Pearson (Ed.), *The transforming leader* (pp. 102–109). Berrett Koehler.

Reams, J. (2016). Immunity to change revisited: Theoretical foundations for awareness based practices for leadership development. *Integral Review, 12*(1), 65–110.

Reams, J. (2017). An overview of adult cognitive development research and its application in the field of leadership studies. *Behavioral Development Bulletin, 22*(2), 334–348. https://doi.org/10.1037/bdb0000032

Reams, J., Fikse, C., & Ness, O. (2020). Leadership development laboratory. In J. Reams (Ed.), *Maturing leadership: How adult development impacts leadership* (pp. 37–57). Emerald Group Publishing.

Robertson, J., & Timperley, H. (2011). *Leadership and learning*. Sage.

Rooke, D., & Torbert, W. R. (1998). Organizational transformation as a function of CEO's developmental stage. *Organizational Development Journal*, *16*(1), 11–28.

Rowson, J. (2008). *From wisdom-related knowledge to wise acts: Refashioning the conception of wisdom to improve our chances of becoming wiser*. [Doctoral dissertation, University of Bristol].

Scharmer, O. (2002). Illuminating the blind spot. *Leader to Leader Journal*, (24), 11–14.

Scharmer, O. (2007). *Theory U: Leading from the future as it emerges*. The Society for Organizational Learning, Inc.

Senge, P. (1990). *The fifth discipline. The art & practice of the learning organization*. Random House.

Snowden, D. J., & Boone, M. E. (2007). A leader's framework for decision making. *Harvard Business Review*, *85*(11), 1–8.

The Arbinger Institute. (2006). *The anatomy of peace: Resolving the heart of conflict*. Berrett Koehler.

Torbert, W., & Associates. (2004). *Action inquiry. The secret of timely and transforming action*. Berrett-Koehler.

Vygotsky, L. S. (1978). *Mind in society: The development of higher psychological processes*. Harvard University Press.

Part II
Adaptive Leadership in Action

6 Adaptive Practices on Global Virtual Teams

Lejla Bilal

The current global pandemic has created new challenges in an already complex world. Our increased reliance on technology, hurried responses to rapid change, and awareness of global interconnectedness continue to evolve and create new uncertainties for organizations, teams, and leaders. Under such circumstances, new capabilities and problem-solving techniques are required, calling for an adaptive leadership approach. Adaptive leadership is a way of practicing leadership that helps groups, organizations, and societies deal with adaptive challenges (Heifetz, 1994). Adaptive leadership requires identifying technical and adaptive challenges. Technical challenges often have an existing solution whereas adaptive challenges require a mindset shift, learning, and a new set of actions. With remote and virtual work becoming the norm, current ineffective solutions need to be abandoned and new approaches to encountered problems will be needed.

Global Virtual Teams (GVTs) are an example of an adaptive response to an adapted environment, where teams must operate within the constraints of working virtually. Their work is conducted across barriers such as space, time, and cultures. At the start of the twenty-first century, adaptability was not only deemed a desired employee and organizational trait, but a required one in a globalized business environment (Silverthorne, 2000). During pandemic-related office closures in many parts of the world, members of GVTs were truly able to work from anywhere and it seems likely that organizational reliance on virtual teams as a solution to new work norms will only continue to increase. Even though the degree of virtuality across such barriers will vary, GVTs will continue to offer both temporal and geographic flexibility with the focus on retaining the best talent. In a recent study from the Academy of Management, work-from-anywhere produced a productivity effect of a 4.4% increase in output (Choudhury et al., 2020).

By their very nature, GVTs often face unpredictable work experiences that call for adaptive leadership practices, with ever-changing work and priorities that introduce new types of problems. Some obstacles have solutions that can be mandated, whereas others require a commitment to learning and reframing the difficulties the team faces. Furthermore, GVTs

DOI: 10.4324/9781003099109-6

are said to exist in environments capable of facilitating innovative solutions, making these teams essential for business going forward. Wergin (2020) proposes, however, that adaptation is not a natural response for most organizations which prioritize production over innovation. Interventions that focus on the needs of organizations, teams, and team members that curb anxiety induced by uncertainty can encourage change-capable business practices within organizations and beyond.

GVTs in the Era of COVID-19

While the global economy was forced to adapt quickly in the midst of a global pandemic, it experienced a crisis that will carry its effects long into the recovery period. According to research from the Brookings Institute, in 2020 the global economy experienced its deepest recession since World War II, disrupting not only economic activity, but travel, supply chains, and much more (Dieppe & Kose, 2020). The human element of this pandemic will likely see longstanding mental health and wellbeing concerns that companies will need to address with their workforce including collective grief, prolonged physical distancing, and associated social isolation (Goldmann & Galea, 2014). GVTs provide a team structure that supports a digital-first approach to conducting business and education. Digital-first approaches address a world engaged in rapid adaptation as well as respond positively to the COVID-19 crises. The time has come to adopt a digital-first approach, one that prepares world citizens instead of leaving even more behind as the world continues to globalize.

This chapter will discuss research on GVTs and their capacity to address the adaptive challenges of the 21st century. It includes key takeaways from the scholarship and practice that may inform adaptive leaders and international cooperation as the global economy mends and prepares for a crisis-primed workplace in the future, one that includes appropriate infrastructure and preventive measures to support potential shifts such as those which occurred through the COVID-19 pandemic. GVTs existed pre-pandemic and, particularly with the trajectory of projected work-from-anywhere practices, these teams are here to stay and may soon represent the norm.

Adaptive Leadership Practices on GVTs

The basic structure of teams supports the theoretical underpinnings of adaptive leadership, which assumes a more flexible power structure. To employ adaptive leadership practices on GVTs, leading from a new perspective is required, with a team leadership process that enables all members of the team to exhibit leadership as situations call for their individual expertise. Heifetz et al. (2009) provide some guiding principles for leading adaptively:

- Moving between the balcony view and the practice field (on the ground);
- Relying on distributed knowledge and expertise (knowledge capital or collective knowledge); and
- Encouraging leadership from all team members (team leadership).

GVTs and the Balcony

A key principle of adaptive leadership is the reference to the metaphor of "getting on the balcony" (Heifetz et al., 2009, p. 7) to describe a perspective that can be gained from afar. A balcony view provides a vantage point of the whole system to inform action and strategies needed on the ground. Often when there is a disturbance in day-to-day work, a distanced perspective offers insight to inform direction. When all work is conducted virtually, however, finding this vantage point can be challenging. The role of team members becomes increasingly important as each will have their own perspective on any given situation that will likely differ from others. This is especially vital when working cross-functionally.

Constant changes and shifts in priorities are a common occurrence for GVTs. Shifting between the overall objective and day-to-day tactical work ensures that a team's tasks are on track and in line with established goals and project deliverables. In times of crisis, individuals tend to focus their time and efforts on tactical work (McGregor & Doshi, 2020), potentially missing the need to adapt to new obstacles and focus on larger challenges that deserve attention. Gaining fresh perspective from the balcony can offer new approaches that can then become action. With cross-functional teams, perspective-taking is a useful strategy for considering different points of view. Perspective-taking is a technique to step outside one's own experience and imagine the emotions, perceptions, and motivations of another (Livermore, 2016). It begins with the realization that two individuals presented with the same information might have two completely different perspectives. Perspective-taking is an essential part of cultural intelligence and culturally intelligent innovation. A globally dispersed, diverse team offers built-in opportunities to take on the perspectives of others, including clients and product users from around the world.

Distributed Expertise

GVTs naturally build collective knowledge through the social capital gained from members' external networks. Each team member provides expertise from their own function, experience, and skill set to contribute to problem-solving and perspective-taking. Formal leaders do not have all the answers necessary to address an identified problem in adaptive work. GVT members contribute project knowledge and abilities, allowing solutions to be determined collectively and in response to adaptive environments that include complexities such as culture, time, geography, and functions.

It was at one time unthinkable for leaders to admit they did not possess all the answers. In today's globalized and fast-paced world, it is equally unthinkable for one person to remain the sole authority and resource for knowledge and effectively resolve adaptive challenges. Adaptive leaders instead tap into their networks for solutions and direction. The nature of adaptive work requires leaders to exercise and model learning agility, to be comfortable with the unknown (Pico, 2018). Learning agility refers to the ability and willingness to learn from experimentation, using new strategies to prepare for an increasingly complex world (Mitchinson & Morris, 2020). It is key to the ability to adapt to change on a personal and organizational level.

Shared Responsibility for Team Leadership

GVTs are heterogeneous across national and regional cultural dimensions. The role of leadership can be viewed as more authoritative when team members represent cultures that value higher degrees of titular power distance and hierarchy (Hofstede, 2001). Whereas hierarchical culture will permeate organizational and team culture, teams can still establish their own norms and practices that value a shared model of leadership. A team culture that values distributing leadership in more lateral, less hierarchical, ways will encourage leadership from all members (Northouse, 2018). Duarte and Snyder (2006) suggest redistributing leadership roles in relation to the problem at hand and team members' areas of expertise. This is especially important for the complex projects GVTs are assembled to complete.

Distributing leadership across a team means that each team member must be encouraged to lead and adopt a leadership perspective. Informal leadership on teams is emergent, given the immediate needs of specific situations. Within a team, a formal leader may not always be the *real* leader in a particular setting (Northouse, 2013). Emergent, or informal, leadership is not assigned; it is acknowledged by others through acceptance of the emerging leader's behavior and the degree of influence that the individual holds within the group or organization. In a healthy GVT, formal team leaders are willing to encourage and even facilitate shared leadership and responsibility across team members. Shared responsibility on teams, like organizations, equates to high adaptive capability.

The more shared responsibility is standardized and nurtured, the more likely team members will contribute to the organization as a whole. On GVTs, shared responsibility can take the form of cross-functional problem-solving and resource sharing across functions or departments. Heifetz et al. (2009) offer some indicators of shared responsibility for

Table 6.1 Shared Responsibility Signals for Organizations Employing GVTs

Indicator	Implication
Rewards established on a team level, not just individual contributions.	This stresses a team dynamic which is based on a shared purpose and outcome
Sharing resources across functions and departments.	Providing an opportunity to engage in something different at work can help keep team members engaged and actively involved across their organization(s).
Sharing ideas and lessons learned across various boundaries.	Knowledge banks or resources (documents, videos, meeting minutes, etc.) can provide the historical knowledge needed to save time and energy for new hires on GVTs, whose dispersed members work around-the-clock cross-functionally.
Promoting individuals who have acquired a wide range of experiences working in different areas.	Creating a team profile that includes individual members' skills and expertise can empower members of a team to contribute to other organizational projects or functions, and at the same time highlight knowledge gaps.
Promoting learning and "job shadowing" (p. 169) to acquire best practices and experiences	Normalizing learning should be viewed as an essential task during a workday or week given the course of globalization and digital innovations shaping the future of work organizations as we know it.

organizations, which can be applied to a GVT or a sector to which a GVT belongs. These indicators are listed in Table 6.1 with additional implications for GVTs to consider.

These indicators serve as guides that can inform leadership interventions, mindset shifts, and solutions to what Heifetz et al. deemed adaptive challenges. These guides are fluid due to the continued trajectory of virtual work, as well as the evolving landscape of the global workforce that brings considerable diversity to GVTs, including members' values, work styles, and points of view. These differences impact the ways in which GVTs approach technical and adaptive challenges.

Technical and Adaptive Challenges on GVTs

In a recent study examining the experience of working on a GVT, technical and adaptive challenges were identified as barriers to successful GVTs. These included working with others who are globally dispersed across distance, time, and culture, technology as a medium for communication, people and project management, knowledge sharing, and appropriate tools (Maley, 2020). Of particular note was that technical

Table 6.2 Technical and Adaptive Challenges on GVTs

Theme	Technical Challenge	Adaptive Challenge
Team Design		
Physical dispersion	x	x
Project specifics	x	x
Roles	x	x
Cross-cultural Communication		
Language	x	x
Error-recognition	x	x
Asking for/receiving help		x
People Dynamics		
Trust	x	x
Relationship building		x
Knowledge sharing		x
Technology		
Appropriate tools	x	x
Tech challenges	x	x
Adequate bandwidth	x	

problems, with seemingly simple solutions, took on more adaptive aspects in a GVT environment, requiring additional learning and full team member involvement. Table 6.2 provides four categories of challenges experienced by GVTs (Maley, 2020), classified here as technical or adaptive to serve as a guide to GVTs as they develop best practices. These themes are explained below.

Team Design

This theme refers to the team membership in terms of (1) member location, (2) project specifics such as meeting frequency, deadlines, and priorities, and (3) roles and role clarity when working cross-functionally. Within this theme, solutions for encountered problems such as time zone inconveniences, meeting logistics, and role clarity/reporting structures can be reinforced through team charters and formal announcements. However, time zones is one element that requires adaptability and special considerations to meet the needs of team members. For example, rotating who on the team is inconvenienced due to extreme time zone differences can help convey the value placed on individuals and their time. Future project planning should take into account the severity of the burden time zones place on team members, their functioning, and project demands. A more regional team design, or one with a decreased degree of dispersion where possible can be helpful. Working virtually does not have to be detrimental to team functioning, but it should be made clear to teams, early on, that certain criteria must be established to guide virtual facilitation to ensure all voices are heard, everyone is using shared language, and talk times are established and cued.

Cross-Cultural Communication

For organizations seeking to become more innovative and adaptive, culture is often the biggest challenge. It cannot be achieved through mandate or top-down approaches; culture lies in the team's shared perceptions (Walker & Soule, 2017). Error recognition, for instance, can be experienced in a cultural context where participants specifically do not bring attention to errors until they are noticed by others (Maley, 2020). Formal leaders play an essential role in creating and modeling psychological safety on a GVT, where acknowledging errors is part of the learning and regular work process. A psychologically safe environment refers to the ways in which members of a team work together, where they value each other's knowledge and input, share information openly, and discuss mistakes without feeling threatened, or fear being penalized (Edmondson, 1999).

It is important for GVT members to encourage communication practices that reinforce interpersonal communication skills and cultural awareness, as certain cultural aspects can influence, as examples, error recognition or a willingness to ask for help. There is a link between relational interaction and communication practices in the workplace and learning and organizational effectiveness. (For greater emphasis on the role of learning in adaptive leadership, see Chapter 2). Leaders of GVTs need to ensure differences that create tensions are managed, or work to maintain creative tension to facilitate team members' individual awareness of cultural competence as preliminary to team level cultural intelligence. Success on a GVT extends well beyond mastering technical skills. It requires people skills and primary challenges on GVTs relate to knowledge sharing and trust (Maley, 2020). These are explored in more depth next.

People Dynamics

As noted above, two aspects of people dynamics are primary: knowledge sharing and trust. Knowledge sharing is an essential part of team functioning. When team members do not have access to information, it hinders productivity. The lack of proper knowledge sharing between team members may cause projects and even organizations to fail if successful strategies are not implemented (Davidavičienė et al., 2020). Knowledge sharing refers to internal and external sources of knowledge and information. Effective team members work together to implement sustainable practices for knowledge and information sharing. Knowledge sharing practices are influenced by culture, motivation, leadership, information communication technology, conflict, low trust, and language barriers and differences (2020).

Trust is an essential building block to relationships and is adaptive in nature, as it is personal and involves emotion. Trust is vital to maintain what Heifetz (1994) refers to as a holding environment and takes time to develop. Trust is also one of the most studied variables of virtual teams (Gilson et al, 2015). Working virtually is itself an impediment to human interaction and the development of trust because the scope for building trust relies on psychological safety and ongoing (tacit) interactions (2015), not possible in GVTs. As well, GVTs are typically task oriented (Jarvenpaa et al., 1998); confidence in team members' abilities to perform the functions of their role competently is required early on to build trust. "Swift trust" is a type of trust with "less emphasis on feeling, commitment, and exchange and more on action" (Meyerson et al., 1996, p. 191). It is dependent upon the establishment of intrapersonal competence, interpersonal confidence, and trust in the system in which the team dynamics take place. Swift trust allows for vagueness and uncertainty as a unique form of collective perception, while team members focus on tasks at hand, assuming confidence in team members' abilities from the onset. The quicker team members can display honesty and goodwill, the quicker swift trust can be prompted. Zakaria and Mohd Yusof (2020) further support the notion of competence-based trust on task-oriented teams and contend that they "perceive trust as dependent on the quality of the performance and deliverables produced by team members; they are most concerned with the tasks and roles being performed by the team" (p.14). Importantly, swift trust is conditional and not necessarily a substitute for trust that is earned through ongoing interaction. It asks team members to give their colleagues the benefit of the doubt to get the job done.

Opportunities for small talk were identified as a need as well as an outcome of collaborative work processes (Maley, 2020). Because diverse teams struggle with building inter-member trust, planned efforts such as opportunities for informal conversations integrated into regular communication are surprisingly beneficial. Although challenging, successful GVTs have found ways to navigate technology-supported informal communication through strategies associated with media richness theory, discussed later in this chapter.

Technology

The availability of information communication technology is a logistical solution to knowledge sharing and trust-building. Technology itself may suggest forthright solutions, but it is people who interact with technology. On a GVT, technology is the medium for communication and project and team management, which adds layers of complexity to teamwork. Explored later in this chapter through adaptive structuration theory (AST), what is notable here is the basic provision of appropriate tools and adequate bandwidth so that team members feel equipped to meet the technical demands of their function. Also critical to GVTs are systems to address the inevitable challenges that arise, that require learning, adaptability, and coordination. Policies and procedures to support a culture that integrates expertise to create a collaborative and highly functioning team can provide guidelines to ensure team members have access to information they need to fulfill the duties of their role and feel valued as contributing members. This requires cohesion, an understanding of the importance of working collaboratively, and valuing varying expertise across the team, business unit, and organization, all while operating virtually.

Generally, technical challenges can be corrected by mandate, such as scheduling meetings across space and time, establishing roles, and offering opportunities for learning and professional development. Adaptive challenges require input from the team as a whole, not just leadership. These may include how the team responds and handles constant changes in priority and scope, knowledge sharing, relationship building, cultural communication factors, personal and work-style preferences that can create conflict, decision-making practices, error-recognition, and asking for/receiving help as identified in research on the experience of working on a GVT (Maley, 2020). This next section examines potential intervention strategies.

Interventions to Technical and Adaptive Challenges on GVTs

The top challenges on teams include both structural (task-based) and those that are more people-oriented, both of which exist on GVTs. I suggest that task-based challenges have more technical solutions, whereas those that are more people-oriented require adaptive practices. GVTs require more structure and formal processes to perform their work (Lurey & Raisinghani, 2001). Individual team members' roles, primary objectives, and priorities, and processes for knowledge sharing and trust-building must be explicit, not simply assumed. Without clear understanding of goals and roles, the progress of members may become stymied.

Adaptive Structuration Theory

Clarity is especially critical in a GVT; ambiguity may impede understanding and functioning. Thus, organizational leaders who try to improve the performance of virtual teams by simply providing them with more advanced technologies may be misdirecting their resources. Deliberate technology tools can be considered, but also team engagement strategies. Adaptive structuration theory (AST) describes the interplay between advanced information technologies, social structures, and human interaction, with specific attention to the role GVT members play in their social system. It calls for group members to actively adapt rules and resources in order to accomplish decision-making goals (Griffin, 2008). How technology is brought into human interaction for purposes of accomplishing team-based tasks, and how groups organize themselves can also be examined through AST.

AST scholars DeSanctis and Gallupe (1987) examined group decision support systems (GDSS), interactive technologies that facilitate group discussion and decision making, remove communication barriers, provide techniques for structuring decision making, and offer systematic direction, guiding timing and content. Video conferencing tools such as Zoom, WebEx, or GoToMeeting can support virtual decision-making processes with features such as breakout rooms, whiteboards, and private messaging to stimulate brainstorming. These functions offer less intimidating environments than whole group meeting rooms where participants may compete for airtime and speak over one another. GDSS can play an important role in adaptive work in a virtual environment as their use, as in the examples above, can facilitate a more psychologically safe holding environment, one that provides safety and structure for individuals to share and discuss their ideas regarding challenging, adaptive work.

More advanced collaboration technologies, such as web-based GDSS, have various origins. Chen et al. (2007) designed TeamSpirit to support decision-making on virtual teams. This GDSS includes (1) the provision of anonymous input of ideas and votes from those less likely to speak up about a controversial idea, (2) ratings or rankings of suggestions, (3) simultaneous display of multiple items on a shared screen, such as the agenda or a timer, and (4) analytic aids such as probability assessment models, decision trees, and social judgment models to preference tasks (DeSanctis & Gallupe, 1987).

Media Richness Theory

Media richness theory is a framework that describes a given communication medium's ability to achieve the intended communication exchange (Daft & Lengel, 1984). To assess the richness of proposed media, immediate feedback mechanisms, number of cues used, number of channels, and personalization of the message and variety of language used are considered. Particularly important is that the more ambiguous the task, the greater the need for richer technology selection; adaptive challenges are frequently ambiguous. Media richness is ranked from high to low, with the highest-ranked medium being face-to-face opportunities, for instance, videoconferencing, and the lowest document sharing

(Gu et al., 2011). Multiple types of media may be appropriate to meet the needs and preferences of team members, an example being a follow-up written text after a video call when some team members may not be as versatile in the spoken language as others.

In a GVT, it is important to note that tolerance for ambiguity will vary as it is influenced by culture (Hofstede et al., 2001). Media richness thus becomes a key consideration in a GVT's holding environment. Reliance on visual cues and personalizing messages will guide the delivery of intended meanings; they can also strengthen a GVT's group cohesion. Successful GVTs establish elements identified by Heifetz et al. (2009) to strengthen team bonds and equalize tensions as they appear. These include creating shared language around issues and topics, identifying shared values and purposes, and deliberate focus on trust among team members and authority figures. On a GVT, such norms and practices can be conveyed using a team charter in which all members of a team contribute desired expectations they wish to codify. These team-contributed norms can and should be revisited as gentle or explicit reminders to reinforce the value of team members' contributions and established best practices.

Many characteristics inherent in a physical space that trigger fresh perspectives outside of the workplace cannot be replicated in a virtual environment, but careful design can use the notion of "offsite" to establish new processes and norms (e.g., virtual photo backgrounds or working outdoors). Today's technological interactions include visual cues (e.g., "raise hand" function) and, as another example, the ability to mute all attendees. These features help minimize disruption and interruption where there are multiple attendees as long as everyone is paying attention to the screen. Important from the outside is the establishment of these types of logistics so as not to disrupt team members' engagement in adaptive work. It can be helpful to survey team members about their preferred communication, knowledge sharing, and project management tools in order to establish commitment. These tools allow the creation of team channels, file sharing, direct messaging, and platform integration, enabling virtual work to replace or supplement traditional "brick and mortar" work practices. Furthermore, communication through electronic connectivity is possible at any time of day and from any place, assuming quality and reliable technical support is available as needed.

Embracing Adaptive Work on GVTs

Adaptive work frequently involves disequilibrium. People's natural tendencies are to avoid situations and conversations that cause distress and, in a virtual environment, it is easy to remain invisible. However, adaptive challenges often cannot be addressed without facilitating some level of distress in order to stimulate learning.

For GVTs, uncertainty is the norm; change and reprioritization are constant as is the need to learn (Maley, 2020). Approaching adaptive work on a GVT through a learning stance generates some amount of disequilibrium, driving team members from their comfort zone with small amounts of pressure applied until sufficient uncertainty is established to enable deep learning and reconsideration of pre-established patterns. The ways in which learning opportunities are framed can foster commitment to embrace the uncertainty and discomfort that accompanies adaptive work. Successful engagement in adaptive work cannot be forced upon a team. Embracing adaptive change requires, above all, a strong holding environment. In GVTs holding environments involve, in addition to the types of support that would occur in a face-to-face environment (e.g., categorizing challenges as technical or adaptive, psychologically safe practices, etc.) media-rich technology and strong team norms that account for the unique complexity inherent in GVTs to drive desired, collective outcomes.

A final consideration to addressing adaptive work on GVTs relates to the values that guide problem-solving and decision-making. It is essential that these values be identified and remain explicit. Naming default interpretations, such as familiar and comfortable ways of problem-solving (Heifetz et al., 2009), can help kickstart adaptive work on GVTs. Once a GVT has a reliable and strong holding environment cultural norms and values, potential losses associated with adaptive work (i.e., time, comfort), hidden alliances (sub-groups within a GVT), default interpretations (i.e., placing blame on vendors or lack of clarity from team leaders), and other sensitive topics can be named and openly discussed. Adaptive leaders can use political savviness to unpack relationships and concerns between team members while building awareness into team members' interests, loyalties, and losses, including those that spark resistance to change. Multiple interpretations of values and default behaviors can be encouraged in ways that drive creative brainstorming and share viewpoints that consider potential, often non-obvious solutions. Here the diversity on a GVT can be harnessed to its fullest potential, drawing perspective across national boundaries and cultures to contribute unique and flexible responses to adaptive challenges (Sole & Edmondson, 2002). Thus, with the right structural and people-centered support, GVTs are well equipped to perform in tomorrow's world, an environment with ongoing uncertainty and inevitable change.

References

Choudhury, P., Foroughi, C., & Larson, B. Z. (2020). Work-from-anywhere: The productivity effects of geographic flexibility. *Academy of Management Proceedings*, 1, 655–683. 10.5465/AMBPP.2020.225

Chen, M., Liou, Y., Wang, C.W., Fan, Y. W., & Chi, Y. J. (2007). TeamSpirit: Design, implementation, and evaluation of a Web-based group decision support system. *Decision Support Systems*, *43*(4), 1186–1202.

Daft, R. L., & Lengel, R. H. (1984). Information richness: A new approach to managerial behavior and organization design. *Research in Organizational Behavior*, *6*, 191–233. 10.21236/ada128980

Dieppe, A., & Kose, A. (2020). The global productivity slump: What policies to rekindle. Global Economy and Development at Brookings. https://www.brookings.edu/multi-chapter-report/reimagining-the-global-economy-building-back-better-in-a-post-covid-19-world/

Davidavičienė V., Al Majzoub K., & Meidute-Kavaliauskiene, I. (2020). Factors affecting knowledge sharing in virtual teams. *Sustainability*, *12*(17), 1–15. 10.3390/su12176917

DeSanctis, G., & Gallupe, R. B. (1987). A foundation for the study of group decision support systems. *Management Science*, *33*(2), 589–609. https://pubsonline.informs.org/doi/abs/10.1287/mnsc.33.5.589

Duarte, D. L., Snyder, N. T. (2006). *Mastering virtual teams: strategies, tools, and techniques that succeed* (3rd ed.). Jossey-Bass.

Edmondson, A. (1999). Psychological safety and learning behavior in work teams. *Administrative Science Quarterly*, *44*(2), 350–383. 10.2307/2666999

Gilson, L. L., Maynard, M. T., Young, N. C. J., Vartiainen, M., & Hakonen, M. (2015). Virtual teams research: 10 years, 10 themes, and 10 opportunities. *Journal of Management*, *41*(5), 1313–1337. 10.1177/0149206314559946

Goldmann, E., & Galea, S. (2014). Mental health consequences of disasters. *Annual Review of Public Health*, *35*, 169–183. https://www.annualreviews.org/doi/10.1146/annurev-publhealth-032013-182435

Griffin, E. (2008). *A first look at communication theory* (7th ed.). McGraw-Hill Companies, Inc.

Gu, R., Higa, K., & Moodie, D. R. (2011). A study on communication media selection: Comparing the effectiveness of the media richness, social influence, and media fitness. *Journal of Service Science and Management*, *4*(03), 291–299. 10.4236/jssm.2011.43035

Heifetz, R. A. (1994). *Leadership without easy answers*. Harvard University Press.

Heifetz, R., Grashow, A., & Linsky, M. (2009). *The practice of adaptive leadership: Tools and tactics for changing your organization and the world*. Harvard Business Press.

Hofstede, G. (2001). *Culture's consequences: Comparing values, behaviors and institutions across nations*. Sage.

Jarvenpaa, S. L., Knoll, K., & Leidner, D. E. (1998). Is anybody out there? Antecedents of trust in global virtual teams. *Journal of Management Information Systems*, *14*(4), 29–64. 10.1080/07421222.1998.11518185

Livermore, D. (2016). *Driven by difference: How great companies fuel innovation through diversity*. AMACOM.

Lurey, J. S., & Raisinghani, M. S. (2001). An empirical study of best practices in virtual teams. *Information & Management*, *38*(8), 523–544. 10.1016/s0378-7206(01)00074-x

McGregor, L., & Doshi, N. (2020). How to keep your team motivated, remotely. *Harvard Business Review*. https://hbr.org/2020/04/how-to-keep-your-team-motivated-remotely

Maley, L. (2020). Maley, L. B. (2020). *Teaming at a distance: The work experience on global virtual teams* [Doctoral Dissertation, Antioch University]. AURA. https://aura.antioch.edu/etds/566

Meyerson, D., Weick, K. E. & Kramer, R. M. (1996). Swift trust and temporary groups. In Kramer, R. M. & Tyler, T. R. (Eds.), *Trust in Organizations: Frontiers of Theory and Research* (pp. 166–195). Sage. http://dx.doi.org/10.4135/9781452243610.n9

Mitchinson, A., & Morris, R. (2020). Learning about learning agility [White paper]. Center for Creative Leadership (CCL). https://cclinnovation.org/wp-content/uploads/2020/02/learningagility.pdf

Northouse, P. G. (2013). *Leadership: Theory and practice* (6th edition). Sage.

Northouse, P. G. (2018). *Leadership: Theory and practice* (8th edition). Sage.

Pico, J. (2018). *The importance of learning agility* [Video File]. https://www.linkedin.com/learning/creating-a-culture-of-change/the-importance-of-learning-agility?u=2207324

Silverthorne, C. (2000). Situational leadership theory in Taiwan: A different culture perspective. *Leadership and Organization Development Journal*, 21(2), 68–74. 10.1108/01437730010318156

Sole, D., & Edmondson, A. (2002). Situated knowledge and learning in dispersed teams. *British Journal of Management*, 13(2), 17–34. 10.1111/1467-8551.13.s2.3

Walker, B., & Soule, S. (2017). Changing company culture requires a movement, not a mandate. *Harvard Business Review*. https://hbr.org/2017/06/changing-company-culture-requires-a-movement-not-a-mandate

Wergin, J. (2020). *Deep learning in a disorienting world*. Cambridge University Press.

Zakaria, N., & Mohd Yusof, S. A. (2020). Crossing cultural boundaries using the internet: Toward building a model of swift trust formation in global virtual teams. *Journal of International Management*, 26(1), 1–19. 10.1016/j.intman.2018.10.004

7 Leading from Betwixt and Between: Exploring How Liminal, Rhizomic Spaces Shape, Deepen, and Sustain Adaptive Leadership Mindsets within Complex Healthcare Systems

Renee Charney and Lisa Gick

We are standing on a precipice of seismic change. In many ways we have already crossed that threshold and have reexperienced what we know to be true—that change is a constant. Our lives are challenged by environmental, physical, and emotional provocations—social upheaval, mental illness, a warming climate, and a global pandemic—all creating stress about our present and our future. As we long for a return to normal, how might that be redefined? How will we find sure footing to navigate what is before us? Who will we become? We long for what is familiar, certain, and stable; we wonder if we have the means to adapt to what is unknown and uncertain.

But we also know that life is never certain or stable; change happens, often abruptly and unexpectedly and, when it does, we have a choice—shift and adapt, or resist and ignore. For example, the recent COVID-19 pandemic, stealthy and ubiquitous in its spread, steered us into a state of liminality, teetering on an edge of global uncertainty. News about the pandemic's spread and guidance for how to navigate individual and societal care was inconsistent, if not actively harmful. Countries, regions, and cities were exposed to the outbreak, received uneven updates, and instituted precautions that were inconsistently loose or tight, breeding a lack of confidence in what was true or untrue regarding how to protect ourselves and others—or how to navigate life overall. This liminal place has forced us to learn new ways of being and to shift mindsets and actions for humanity's sake.

Liminality, a term that originated in the field of anthropology (Gennep, 2013), describes an existence between two stages or places, a fold of time and space that is a gateway to another state of being, an offer to consider and become other. According to Richard Rohr, "liminality is a form of holding the tension between one space and another. It is in these transitional moments of our lives that authentic transformation can happen"

DOI: 10.4324/9781003099109-7

(2020, p. 17). Living in liminality can feel chaotic and disruptive; it can also present new learning (and unlearning) opportunities for leaders to develop other ways of being and leading. Volatility provides leaders a chance to deepen capacities for adapting to uncertainty and to provide firm footing for others even during wrenching times of transition and uncertainty. Liminal times offer opportunities for leaders to demonstrate their greatest impact.

Healthcare leaders and practitioners were ushered into a pandemic-chaotic world that called for adaptive thinking and being in ways that are often tough, tender, and turbulent, resulting in making decisions about, and executing, care procedures that are far less dependent on what has been done in the past. Tried-and-tested procedures became less reliable, driving practitioners to break from tradition and improvise on a less-tested or un-tested path. Doctors, nurses, and lab technicians were forced into a liminal space, in the middle of uncharted territory, crafting innovative solutions on the fly in an effort to care for the sick and dying. This way of working increases stress and imparts even more uncertainty; breaking away from well-charted territory and finding a way around unknowns does not often align with their medical training.

This way of learning, unlearning, testing, retesting, thinking, acting, and being becomes what Deleuze and Guattari (1987) described as rhizomic nonlinear, nonhierarchical, and nonbinary. Deleuze and Guattari developed rhizome theory as a philosophical lens to describe how culture and society thrives by appreciating and incorporating multiplistic and heterogeneous perspectives, a way to engage with problems or situations in a cartographic, maplike way, where an individual can encounter a problem from various access points and not be locked into a singular solution or direction. It is a theory that invites creative and curious pursuit rather than the stasis of rote or fixed methods.

Rhizome theory, based on the metaphor of a rhizome's growth, is inspired by horticulture; grass, ginger, quaking aspens, and bamboo are all rhizomes. Such growth is described as directionally adventitious and is considered resilient, connected, multidirectional, and somewhat unpredictable (Deleuze & Guattari, 1987). Rhizome theory offers a lens through which to consider (and observe) ways for leaders to engage, adapt, and act that reach beyond legacy and traditional adaptive theories and frameworks, and is particularly suited as a lens to examine the changes that occur within liminal space. This provides access to greater creativity, curiosity, and the multiplicity of ideas. It is a way of thinking and being that is less directed or narrativized and more fluid or multidirectional. Deleuze and Guattari (1987) describe this way as "being in the middle" of things, thus allowing for new thought to promote new perspective; it conjures a more dynamic approach rather than one that is fixed. A disease such as COVID-19, which emerged like a battlefield ambush, calls for an immediate reframe, a step back before stepping forward, a remaining in the middle to allow space to observe its attack and to consider heterogeneous perspectives and solutions by which to address its spread.

Throughout the COVID-19 pandemic healthcare practitioners and leaders needed to reframe in the moment, make quick (and often untested) decisions, and deliver care in unconventional and extraordinary ways. Patients were treated for symptoms that were disguised as common malaise only to learn that their bodies were unresponsive to well-practiced, proven treatments, thereby prompting abrupt and experimental shifts in care. The need for clear thinking while in the throes of life-and-death situations increased enormously.

One example was the treatment of patients who had difficulty breathing. In the beginning of the pandemic, healthcare practitioners followed standard accepted procedures: providing oxygen and propping patients up on their backs. Over time, physicians came to realize that the low-oxygen symptoms patients experienced were unlike what they had treated in the past and were not sufficiently alleviated using standard methods. They learned, through experimentation, that by turning patients on their stomachs (a procedure called "proning"), they were able to breathe more easily without the immediate intervention of additional oxygen (Astua et al., 2020). If healthcare practitioners had stayed the course and focused on following past procedures, they would have never discovered the alternative. By experimenting, reframing, and adapting a different approach, they discovered one that was more effective and lifesaving.

The goal of this chapter is to demonstrate that healthcare is encountering seismic change in new ways and that we can use the changes that healthcare is experiencing as examples of how we can all effectively shape, deepen, and sustain curious, adaptive leadership mindsets. We offer a way to see possibility in examining how to navigate those changes, a way that is nonlinear, holds fewer boundaries, and is opportunistic. We present this landscape within a context of liminal and rhizomic sensibilities (Deleuze & Guattari, 1987; Gennep, 2013), while recognizing contextual elements across and within systems that offer a foundation to expand capacity for curious and adaptive mindsets.

It is through the aperture of liminal, rhizomic, and adaptive leader mindsets and behaviors, and from themes collected and analyzed from healthcare practitioners' and leaders' experiential stories within their ever-changing environments, that we offer an alternative to consider how to lead and adapt within complex systems. The authors will place in the context of complex healthcare systems how leading in the liminal space intersects and extends opportunities for leaders to engage differently in the modern world through the experiences of adaptive leadership and its practice.

Healthcare Organizations as Complex Systems

In their review of complexity leadership in healthcare, Belrhiti et al. (2018) indicate that health systems are acknowledged to be complex systems, even though complexity theories for the study of leadership inside of healthcare have received limited attention. Even so, the authors identify in their research a reluctance in the healthcare industry to self-establish a mindset of inherent operational or systemic complexity; rather, some posit that complexity in healthcare is only situational (Belrhiti et al., 2018), or driven by a particular circumstance versus the contextual experience. For the purpose of this chapter, we will anchor healthcare systems in the contextual domain of the discussion, holding that the landscape in which healthcare systems operate today invites a more expansive and overarching mindset to navigate the experiences of the day in an open, emergent, creative, and curious way. In this view, we can say a healthcare organization is a complex adaptive system, comprised of a diverse group of people who interact spontaneously through self-organization (Bailey et al., 2012). In 2007, Uhl-Bien et al. developed an overarching framework for studying complexity leadership theory, "a leadership paradigm that focuses on enabling the learning, creative, and adaptive capacity of complex adaptive systems within the context of knowledge-producing organizations" (Uhl-Bien et al., 2007, p. 298). Complex adaptive systems are dynamic systems able to adapt and evolve in a changing environment (Uhl-Bien & Arena, 2017). Leadership arises in the interactions among the system members as they adapt through their work together; in this way, all members of the system have leader capacity (Bailey et al., 2012). (For an in-depth description of organizational complexity concepts, see Chapter 1.)

Effective clinical decision-making requires a holistic approach (which is generally lacking) that accepts unpredictability and builds on subtle emergent forces within the overall system (Wilson, et al., 2001). In a healthcare system, the development and application of clinical guidelines, caring for the multiple clinical and social needs of a patient, and coordinating development of education needs within a department are all examples of complex experiences that require adaptive focus (Wilson, et al., 2001). Linking the experience of complexity with adaptive behaviors reinforces the notion of healthcare organizations as complex adaptive systems. Whereas initial instincts may be to apply reductionist thinking in an effort to "fix," or narrow in on a "certain" outcome, complexity principles suggest it is often better to try multiple approaches and see what emerges and develops as meaningful (Plsek & Greenhalgh, 2001). To get comfortable with deepening complexity in healthcare, practitioners must set aside linear pathways and models, embrace the unpredictable, respect autonomy and creativity, and hold emerging patterns and discoveries with flexibility (Plsek & Greenhalgh, 2001).

In healthcare, complexity leadership is foundationally meaningful to the practice landscape for all professionals, regardless of role, and therefore a compelling context for focusing on the liminal space in leading.

Leading in the Liminal Space

Whereas living in liminality can be chaotic and disruptive, leading in liminality offers even greater challenges. Leadership self-awareness and capacity for adapting along with other-awareness while one leads within a liminal space calls for a willingness to shift from addressing challenges with proven methods to a mindset of the new and untested.

Characterizing the Liminal Space

When mindful of operating in the liminal space, the leader experiences extend beyond what is available when only applying the adaptive leadership framework. The liminal space is framed as generative, meaning the environment is perceived to be open, full of possibilities, inventive, and opportunistic. Much like a rhizome's multidirectional characteristic, it encourages disconnecting with the past to make space available for newness with no anchors to tether the leader to historical or ceremonial weight, eliminating the hovering of distracting organizational traditions or sacred cows. It is dynamic in that it is adventurous; real-time experimentation honors emergence and resonates a *craft-as-you-go* capability, or what rhizomic theory describes as *asignifying rupture,* a perpetual, regenerating movement of connections breaking (deterritorializing) and reforming (re-territorializing). It makes room for everyone to self-identify as a leader, taking ownership for creative contributions that advance learning and the condition engaged. This action takes place in what we call the *liminal fold.*

Liminal Folds

We define the new concept of *"liminal folds" as* the space and time between provocative events where one releases attachment to what is previously known to allow oneself to enter a new fold of thinking or way of being. It holds an equal or neutral space for all to develop fully, a space where noticing, getting curious, opening to possibility or change, and attempting new pathways are sought and experienced.

Imagine jazz and its musical elements. Distinct from symphonic ensembles, the jazz ensemble is typically comprised of several or so individuals, each approaching the stage with their instrument, their talent, and a curiosity about where their collective notes will take them. Jazz depends on each player being open to what each musician will bring to the composition. A musician begins to play and others listen for when their contribution will add and enrich the piece. Each player does the same and a medley is created within the folds of notes, a melodic "yes, and" example of partnership, play, and performance that is new, fresh, and classically rhizomic in its adaptation. Its rhizomic nature centers in how players adapt, flow, and expand from each other's notes. Arrangements fold and unfold within the moments of play.

Dr. Sanjay Gupta, a neurosurgeon and CNN's chief medical correspondent, shared how he and his team quickly entered a new fold of thinking while covering the war in the Middle East as a reporter for several weeks, traveling with a group of naval doctors known as the Devil Docs. One day a lieutenant arrived at their camp with a severe head injury, no apparent pulse, and was thought to be dead. Even though Dr. Gupta was functioning as a correspondent during that trip, the group knew he was a neurosurgeon and, when the Devil Docs examined the lieutenant and found a faint pulse, they looked to Dr. Gupta to help relieve the lieutenant's brain swelling.

The conditions in the dusty desert tent were unsanitary for a craniectomy, the procedure needed to remove a part of the skull to relieve pressure, and Dr. Gupta had not packed surgical equipment to optimally perform such a delicate and precise procedure. He needed to quickly improvise. Finding a Black and Decker drill and holding it steady with sterile gloves, he sanitized the drill bits with a chemical sterilant and then used the drill to remove a layer of skull, relieving the pressure building in the lieutenant's brain. Then, to protect the brain from infection, Dr. Gupta needed to find a substitute material to line the exposed brain. The only material available that was sterile and pliable enough to do the job was the inside lining of an intravenous bag. So, he cut the bag open, fashioned a substitute lining, spread the lining over the brain to protect it from any external contaminants, and closed the opening. The young lieutenant's brain fully healed over time, and he went on to live a normal, productive life.

Dr. Gupta was betwixt and between a series of life-saving steps. He was faced with a liminal fold of choice, one that required him to adapt to a nonroutine challenge that held conditions beyond the ordinary or optimal, and offered an opportunity to go beyond what was known to be possible—new territory was taken and breakthroughs of significant magnitude waited to be discovered. His decision, in that moment, was critical to the care and survival of a life (Gupta, 2020).

Nonroutine challenges present an opportunity to go beyond what we have known to be possible. Amid nonroutine challenges, new solutions materialize, new territory is taken, and breakthroughs of significant magnitude wait to be discovered. This kind of opportunity does not present itself inside of known challenges demanding nothing more than an application of already discovered, established solutions.

The steps that Dr. Gupta took to save the young man's life align with rhizomic principles of connection, heterogeneity, asignifying rupture, and cartography. His affiliation to journalism and healthcare sparked a connection to what might be possible in a life-or-death situation. He was able to put aside his attachment to what a Black and Decker drill is most used for–to drill holes for woodworking or building–and to look beyond what he and others knew as a "drill" to then be able to see it as a surgical tool. Dr. Gupta's capacity to reach beyond his long years of training, the fixed idea that surgery is performed with certain tools and in certain rooms, demonstrated lines of flight thinking and action, an unlearning and relearning to perform surgery and save a life with a common drill on the brain of a dying man.

The transformative flight of unlearning and relearning moves individuals to become other, to move beyond what is known or fixed; it is an opportunity to invent, create, and experiment, to grasp the opportunity to transform life (Colebrook, 2002; Deleuze & Guattari, 1987).

Figure 7.1 illustrates a visual model of liminal leadership, holding the opportunistic liminal folds and rhizomic principles.

In the model, the spherical movement indicates the recursive opportunities that arise day in and day out, giving way to the provocative events that reveal a liminal fold. Rhizomic context and adaptive capacity feature leader opportunity within the liminal leadership model.

Rhizomic Context

Rhizomes are continuously growing horizontal underground stems that push out interval adventitious shoots. These multidirectional, highly resilient stems connect as they grow and can be somewhat unpredictable in the directions they take. They bend their way around, under, and over boundaries that stand in the way of their movement, finding new paths that allow them to multiply. Botanists have recognized that plants that rely on rhizomes have an evolutionary advantage in surviving harsh and changeable external conditions (Bell & Tomlinson, 1980; Hutchings & de Kroon, 1994). One only needs to attempt to change a lawn's border to know that it takes patience and determination to tame and redirect its growth. Free, expansive movement connecting with random and infinite points provide a powerful metaphor for how being curious, detaching, and reimagining are factors that develop comfort with adapting.

New ways of thinking derived from rhizomic principles offer consideration about how healthcare practitioners learn, consider options, unlearn, adapt, make decisions, and act when faced with uncertain, complex, and often dire, conditions. Like a rhizome's tenacious, multidirectional growth, it takes a willingness to step away from processes anchored in prior learning and practice and pursue new ways of serving by getting curious and exploring beyond to allow for expansive ideas to emerge. Awareness about how practitioners learn and adapt while in the midst of turmoil is important work; learning, unlearning, curiosity, and adapting often occur implicitly within the liminal folds of explicit work.

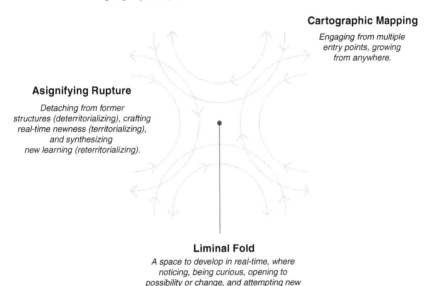

Liminal Leadership Model

The spherical movement indicates the recursive opportunities that arise day in and day out, giving way to the provocative events that reveal a liminal fold.

Cartographic Mapping

Engaging from multiple entry points, growing from anywhere.

Asignifying Rupture

Detaching from former structures (deterritorializing), crafting real-time newness (territorializing), and synthesizing new learning (reterritorializing).

Liminal Fold

A space to develop in real-time, where noticing, being curious, opening to possibility or change, and attempting new pathways are sought and experienced.

Figure 7.1 Liminal Leadership Model.

Allowing oneself to detach from what is proven moves one away from a "yes, but" mindset to a mindset of "yes, and," a mindset of perpetual inquiry, exploration, and creativity. Real learning has neither beginning nor end; in a rhizomic sense, true learning resides in the middle of things, a powerful intermezzo, linking past learning, tacit learning, and new learning thereby creating powerful perspectives that influence ongoing learning and adapting.

Consider procedures learned in medical school and practiced routinely within our healthcare systems. Often, while carrying out procedures, other possibilities that might accelerate a patient's survival rate may emerge. Instead of anchoring to what is previously learned, when we allow ourselves to stand on the threshold of what is and what might be, to open ourselves to discoveries that exist within the liminal folds of curiosity and possibility, we enable new, potentially undiscovered ways of being, thinking, serving, and healing to emerge. Creative, innovative discoveries disrupt what was previously known.

When a practitioner develops and practices flexibility in tandem with stable, fixed processes, where they dwell in the middle of things, allow for centering and comfort with the unknown, crafting solutions as they go, it is in that liminal fold that learning and adapting become emergent, generative, and rhizomic. Dwelling in the middle of flow and liminality allows for what may become, what may be discovered, what may change (Csikszentmihalyi, 1990).

The opportunity that extends beyond new ways of being and learning is furthered through intentional practice, and becoming other (Clegg et al., 2005; Deleuze & Guattari, 1987). We are changed when we open ourselves to the other–comfortably connecting to what dwells within the folds of what might be, seeking to understand other perspectives and meaning. A rhizomic lens offers a means through which to view (and from which to observe) ways of engaging with others within healthcare systems that expand beyond legacy and traditional adaptive theories and frameworks.

Enduring Concepts of Adaptive Leadership in the Liminal Space

As the world was thrust into the complexity of the 2020 COVID-19 pandemic, leaders in healthcare organizations found themselves betwixt and between in meeting the uncertainty of the patient experience with their standard care approaches honed over time. Often, what served in the past failed in the moment, as with the proning example mentioned earlier. Both operational and strategic challenges (Laurie, 2000) leapt to the forefront requiring "craft-as-you-go" sense-making akin to the telling metaphor, "build the plane while you're flying it." Perplexing, stunning, overwhelming, and emotional are all words healthcare professionals offer that define the tension of the time.

When peering through the leader lens, time-favored behaviors for operating in uncertainty are easily associated with the theory and principles of adaptive leadership. Defined as the practice of mobilizing people to tackle tough challenges and thrive (Heifetz et al., 2009b), concepts and practices of adaptive leadership endure in the liminal space within which leaders operate. The following are key concepts in adaptive leadership:

- Technical versus adaptive issues: In the adaptive leadership framework, distinctions are made between the presence of technical and adaptive issues. Technical concerns generally have clear pathways to offer fixed solutions. Adaptive challenges can only be addressed through changes in beliefs, priorities, habits, and loyalties (Heifetz et al., 2009). Heifetz et al. further offer that making progress requires mobilizing discovery, shedding entrenched ways, tolerating losses, and generating new capacity to thrive. This takes an openness to learning throughout the continuum of the challenge, not just simply clarifying perspective and direction. We find these attributes consistent with a leader approach in the liminal space.

- Leadership versus authority: Leading through adaptive challenges is not incumbent upon authority; in fact, authority can get in the way of successfully leading through adaptive challenges. As defined by Heifetz et al. (2009), regardless of leader identity, authority gives us three core responsibilities: to provide direction, to provide protection, and to provide order. As we consider both our opportunities with adaptive challenges and leading in the liminal space, a posture of authority is confining, restricting our ability to take advantage of the messiness of uncertainty, and exist in the possibilities of what is not yet known.
- Adaptation relies on diversity: To tackle adaptive challenges, organizations must embrace the collective genius of their communities, as opposed to relying on centralized planning (Heifetz et al., 2009). Constructing the employee experience in ways where diverse perspectives are naturally encouraged and celebrated, relational engagement moves beyond traditional pathways and instead is embedded through a network of intersections. This enables transformational discovery on many levels, from unlearning and learning to experience sharing, together crafting ways for newness. Openness without real or perceived boundaries generates more fully.
- Experimental mindset: Adaptive challenges are perplexing and situate among possibilities. When we approach them as experiments, we are open to learning, honoring the present context rather than applying fixed solutions drawn from the past. We also lighten our commitment to any one solution in favor of noticing when new thinking and action are needed. When called to lead adaptively in the liminal space, we are *further* invited to explore experimentation through the rhizomic opportunities that emerge, noticing the asignifying ruptures that offer recursive engagement in experimenting for discovery of what will be relevant and compelling in the moment. The experiments help us break and reform ineffective ways, again and again, leading with meaning in the perpetual flow of our experience.

In carrying out these imperatives of adaptive leadership, leaders mobilize people to bring the change that is needed in the system (Heifetz, 1994; Heifetz et al., 2009a, 2009b), as opposed to exerting influence in more traditional leader/follower relationships. Leaders create a holding environment (Heifetz, 1994) in which the adaptive measures can effectively unfold, while artfully providing a meaningful balance of challenge and support to see the system through the change. As we extend our thinking beyond adaptive leadership and appreciating the concept of leading in the liminal space, we contend that all members of an organization have the ability to lead to bring the change that is needed in the system.

Leading in the Liminal Space

The current landscape is calling us to extend our thinking and practice beyond the existing adaptive leadership framework. New considerations focused on caring for the perpetually dynamic, recursive nature of change emphasize the need to recast perspective and practice with certain perceived limiting structures to shift and optimally shape the leader context of the day. Our focus on the liminal space enriches the experience of adaptive leadership in several ways, with considerations for new thinking and practice for modern leading as is demonstrated in Table 7.1.

In this conceptual offering, the authors invite consideration for a fresh mindset of leading in a liminal, rhizomic space as a new and generative

Table 7.1 Distinctions of Adaptive Leadership and Leading in the Liminal Space

Adaptive Leadership Suggests	*Leading in the Liminal Space Advances This By*
Adaptation takes time; it is event-driven.	Acknowledging the experience of change in the contemporary world is perpetually dynamic, requiring leaders be open to the "real time" recursiveness of adaption, and all that comes with it.
Successful adaptive changes build from the best of the past.	Acknowledging this may or may not be true. In the liminal space, leaders are more likely to design in openness rather than assume perceived DNA is inherent in the solution. "Presence" is prioritized to be freed from anchors to former structures.
Becoming an objective viewer by "getting on the balcony" to assess adaptive challenges.	Acknowledging that the leader is integrally connected to their experience, honoring their immersion and identity with it, versus distancing from it.
Yesterday's adaptations may become today's routines.	Acknowledging that routines are not assumed as part of the lexicon.
Acknowledges "loss" for stakeholders and factions in the system.	Acknowledging adaptations are creating generation for the system versus loss. Operating in the liminal space redefines "what is normal;" deterritorializing over territorializing opens generative "lines of flight" thinking.
Leaders in authority empower followers to participate in the experience of change.	Deemphasizing authority over self-leadership. A focus on self-leadership accelerates and optimally enriches generation in the liminal space.

framework that opens thinking and practice opportunities beyond those available in the adaptive leadership model. It is the capacity to operate rhizomically in the liminal space that raises performance opportunity and lays a foundation for a new leadership model.

Weaving Organizational Stories, Narratives, and Plotlines within the Liminal Leadership Framework

As scholar-practitioners in the consulting industry, our leadership focus gives us an opportunity to engage regularly in qualitative assessments through organizational storytelling to inform learning and practice. Organizational storytelling provides a lens through which individuals' stories reveal how their learning experiences might be grounded (or not) in fixed (territorialized) systems, if they are free to take flight with new ideas (lines of flight or deterritorializing), thereby becoming other (re-territorializing), and if, through their experiences, relational and nomadic learning are practiced.

For this work, we used semi-structured interviews to engage professionals self-identifying as leaders in healthcare, inviting them to individually share their stories of leading through the trajectory (liminal space) of the 2020–2021 COVID-19 pandemic. In learning about their experiences, we wanted to know (1) What they noticed about the experience of their organizations during this time? (2) What was a peak moment of "aha" as they led through the year? (3) What experiences did they have of being "betwixt and between" or generating in the space of not knowing?

Consistent with what we offer about rhizomic ways of being and advantaging leaders in the liminal space, one leader shared that on many levels, asignifying ruptures were occurring at a rapid pace. Changes the organization had ruminated over for some time were immediately engaged, a form of de-territorializing and reterritorializing:

> Before the pandemic, we were holding back on promotions as we assessed the professionals were not ready for their next assignment, but with the early onset of the pandemic, we needed help to mobilize around the incoming uncertainty. We moved on the promotions right away, and quickly noticed how beautifully the new leaders were performing. I immediately wondered why I was previously holding them back. I was stuck in my own structure of what should be. That got in my way of creating a better experience for employees and our organization.

By letting go of fixed thinking and accepting the need to "reterritorialize" in the moment, new pathways were launched uplifting the experience for all.

In her professional life, another leader comforted hospital patients by meeting them in their dire moments with hand-holding and prayer. As the pandemic overwhelmed her hospital, and she comforted critically ill COVID-19 patients with her prayerful approach, she was quickly redirected by these patients from the posture that had served her so well to that point. What she had known to be comforting was not so in that moment; these patients surprised her by rejecting her professional routine and requesting her to join them differently:

> For them, I learned I needed to change my approach and simply be present to hold meditative space, to listen, to take in everything they wanted to say to allay the fear that they would not have anyone else to share their most precious thoughts within what was expected in their final days and moments.

This leader learned that what had been her best professional practice was certainly not what was needed in that moment, and she wondered if she had made assumptions about her prior patients: "I gave them what I thought they needed. This experience has changed how I show up for my patients going forward; I now invite the needs of each patient, so I can more deeply deliver true person-centered care." She was called to improvise, to notice that the traditional pathway she so confidently paved required an urgent detour. And while deviating from her expertise was unsettling in this real-time crisis, her openness and willingness to experiment in the moment enabled her to authentically hold and honor her patients.

In the stories of healthcare leaders in the throes of dynamic uncertainty, we find vivid examples of transformation available when leading in the liminal space. In each of these examples, new lines of flight resulted from being present and open to the experience unfolding, making moves in real time while noticing the emergent landscape, untethered and suspended from fixed and familiar structures that might otherwise get in the way.

Adopting a Rhizomic Way of Being when Leading in the Liminal Space

Adaptive leader practices take intention to embody in meaningful ways. To consider adopting more emergent and rhizomic ways of being to thrive as a leader in the liminal space, the authors invite the reader to experiment with and build practice around new behaviors.

Engage in Reflective Practice

The honoring and practice of self-leadership are integral to engaging leaders optimally in the richness of the liminal space. And yet, more traditional leadership perspective focuses on the ability to lead others versus self. In reframing this focus, a core opportunity for leaders is in building a reflective practice.

Making room for reflective practice may initially feel counterintuitive to the real-time dance in which leaders engage in the liminal space. Holding a reflective practice, however, brings a posture to leading in the liminal space that encourages transformational thinking and being. In *The Reflective Practitioner* (1983), Schön expands the concept of reflection beyond the retrospective (reflection-on-action) and into the synchronal (reflection-in-action). Having a reflective practice, "coaches" leaders to be open, available, and ready to receive experiences for the meaning they make in the moment. In this way, they are fortified to optimize their experience and the sensemaking liminal space provides. A strong reflective practice also strengthens our ability to notice the dynamics of the changing landscape and be better prepared for, able, and willing to actively improvise, create, and experiment in the continual experience of unlearning and learning.

Questions for leaders:

- What might a meaningful reflective practice look like for you? How might you experiment with integrating it into your experience?
- What do you notice about your ability to quiet your mind, so it is available and open to craft and/or consider something new?
- What behaviors may you need to change in order to benefit from a meaningful reflective practice?

Build Curious Capacity

There is no question that curious leader behavior can offer dividends to people and organizations in the contemporary work environment. As Weick (1993) once argued, in a fluid world, wise people know that they do not fully understand what is happening right now. He further articulated that curiosity is what organizations need most in changing times. With the fluid nature of change, prompted by the complexity of the organizational experience today, Weick's words may have never been more meaningful.

Whereas many definitions of curiosity exist, Kashdan and Silvia (2009) frame it well for this discussion as the recognition, pursuit, and intense desire to explore novel, challenging, and uncertain events. Curious leadership is a behavior that serves as a connective enabler among complexity leadership theory (Lichtenstein et al., 2006; Uhl-Bien et al., 2007) and the adaptive leadership framework (Heifetz et al., 2009), and continues to have generative meaning in a rhizomic context. When situated in the liminal space, curious behavior offers leaders a meaningful and accessible channel through which uncertainty and ambiguity can be intentionally and patiently held. The idea of sitting in the not knowing state of curiosity also implies we respect what is offered outside of ourselves, key in what the rhizomic context brings with its emphasis on the interdependencies or social integration in our environment.

How might curious capacity be delivered to extend the adaptive experience in the context of a complex adaptive system to generate within the liminal experience? When applied within a liminal fold, a curious mindset and behavior awakens intentionality for the leader to comfortably and confidently situate in the movement associated with learning and unlearning, letting go of previously learned anchoring beliefs to make way for what is not yet known. Being comfortable in not knowing is inherent in the notion to adapt. One's ability to say yes to not knowing, being willing to replace expertness with openness, is required to be available and generative in the liminal fold. Certainly, within a context of a global pandemic where untested challenges can be overwhelming with how to encounter and address new diseases, healthcare workers need to be prepared to do adaptive work, which often calls for them to adjust their values, attitudes, habits, priorities, and practices (Heifetz, 1994; Williams, 2005).

Questions for leaders:

- When have you been willing to step away from what you know to consider the unknown?
- In what situations are you willing to set aside your own expertise to be open to the thoughts and ideas of another?

Build a Network of Relational Intersections

In both adaptive leadership and leading in the liminal space, recrafting our relational networks inside our organization becomes an imperative. Depending on traditional structures and their engagement expectations becomes weighty and ineffective. Formal and informal boundaries become limiting when leading in the liminal space. Leaders taking full advantage of the liminal space rethink the possibility of relationships. Stretching throughout the organization to create relational pathways that may be unchartered and unexpected, or deterritorialized as expected in the rhizomic experience of operating in the liminal space, advances knowledge generation, diversity of perspective, contribution, and shared ownership arising from creatively networked partnering.

Questions for leaders:

- In reframing your relational network, what may be one new connection you are curious to enable?

- What relational opportunities might you have in extending beyond your current line of sight?
- How might you break through your more traditional pathways by unlearning what has served you in the past, and newly learning what may be possible in this way?
- What relationships are available to you today that may not have been before?

Posture "Craft-as-You-Go" Agility

The liminal space is dynamic. It holds the construction of the landscape that we are building every day, every hour, every minute. It is in this perpetual construction of context that we call ourselves to be agile and open to the shifts in thinking and practice that enable what is called for now. We call this craft-as-you-go or being present to take action as you lead that will elevate learning in service to uplifting the experience.

The pandemic has offered us a sound laboratory where "craft-as-you-go" unfolded in real-time, showing us our capacity for holding this as fundamental to leading in the liminal space. The imperative of the day showed us what we are capable of, redefining rules of engagement. By offering the framework of leading in the liminal space, holding the possibility for craft-as-you-go sense-making to produce meaningful and viable outcomes.

Questions for leaders:

- What do you know about yourself that prevents you from operating in a "craft-as-you-go" way?
- What is one thing you are willing to set aside that will encourage you to freely experiment within the emerging scene?
- What have you created and experimented with "in the moment" that was raw, new, and untested? What was learned from that experience?

Conclusion

The features of adaptive leadership provide a foundational underpinning to the capacity of leaders to engage an organization in reframing opportunistically through change. The authors contend, however, that the concept of leading rhizomically in the liminal space brings new considerations and mindsets for holding the fluidity of change we experience in the contemporary organizational landscape. When we amplify the nurturing of self-leadership, consider our experience for what it is in the present with our fullest and most empathetic connection, and experiment in a craft-as-you-go way, we allow ourselves to set aside the objective, deliberating space of deciding what move to make, and instead courageously walk enjoined with our experience and accept the move that emerges in real-time. It is this action that constructs the experience and informs us of what will come next. While our healthcare systems have given life to this posture through the pandemic, the embodiment of leading in the liminal space brings new opportunities for leaders everywhere. The authors invite all leaders to live into and cultivate these reframed mindsets and pathways that will bring unexpected newness and innovation as we're called to lead differently in the contemporary world.

References

Astua, A. J., Michaels, E. K., & Michaels, A. J. (2020). Proning during pandemic: The rapid institution of a safe, transferable, and effective prone positioning program at NYCHHC/Elmhurst Hospital: A situationally resource limited facility, during the peak of the Covid 19 surge. *Research Square.* https://www.researchsquare.com/article/rs-29653/v1

Bailey, D., Docherty, S., Adams, J., Carthron, D., Corazzini, K., Day, J., Neglia, E., Thygeson, M., & Anderson, R. (2012). Studying the clinical encounter with the adaptive leadership framework. *Journal of Healthcare Leadership, 2012*(4), 83–91. https://www.ncbi.nlm.nih.gov/pmc/articles/PMC3883363/

Bell, A. D., & Tomlinson, P. B. (1980). Adaptive architecture in rhizomatous plants. *Botanical Journal of the Linnean Society, 80*(2), 125–160. 10.1111/j.1095-8339.1980.tb01662.x

Belrhiti, Z., Nebot Giralt, A., & Marchal, B. (2018). Complex leadership in healthcare: A scoping review. *International Journal of Health Policy and Management*, 7(12), 1073–1084. https://www.ncbi.nlm.nih.gov/pmc/articles/PMC6358662/

Clegg, S. R., Kornberger, M., & Rhodes, C. (2005). Learning/becoming/organizing. *Organization, 12*(2), 147–167. 10.1177/1350508405051186

Colebrook, C. (2002). *Gilles Deleuze.* London, UK: Routledge.

Csikszentmihalyi, M. (2009). *Flow: The psychology of optimal experience.* HarperCollins.

Deleuze, G., & Guattari, F. (1987). *A thousand plateaus: Capitalism and schizophrenia.* University of Minnesota Press.

Eichholz, J. C. (2017). *Adaptive capacity: How organizations can thrive in a changing world* (2nd ed.). Lid Publishing.

Gennep, A. V. (2013). *The rites of passage.* Routledge.

Granger, K., & Hanover, D. (2012). Transformational performance-based leadership: Addressing non-routine adaptive challenges. *Ivey Business Journal*, 76(1), 41–45. https://iveybusinessjournal.com/publication/transformational-performance-based-leadership-addressing-non-routine-adaptive-challenges/

Gupta, S. (2020). *Keep sharp: How to build a better brain at any age.* Headline.

Heifetz, R. A. (1994). *Leadership without easy answers.* Harvard University Press.

Heifetz, R. A., Grashow, A., & Linsky, M. (2009a). Leadership in a (permanent) crisis. *Harvard Business Review*, 87(7/8), 62–69. https://hbr.org/2009/07/leadership-in-a-permanent-crisis

Heifetz, R. A., Grashow, A., & Linsky, M. (2009b). *The practice of adaptive leadership: Tools and tactics for changing your organization and the world.* Harvard Business Press.

Heifetz, R. A., & Linsky, M. (2017). *Leadership on the line, with a new preface: Staying alive through the dangers of change.* Harvard Business Press.

Hompe, L. (2019). *Executive coaching in a healthcare setting: An exploration of the impacts, outcomes, and challenges in a changing, complex environment* [Master's thesis, University of Pennsylvania]. University of Pennsylvania Scholarly Commons. https://repository.upenn.edu/cgi/viewcontent.cgi?article=1091&context=od_theses_msod

Hutchings, M. J., & de Kroon, H. (1994). Foraging in plants: The role of morphological plasticity in resource acquisition. *Advances in Ecological Research, 25,* 159–238. 10.1016/S0065-2504(08)60215-9

Kashdan, T. & Silvia, P. J. (2009). Curiosity and interest: The benefits of thriving on novelty and challenge. In S. J. Lopwz, & C. R. Snyder (Eds.), *Oxford handbook of scholarly psychology* (pp. 367–374). Oxford University Press.

Laurie, D. L. (2000). *The real work of leaders: A report from the front lines of management.* Basic Books.

Lichtenstein, B., Uhl-Bien, M., Marion, R., Seers, A., Orton, J., & Schreiber, C. (2006). Complexity leadership theory: An interactive perspective on leading in complex adaptive systems. *Emergence: Complexity & Organization, 8*(4), 2–12.

Plsek, P. E., & Greenhalgh, T. (2001). Complexity science: The challenge of complexity in health care. *BMJ, 323*(7313), 625–628. 10.1136/bmj.323.7313.625

Rohr, R. (2020). Introduction. *Oneing, 8*(1), 17–21.

Schön, D. (1983). *The reflective practitioner: How professionals think in action.* Basic Books.

Uhl-Bien, M. & Arena, M. (2017). Complexity leadership: Enabling people and organizations for adaptability. *Organizational Dynamics, 46*(1) 9–20. 10.1016/j.orgdyn.2016.12.001

Uhl-Bien, M., Marion, R., & McKelvey, B. (2007). Complexity leadership theory: Shifting from the industrial age to the knowledge era. *The Leadership Quarterly, 18*(4), 298–318. 10.1016/j.leaqua.2007.04.002

Weick, K. (1993). The collapse of sense-making in organizations: The Mann-Gulch disaster. *Administrative Science Quarterly, 38*(4), 628–652. 10.2307/2393339

Williams, D. (2005). *Real leadership: Helping people and organizations face their toughest challenges.* Berrett-Koehler.

Wilson, T., Hold, T., & Greenhalgh, T. (2001). Complexity science: Complexity and clinical care. *BMJ, 323*(7314), 685–688. 10.1136/bmj.323.7314.685

8 Modifying the Stories We Tell: Discourse as Racial Justice Capacity Building in the Helping Professions

Cherie Bridges Patrick and Lindsay Lyons

The very public exposure of enduring gruesome American racism and White supremacy was foregrounded throughout 2020, yet efforts to address their presence and impact are frequently treated as if race is separate from all aspects of American social life. The perpetual denial of racism in the presence of ongoing White supremacy has resulted in a profound social response that now refuses to be ignored. Heeding these demands, universities and organizations are pivoting towards diversity, equity, inclusion, and antiracism action, emphasizing the need for organizational change. A proliferation of antiracism education, dismantling-White-supremacy symposiums, and workshops espousing racial equity and justice have emerged, more often than not conducted as stand-alone, cognitively-focused, one-time events. Implicit in the one-time-event is a return to business-as-usual mentality that does not integrate this often highly-charged material into practice and thus cannot bring about substantive change. Rather, these efforts often reproduce the very dynamics racial justice actions intend to change, leaving issues of race separate from all else. Introducing the topic of race to the classroom or workplace when it is not the primary subject reveals the implicit boundaries that resolutely govern racial dialogue and thus sanction racial dominance to determine the terms and conditions of when and where conversations can occur. Despite the omnipresent nature of racial dominance and the harm it continues to inflict, routine and explicit dialogue about race remains taboo in many institutions. These dynamics support the need for racial justice work in schools and organizations.

Our backgrounds are in the education and social work professions and our discussion highlights our work experiences and research. In our racial justice efforts, the most common concerns hover around *how* to have conversations about race. As such, the spaces for generative racial dialogue we endeavor to create are deliberate and draw attention to the ways in which race is usually the "elephant in the room," whether it is acknowledged or not. Although having intentional dialogue around race is challenging for a host of reasons, its purpose is clearly defined. In workshops and symposiums, for example, while participants may not

DOI: 10.4324/9781003099109-8

have the same level of comfort, skills, or desire to be present and engaged, they all know why they are there. On the other hand, inserting the topic of race into academic or workplace discussions where race is *not* the explicit focal point is an entirely different undertaking. Although race is a social construction, racism is a social reality, often operating without our implicit awareness (Miller & Donner, 2000).

Grounded in the canons of White supremacy is a racial hierarchy that is the basis for the racialized White group to be the standard from which all other racialized groups deviate and are evaluated (Frankenberg, 1993; hooks, 1992; Levine-Rasky, 2016). We believe that racial justice presupposes elimination of the injustice created when differences are sorted and ordered in a racial hierarchy that confers illegitimately gained power, social, and economic advantages to groups based on their racial locations in that hierarchy. Moreover, racial justice extends beyond the absence of discrimination and inequities. Broadly speaking, racial justice is the presence of deliberately created systems and relevant supports to achieve and sustain equity through proactive and preventative measures. Once established, policies, practices, attitudes, and actions that produce racially equitable power, access, opportunities, and treatment are proactively reinforced. Consequences of equity produce leaders who have a sense of their own agency as well as a sense of social responsibility toward and with others. Creating racially just classrooms and workplaces is an ongoing process of adaptation.

Our primary goal for this discussion is to map a route to building adaptive capacity for actors to engage in generative, organic conversations about race (that include consideration of its history, complexity, and its associated perpetual injury) in team and board meetings, classrooms, and workplaces. We intend to chart a course of action that normalizes the practice of generative "mobilizing discourses" (Eichholz, 2017, p. 110) about race within organizations for the purpose of achieving racial justice. According to Eichholz (2017), mobilizing dialogue acknowledges "the elephant in such a way as to create enough disequilibrium to make progress on the issue" (p. 110) that ultimately produces conversations "where people feel the tension yet remain engaged in the conversation" (p. 110). We present four communication patterns that gauge an organization's dialogic and adaptive capacities. Critical to engagement in generative racial dialogue are many individual capabilities, yet most relevant is the environment that invites and enables these thorny, yet essential, conversations (Eichholz, 2017). Along with Eichholz's (2017) treatise on adaptive capacity, our discussion will include adaptive leadership capacity-building practices offered by Heifetz et al. (2009). We situate the facilitation of racial justice within Mitchell and Sackney's (2011) three dimensions of capacity building—personal, interpersonal, and organizational—using real-life stories and integrate Bridges Patricks' (2020) four elements of fruitful racial dialogue: readiness and willingness; vulnerability;

adaptability; and a positive, encouraging, liberating dialogic environment into each of the three dimensions. Finally, we describe the elements for creating a holding environment and building organizational capacity. At the heart of racial justice is its concern for eliminating barriers that stand in the way of the full expression of human potential.

A looming question for academia and organizations intentionally navigating uncharted and often turbulent racial waters is, how do they "survive and thrive under conditions of internal and external uncertainty they've never experienced before?" (Eichholz, 2017, p. xv). The question directly points to the need for individuals to collectively "concentrate on becoming very good at learning to do new things" (Eichholz, 2017, p. xv) within their organizational settings.

Adaptive Leadership: The Importance of Diagnosis

Many individuals, communities, and organizations will attempt to address racism as a technical problem—utilizing their current problem-solving knowledge to tackle its intransigent affront (Harbin et al., 2019; McCready & Soloway, 2010). Approaching racism as a technical problem solidifies a gap between actors' espoused values and their capacity to live out those values in their environments; it also illustrates what Heifetz et al. (2009) refer to as work avoidance. Taking an adaptive approach requires leaders and the stakeholders to interrogate long-held beliefs that may deny the presence of racial dominance and what justice should look like (for further discussion on diversity in adaptive work, see Chapter 1). Using an adaptive lens means critically examining disconnects between what we *say* we value and what our policies, practices, and assessments indicate we *actually* give preference to, or honor. Adaptive solutions require changes to people's values, beliefs, habits, ways of working, or ways of life (Heifetz et al., 2009).

Education and social work have several similarities. First, those in both professions are predominantly White and female. Second, formal education practices in both professions consider issues of race as separate and independent topics. Third, both generally maintain a deficit approach to teaching and helping, giving attention to oppression and its impact on racially marginalized groups, but leaving the sources of dominance unexamined. In response, we briefly present an adaptation of a model for "facing difficult conversations" offered by Eichholz (2017) to examine racial discourse. Like Eichholz (2017), we believe that the ways in which actors communicate about difficult topics within organizations is an effective barometer in gauging adaptive capacity. The converted model (Figure 8.1) captures four common discourses that reflect the nature of an organization's communicative environment.

Talking about race often produces physiological reactions, strongly felt emotions, and mental images that arouse defenses. Polarizing

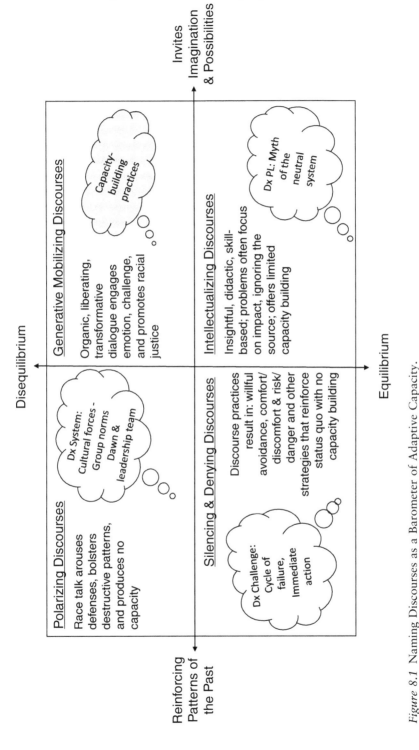

Figure 8.1 Naming Discourses as a Barometer of Adaptive Capacity.

Note. Adapted from Eichholz, JC, 2017, p. 11, *Adaptive capacity: How organizations can thrive in a changing world* 2nd edition, London, United Kingdom, LID Publishing, reprinted with permission.

discourses (upper left quadrant) often occur when actors lack desire, skill, knowledge, and/or support. Defenses often bolster harmful communication that inhibits efforts toward capacity building. Polarizing discourses intensify past ineffective patterns, reproduce racial dominance, and result in harmful interpersonal practices (for further discussion on polarization in discourse, see Chapter 9). As shown in the lower left quadrant, silencing and denying discourses block or limit access to productive communication and maintain the status quo. Discourse themes may appear as willful avoidance, silence, comfort/discomfort, and risk/danger, and reinforce past patterns and racial dominance (Bridges Patrick, 2020). These discourse themes suggest the challenge of dismantling racial dominance "may exceed the culture's adaptive capability" (Heifetz, 1994, p. 37). We must acknowledge the tension that exists in this statement when juxtaposed against the intention of the system of White supremacy that undergirds its maintenance.

Moving rightward toward more invitational discourses, but still operating in a comfort zone, the graphic shows intellectualizing discourses as insightful, informative, sometimes skill-based, and reflective (lower right quadrant). Intellectualizing discourses often focus on the impact of racism while negating crucial attention to its source. These discourses sometimes reveal historic patterns of dominance and invite imaginative possibilities to change but offer limited capacity-building practices. Finally, the upper right quadrant describes generative mobilizing discourses that intentionally seek to develop dialogic capacity and normalize practices that lead to racially just organizations. These discourses draw on multiple issues, among them identity, history, complexity, and the perpetual injury associated with racial dominance. Proper diagnosis of the system, challenge, and political landscape is necessary to create the environmental conditions that result in normative, mobilizing discourse. Organizational discourse patterns in the other three quadrants suggest there is a need for individuals and organizations to improve their capacity to engage in generative discourse around race and White supremacy. Thus, capacity-building interventions are warranted.

We follow the insistence of Heifetz et al. (2009) on diagnosing first, then acting. Taking this advice allows leaders to examine an array of system operations such as cultural norms and forces, structural implications, and underlying values that drive behavior. The diagnostic process involves three components: the organizational system, the adaptive challenge faced by the organization, and the political landscape within the organization. A thorough examination of the organizational system is the first step in the diagnostic process.

Diagnosing the System

A framework grounded in adaptive leadership is a divergence from conventional approaches applied to issues of racial dominance and justice.

The process of diagnosis argues for leaders to intentionally analyze their own actions and involvement alongside the organizational diagnostic process. An adaptive approach also directs leaders to interrogate disconnects between desired organizational values and the *actual* practices they undertake and policies that guide them, using emergent data to inform change efforts aimed at building racially just organizations—a systems approach. Diagnosing first, then acting, aligns with an adaptive approach, while supporting antiracist scholar Ibram Kendi's injunction to first identify, name, then dismantle racism (Kendi, 2019).

Adaptive work is deliberate and often slow (Heifetz et al., 2009). Prior to commencing the work, actors will benefit by taking into account the illusion that the system is broken (Heifetz et al., 2009). Heifetz et al. (2009) challenge the thinking that suggests organizations need to be changed because they are broken. They argue that "any social system is the way it is because the people in that system (at least those individuals and factions with the most leverage) want it that way" (p. 16). Both education and social work aim to achieve justice and yet both systems are, in fact, designed to perpetuate racial injustice. The gap in these systems' espoused values versus their lived behaviors is brought about by inattention to the structures and priorities of those in positions of power and authority. Viewing these systems as "dysfunctional" only contributes to maintaining those results. This shift in perspective enables a direct examination of the complex ways in which racial dominance functions with the purpose of retaining control. Understanding the durability of systemic racial dominance may help as actors engage in efforts to dismantle it. A racial justice grounding requires that we look to see how hegemonic forces contribute to organizational functioning by keeping disparities created by the system out of view while their impact receives myopic and intense focus.

Systemic inequities concealed in plain sight are confounded by practices that have historically marked racial dialogue as socially and culturally forbidden, leaving many people ill-equipped to engage in productive, conversations. One of the stories we tell is that we cannot talk about race in the workplace because it is divisive, impolite, counterproductive, uncomfortable, and so forth. Workplace dialogue is often practiced and maintained by employees who take their communication leads from leadership. An adaptive lens allows us to see this as a cultural force that governs how leadership responds to racism. It eventually becomes part of organizational group norms that regulate how people relate to each other (Heifetz, et al., 2009). A social worker's comments first capture her view of leadership fears and then her own around having any form of racial dialogue (Bridges Patrick, 2020):

> I think [the administration is] afraid that if they even mention it, or even acknowledge that there's a racial thing that it puts them at risk

for liability, litigation, and all of that, and nobody wants to touch this issue.

I can think of like two people if we got in the same room, I'd be scared to bring it up because it is so emotionally charged to the point that maybe we couldn't have constructive discourse. And then it's like, how do you do that to change those things, and nobody ends up with a black eye? (p. 132)

Her comments capture an imagined fear of violence and destruction that presupposes talk about race and is reflected in the polarizing discourse quadrant (Figure 8.1). Organizational culture is not often a documented process, so exploring corporate narratives, rituals, and group norms can bring needed awareness to the investigation. An understanding of an organization's culture and group norms is essential and includes identifying elements that "facilitate change" as well as the factors that "stand in the way" of change (Heifetz, et al., 2009, p. 57). Data gathered in a systems-level analysis will inform the diagnostic process of the adaptive challenge.

Diagnosing the Adaptive Challenge

Organizational systems are extremely complex and comprise aspects of both technical and adaptive problems. Adaptive challenges are those problems that have no pre-designed solutions and cannot be fixed by technical expertise; rather, resolutions for adaptive challenges often lie within people themselves. Adaptive challenges are earthed in the "complexity of values, beliefs, and loyalties" and arouse "intense emotions rather than dispassionate analysis" (Heifetz et al., 2009, p. 70). Diagnosing an adaptive challenge requires a willingness to live in uncertainty. Racism is a long-standing social problem and we see it as an adaptive challenge. Traditional "logical" arguments are insufficient for its resolution.

As helping professionals, one of the stories we tell ourselves around creating just and equitable workplaces is that action equals progress. Approaches to address racism within the profession at the 1982 Color in a White Society conference (White, 1984), the first national conference on minority issues, are unsurprisingly similar to the challenges social workers continue to face (Social Work Policy Institute, 2014). A common response is to take immediate action which often leads to a cycle of failure. The burgeoning of antiracism education and workshops referenced in our introduction juxtaposed against racism's relentless evolution illustrates the story that action equals progress. Underlying this action is that productivity requirements and organizational structures create pressures for people to act immediately to solve the problems created by racial dominance (Essed, 1991, 1996). We locate this story in the silencing and denying discourse quadrant of Figure 8.1. Recurring failures are often the result of misreading or simplifying problems, not noticing the changing organizational topography, and, perhaps most importantly when it comes to racial discourse, the desire for technical solutions that minimize or avoid interruption or distress within the agency (Heifetz, et al., 2009). Unexamined or under-examined practices can create cycles of failure which are often key identifiers of an organization's adaptive challenges.

The desire to fix the racial problem is often posited with the question "what can I or we do now?" When asked by White people, it is usually framed as external action to help "those" people to whom race is naturally ascribed. This question reveals four assumptions. First, race (and all that it encompasses) is for non-White people. Second, the question suggests there is a technical fix that can be applied to the centuries-old problem of White supremacy. The third implies that many barriers obstructing racial justice are external thus excluding the essential and painful internal labor. The fourth implication is that issues involving racial dominance are visible and obvious (e.g., violence and extremism). The drive for action supersedes becoming proximate to and diagnosing how racial dominance presents itself in one's context and environment. Analysis of the political dynamics of an organization is the last element in the iterative diagnostic process.

Diagnosing the Political Landscape

Tackling racism requires an adaptive approach that understands the values that motivate behavior, recognizing that resistance to such exploration (and to change in general) can be understood as loss (Heifetz et al, 2009). Understanding political dynamics within organizations requires engagement with stakeholders to hear their perspectives on the challenge.

A White social worker's expression of fear in challenging racism captures issues of identity, capability, and potential damage to collegial relationships:

> … To be perfectly honest, how are my coworkers going to look at me if I'm always the one bringing this up, and… can I take that on myself? …It's hard and you don't want to be that person. (Bridges Patrick, 2020, p. 166)

Her comments suggest concerns with multiple losses and, if left unexamined, the social worker's silence likely to be interpreted primarily as resistance. Adaptive leadership requires an exploration of personal loss for those engaged in systems change. Naming the losses at risk is critical and serves as a reminder that "resistance to change stems from a fear of losing something important" (Heifetz et al., 2009, p. 96).

From the perspective of racial dominance, those constituted as racially inferior must navigate the impact of internalized racism and the host of false ideologies and social practices that have kept them in collusion with a system set up against them (Akbar, 1996; Menakem, 2019). In the context of racial dominance, comfort is frequently found in the familiar and predictable. Those racialized as White face loss of the false internalized goodness and superiority that have allowed for performativity in place of authenticity, access to valued resources, and prioritization of needs and desires. People who resist initiatives, particularly around race, are people who likely feel most threatened by it.

A key leadership role in the context of addressing racism in the workplace is to mobilize people to grapple with the discomfort, fear, risks, and emotions that create barriers to talking about how racial dominance operates to maintain the status quo and reproduce racial power abuse.

Building Capacity for Mobilizing Discourse for Racial Justice Conceptual Model

We have developed a conceptual model to illustrate how organizations can establish practices that normalize generative, mobilizing discourse to transform organizational culture. The model (see Figure 8.2) draws upon Mitchell and Sackney's (2011) three dimensions of capacity building that situate personal, interpersonal, and organizational elements within the

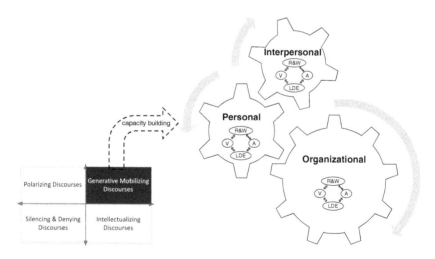

Figure 8.2 Building Organizational Adaptive Capacity: An Integrated Model to Transform Racial Dialogue.

Note: This figure integrates concepts from our Naming Discourses as a Barometer of Adaptive Capacity framework (Figure 8.1), Mitchell and Sackney's (2011) capacity building dimensions, and Bridges Patrick's (2020) racial discourse capacities.

context of an organization. As discourse is central to the labor necessary for achieving racial justice, within each dimension we specify four discourse capacities that support organizational endeavors: a liberating dialogic environment, adaptability, readiness and willingness, and vulnerability.

Efforts toward racial justice necessarily require attention to the notion of race. The nature of race as a social construction is highly relational and demands that people racialized as White derive their identities from racialized non-White group members to form the basis on which to evaluate themselves and other racialized groups (hooks, 1992; Levine-Rasky, 2016). Exposing the dependency of White identity on racially marginalized identity helps deconstruct how our racialized hierarchy is maintained. Complicating matters is that this dependency is always at play and impacts the ways in which people relate to one another.

Our application of an adaptive approach in organizations focused on racial justice requires cognitive and affective investments in order to thrive (Mitchell & Sackney, 2011) with ongoing attention to the core processes of diagnosis first, then action that unfolds in two dimensions: toward the self *and* the organization (Heifetz et al. 2009, p. 6). Organizational members also require an understanding that connection and relationships are the heart of change. Integrated within the three individual dimensions of the framework are four capacities for generative racial dialogue. Starting with the personal, each of the dimensions and capacities are briefly discussed to emphasize optimal adaptive dialogic and diagnostic capacity.

Personal Dimension

The individual dimension is the root of the learning community and is the internal space where reflexive construction and reconstruction (Mitchell & Sackney, 2011) of racial justice knowledge occurs. Building capacity in this domain challenges values, assumptions, belief systems, and practices. An interior focus suggests grappling with and modification of the deeply rooted stories we tell ourselves and the rest of the world about what we "believe in, stand for, and represent" (Heifetz, et al., 2009, p. 23). Distorted narratives are deconstructed through ongoing application of "reflection on action," which Mitchell and Sackney (2011) define as "post hoc analysis of events" (p. 25) and "reflection in action," which they define as "critical analysis of events as they transpire" (p. 25) with the goal of eventually reconstructing professional narratives by marrying new knowledge to practice (Mitchell & Sackney, 2011). New knowledge is practiced and cultivated interpersonally and organizationally.

Interpersonal Dimension

This dimension is concerned with building collective meaning within the learning community. Capacity develops in relationship to others. Thus, capacity is built by bringing people together to develop shared purpose and values, build collective meaning, engage in regular dialogue that includes honest critique, and shared decision-making for community actors (Mitchell & Sackney, 2011). Within the interpersonal dimension is the necessity for optimal cognitive and affective conditions that empower members to engage in collective reflection on and in action and in conversation. Mentally, community members should engage in critical reflection (Mitchell & Sackney, 2011), shared leadership, data-driven improvement, and risk-taking. Effective emotional engagement includes trust-building, support, and care practices (Mitchell & Sackney, 2011). Dialogic learning occurs within relationships and the interpersonal dimension is where racialized identity and its dependencies are challenged through interaction. Interpersonal relationships form the communicative foundation from which elements of organizational life originate, develop, and are preserved and transformed.

Organizational Dimension

At the core of the organizational dimension is the need to assemble structures that support the creation, continuation, and maintenance of sustainable racially-just organizational processes, practices, and policies. This means building flexible systems that support old, yet effective, methods *and* new innovative ideas. Finally, it is important to know that the organizational dimension shapes the personal and interpersonal dimensions (Mitchell & Sackney, 2011). Our intentional focus on discourse offers a new level of awareness to an obvious, yet under-acknowledged resource.

The Primacy of Discourse

As van Dijk highlights (1992, p. 102), "Discourse lies at the heart of racism;" it is also an essential element and invaluable tool in the work of racial justice. First, discourse is a universal social practice that is widely used by most, if not all, societies. Second, the nature of discourse is socially constitutive and socially conditioned (Wodak, 2015) and thus a multifaceted resource that carries with it the potential to not only create and solve social ills but to act as a mediator for everything in between. For purposes of this writing, we use discourse, dialogue, talk, communication, and conversation interchangeably.

With all the history, angst, violence (physical, emotional, and psychological), shame, hegemony, and continual harm that accompanies the concept of race, how do individuals engage in and normalize generative dialogue in their workplaces? Developing and building individual, interpersonal, and organizational adaptive capacity (dialogic and diagnostic) become critical to answering this question. Contributing to an adaptive, healthy learning community are four elements that promote dialogic capacity.

Adaptability

Adaptability supports the development of skills necessary to fill the gap that exists between espoused values and values that are actually practiced. It is developed primarily in the personal realm and refined through interaction with others in the interpersonal dimension. For an in-depth discussion of the related concepts of single-, double-, and triple-loop learning, see Chapters 2 and 9. The adaptive individual or team/organization creates a container or toolbox of sorts that supports new ways of thinking and practicing.

Readiness and Willingness

Readiness and willingness capture the essence of an actor's preparedness to engage in antiracist dialogue, education, and practice for the purpose of unsettling White supremacy. Within this capacity is conscious acknowledgment that one is willing to brave disequilibrium. Whereas readiness and willingness fall within the personal domain, they are practiced and cultivated in the interpersonal and organizational dimensions.

Vulnerability

Vulnerability relates to one's willingness and ability to allow one's true self to be fully seen; its definition literally means "open to attack" (Brown, 2006, p. 48). In the context of racial discourse, vulnerability consists of articulating fears, internal conflicts, one's ability to admit mistakes, and to authentically engage in antiracist dialogue and practice for the purpose of dismantling White supremacy. Building dialogic and adaptive capacity takes desire, time, tenacity, support, various resources, and, most of all, practice. Combined efforts result in the development of an organizational holding environment.

A Positive, Encouraging, Liberating Dialogic Environment

The dialogic environment is the primary vehicle for information transmission and ultimately organizational transformation. Meetings, client sessions, employee trainings, and water cooler conversations all fall under the rubric of the dialogic environment that first begins within the mind (beliefs and values) of the individual. It is within the individual's mental and emotional realms that all antiracism work begins, yet the action of communication occurs interpersonally and organizationally. A positive, encouraging, liberating dialogic environment, then, is one that invites and creates space for venturesome thoughts and conversations.

Facilitating Discourse

Heifetz et al. (2009) write about preparing for single "off-site" events to orchestrate conflict to tackle adaptive challenges. There is value in taking stakeholders out of the business-as-usual environment to engage in orchestrated discussions, but the value of these formal conversations is in their power to build capacity for stakeholders to have generative, unorchestrated conversations about race and racism when they return to their daily professional lives. Facilitated discussions enable stakeholders to establish a holding environment that can eventually develop into informal conversations for stakeholders to engage in generative conversations about race with intentionality, thus normalizing the practice throughout the organization.

Facilitated conversations are necessary because many of us don't know how to talk about race. The holding environment, what we call "a positive, encouraging, liberating dialogic environment" (Bridges Patrick, 2020, p. 171), must stretch people beyond the comfort that is often conflated with the term "safe space" (for further discussion of the term "safe space," see Chapter 9). The assertion that a conversation will be comfortable practically guarantees participants will avoid vulnerability, a necessary ingredient for generative mobilizing dialogue. The dialogic environment is a space where tension, conflict, and challenge are invited and used for information and transformation, where disagreement is needed and must be expected, and "strong emotions are seen as expression rather than personal attacks" (Bridges Patrick, 2020, p. 172). The space must not only be free from actual or threats of physical and/or emotional violence, it must also center around dignity and inherent worth for everyone. Essential to organized conversations is a confident facilitator.

Facilitator Capacity

Facilitated conversations about race and racism require a facilitator who will ensure that the dignity of each person is honored. The facilitator should also be skilled in navigating some hallmarks of racial dialogue: tension, discomfort, and stress. Furthermore, the facilitator's racial literacy—racial competence and the ability to navigate its complex dynamics in a group setting—should be well developed. Given the emotional weight of talking about race and racism, the facilitator should also be able to recognize and embrace appropriate opportunities for laughter. This emotional release is critical to sustaining stakeholders as they labor for racial justice.

Role of Organizational Leaders

Heifetz et al. (2009) distinguish between technical and adaptive approaches to "protection" of an organization and its employees. Exercising uncritical direction in confronting racial injustice (a technical approach) can unwittingly insulate people from disequilibrium and interrupt justice efforts. Practicing leadership (an adaptive approach) alerts employees to external threats so that they can recognize adaptive challenges and begin the adaptive process of addressing the challenge. An adaptive leader will not let an organization ignore the existence of racism and White supremacy; they will, however, establish strong holding environments that invite essential capacity-building discourse. Once members are collectively mobilized and supported to build their understanding of racial dominance and facilitate conversations about racism and White supremacy, a leader can step in to protect employees from unproductive external threats such as being fired for being too "political" or an angry White client claiming the organization promotes "reverse racism." Supporting people who labor for racial justice in this way (spending political capital to ensure job security, preventing a person from berating an employee, and creating educational supports and conversational spaces for the angry individuals are ways in which positional leaders can leverage their authority), keeping the temperature within the "productive zone of disequilibrium" (Heifetz et al., 2009, p. 30) so that the staff can continue their adaptive work.

Increasing a System's Overall Capacity for Continuous Learning

At its heart, adaptive work requires an ongoing commitment to learning and learning is at the heart of capacity-building dialogue. Preskill and Brookfield (2009) describe "learning leadership" as leadership that centers a "commitment to, and practice of, learning" (p. 14). In addition to developing their own capacity to learn, learning leaders see "the learning of members as the most important purpose of an organization" (p. 14). When individual members learn and adapt, they contribute to systems-level organizational learning and adaptation.

A story often told by organizations in the helping professions, which are frequently led and staffed by White women, is that they know what's best for children and families. Historically, Black, Latinx, and Asian students have been legally excluded from educational spaces via segregation, racist admission policies, and dress codes that remove students from class for "unprofessional" dress or hair. In one of many examples, Indigenous children were removed from their homes, cultures, and languages and given to White families or forced to attend boarding schools that were sites of attempted cultural genocide as referenced in Senate Bill

4752, Truth and Healing Commission on Indian Boarding School Policy Act (2020). Today, this assimilationism continues and impacts all minoritized populations as organizations police Black, Indigenous, and People of Color (BIPOC) individuals' dress and hair through racist dress codes, problematize multilingual people through labels relating to English proficiency, and dictate to, rather than partner with, clients and families. Creating a liberating dialogic environment is a necessary part of continuous learning to confront White supremacist organizational culture, building personal, interpersonal, and organizational capacity to advance racial justice.

Heifetz et al. (2009) list several components of building an adaptive culture. In addition to naming the "elephants in the room," an adaptive culture requires all stakeholders to "share responsibility for the organization's future" (p. 103). Heifetz et al. (2009) emphasize the importance of developing leadership capacity to sustain a thriving adaptive culture. Mitchell and Sackney's (2011) capacity building framework highlights the importance of developing leadership capacity on all three levels: growing individual stakeholder capacities for engaging in critical reflection of system and self, building the interpersonal muscles to engage in generative dialogue about race and racism, and structurally providing opportunities for all stakeholders to be leaders in the organization. The cultural aspect of organizational capacity-building that Mitchell and Sackney write about correlates with Heifetz and colleagues' call for institutionalizing reflection and learning. We call this "systematizing the process of diagnosis." It involves a multidimensional approach to capacity building and, using organizational structures, embeds this inclusive diagnostic process into the fabric of an organization's culture. To make this work, sustainable organizations must embed structures that facilitate regular inter-stakeholder discourse and collective decision-making.

Capacity Building Through Shared Leadership

Organizations that do not broaden conceptions of leadership to include more than the leaders at the top of the organizational chart miss an opportunity for exponential transformation. An organization's leadership structure (i.e., how decisions are made and who is involved) influences organizational policy, which types of data will be collected and analyzed, and how money will be spent. If racial justice is not a priority for the leadership team or if the team is not representative of all stakeholders who experience and contribute to the problem, racism and White supremacy will persist.

United States Representative Ayanna Pressley (2019) says, "People closest to the pain should be closest to the power" (para 2). She asserts "that a diversity of voices in the political process is essential to making policies that benefit more Americans" (para. 2). The same is true for an organization's decision-making process. Systems that ensure "people closest to the pain" are equitably represented on leadership teams enable their organization to continuously grow and learn from stakeholders with varied experiences and insights. Such a shift—fundamentally changing the structure of how decisions are made—is a far cry from a one-time focus group. Minor (2019) defines inclusion: "Inclusivity... does not simply mean that 'you are allowed to be present here.' To be included means 'we have changed ourselves and our practices to make 'here' a place where you can thrive,'" (p. 36).

Mary Parker Follet (1924) laid out several reasons for sharing power, asserting that the act of sharing power is generative. She insists that bringing together stakeholders with different ideas and experiences to lift up and confront those various desires "means a freeing for both sides and increased total power or increased capacity in the world" (p. 302), strikingly similar to mobilizing discourse. Follet's example of mobilizing discourse is supported by shared decision-making structures; it also requires individuals to build capacity for this type of discourse both through the individual work of interrogating their own beliefs and loyalties and consistent practice of generative mobilizing discourse at all levels—personal, interpersonal, and organizational.

With regard to leaders who see inclusion as merely asking for feedback in lieu of multi-stakeholder, mobilizing discourse, the application of turbulence theory is instructive. In 2009, Mitra and Gross urged schools to practice building capacity for student leadership, using turbulence theory to support their position. Just like Heifetz et al. (2009) argue that disequilibrium must be in a productive zone, they emphasized that merely listening to stakeholders (in this example, students) actually increases individual and organizational turbulence (i.e., disequilibrium) because it only surfaces problems that were previously ignored; it does not necessarily address them. However, building capacity for sustained stakeholder (e.g., student) leadership decreases turbulence for organizations and individuals as it enables organization-wide communication with real plans to address existing problems. Initially, enabling stakeholder groups to take on leadership roles in organizations when historically they have not held such positions may trigger a default response, such as "they can't lead." However, Eichholz's (2017) framework reminds us that reinforcing patterns of the past pulls organizations away from mobilizing discourses. Mitra and Gross's (2009) analysis illustrates the importance of innovation and capacity building. Their work helped to stabilize educational communities to continuously learn and grow. Furthermore, it supports our approach to addressing White supremacy through the development of sustainable, adaptive capacity, rather than technical fixes. And, as stated previously, organizations and leaders will need to confront the underlying beliefs and loyalties that have heretofore impeded mobilizing discourse and commit to consistently building generative dialogue capacity.

Conclusion

The old ways of addressing racial injustice have not worked. Asking ourselves diagnostic questions inspired by Heifetz et al. (2009), we realize racial dominance to be an adaptive challenge. In the helping professions, are our systems operating to maintain White supremacy, preventing new and imaginative ideas? Yes. Have previous initiatives failed to address the racial injustice? Yes. Do we find ourselves looking to others to tell us how to fix racism instead of looking inward, at our-selves? Yes. Does the political landscape encourage us to avoid talking about race? Yes. On September 22, 2020, then United States President Donald Trump signed an executive order calling antiracist discourse "pernicious," "false," and "destructive," and claiming talking about race "promote[s] divisiveness," and "misrepresent[s] our country's his-tory and its role in the world" (Exec Order No. 13950, 2020). This response to widespread calls to talk about racial justice is just one reason the answer to this question is yes.

The how is less clear. That's the nature of adaptive leadership—there are no clear solutions. We know that the stories we tell are critical–whether they reinforce past patterns or spark generative discourse that charts a new future in which racial injustice is our history, not our present. We know that the power of these stories is aided by tools to address adaptive work. We know that we must first diagnose the challenge. We have to name the previously unnameable before we can address the challenges we face. We must invest in building dialogic capacity across three dimensions (personal, interpersonal, and organizational). We need to create structures of shared leadership to systematize and normalize the process of diagnosis and capacity building. We know that these tools will ultimately sustain the types of discourse that unravel the hold White su-premacy has on our psyches, our lives, and our organizations. And finally, we know that if we can build our personal, interpersonal, and organiza-tional capacity for mobilizing discourse, we can begin to unpack the stories we tell, identify the beliefs we hold, and collaboratively dismantle oppression, transforming organizations into systems that center on justice and healing.

References

Akbar, N. (1996). *Breaking the chains of psychological slavery*. Mind Productions & Associates.

Bridges Patrick, C. (2020). *Navigating the silences: Social worker discourses around race*. [Doctoral dissertation, Antioch University Graduate School of

Leadership and Change]. Antioch University Repository & Archive. AURA. https://aura.antioch.edu/etds/560

Brown, B. (2006). Shame resilience theory: A grounded theory study on women and shame. *Families in Society*, 87(1), 43–52. 10.1606/1044-3894.3483

Eichholz, J. C. (2017). *Adaptive Capacity: How organizations can thrive in a changing.* (2nd ed.). LID Publishing.

Essed, P. (1991). *Understanding everyday racism: An interdisciplinary theory.* Routledge.

Essed, P. (1996). *Diversity: Gender, color, and culture.* University of Massachusetts Press.

Exec. Order No. 13950, 85 Fed. Reg. 60683 (September 22, 2020).

Follet, M. P. (1924). *Creative experience.* Longmans Green.

Frankenberg, R. (1993). *White women, race matters: The social construction of whiteness.* University of Minnesota Press.

Harbin, M. Brielle, Thurber, Amie, and Bandy, Joe (2019). Teaching race, racism, and racial justice: Pedagogical principles and classroom strategies for course instructors. *Race and Pedagogy Journal: Teaching and Learning for Justice*, 4(1), 1–37. Available at: https://soundideas.pugetsound.edu/rpj/vol4/iss1/1.

Heifetz, R. (1994). *Leadership without easy answers.* Harvard University Press.

Heifetz, R., Grashow, A. and Linsky, M. (2009). *The practice of adaptive leadership: Tools and tactics for changing your organization and the world.* Harvard Business Press.

hooks, b. (1992). *Representing whiteness in the black imagination.* Routledge.

Kendi, I. X. (2019). *How to be an antiracist.* One World.

Levine-Rasky, C. (2016). *Whiteness fractured.* Routledge.

McCready, L. and Soloway, G. (2010). Teacher's perceptions of challenging student behaviours in model inner city schools. *Emotional and Behavioural Difficulties*, 15(2), 111–123.

Menakem, R. (2019). *My grandmother's hands: Racialized trauma and the pathway to mending our hearts and bodies.* Central Recovery Press.

Miller, J., & Donner, S. (2000). More than just talk: The use of racial dialogues to combat racism. *Social Work With Groups*, 23(1), 31–53. 10.1300/J009v23n01_03

Minor, Cornelius. (2019). *We got this: Equity, access, and the quest to be who our students need us to be.* Heinemann.

Mitchell, C. & Sackney, L. (2011). *Profound improvement: Building capacity for a learning community.* Routledge.

Mitra, D., and Gross, S. (2009), Increasing student voice in high school reform: Building partnerships, improving outcome. *Educational Management Administration & Leadership*, 37(4), 522–543.

Preskill, S., & Brookfield, S. (2009). *Learning as a way of leading: Lessons from the struggle for social justice.* Jossey-Bass.

Pressley, A. (2019). Meet Ayanna. https://pressley.house.gov/about

Social Work Policy Institute. (2014). *Achieving racial equity: Calling the social work profession to action.* Washington, DC: National Association of Social Workers. http://www.socialworkpolicy.org/news-events/report-on-achieving-racial-equity.html

Truth and Healing Commission on Indian Boarding School Policy Act, S.4752, 116th Cong. (2020). https://www.congress.gov/bill/116th-congress/senate-bill/4752/text

van Dijk, T. A. (1992). Discourse and the denial of racism. *Discourse & Society*, 3(1), 87–118. 10.1177/0957926592003001005.

White, B. W. (Ed.). (1984). *Color in a White society: Selected papers from the NASW Conference, Los Angeles, California, June 1982*. Los Angeles, CA: National Association of Social Workers.

Wodak, R. (2015). Critical discourse analysis, discourse-historical approach. In K. Tracy (Ed.), *The international encyclopedia of language and social interaction*, Vol. I, 275–288. 10.1002/9781118611463.wbielsi116

9 Activism Has Lost Its Way: The Case for Micro-Activism

Jeffery MacDonald Hardesty,
Michael Christopher Boyce, and
Harriette Thurber Rasmussen

Mainstream socio-political discourse in the present day has poised these authors to contemplate the attributes of activism and our collective capacity to authentically engage in the resolution of social issues. A rich body of examples suggests that ideologies have become alarmingly polarized and that the midground for effectively addressing social concerns is diminishing. If we are to realize genuine social progress, leaders must work to build our collective capacity to examine, reflect on, and value the differences inherent in a complex society. We maintain that large-scale activism contributes to polarization and that authentic progress is best realized through small-scale deliberate actions, what we term micro-activism. Through empathic, reflective dialogue, micro-activism can reframe the polarities of society to draw on the power of individual dualities and collective diversity.

This chapter is a call-to-arms for the adaptive leader to perceive activism as a micro-level effort to build community capacity for real dialogue and the social tension that arises between individuals as they wrestle with opposing viewpoints around complex, adaptive problems. We argue, as do others (Eichholz, 2014; Heifetz et al., 2009), that the ultimate purpose of leadership is to build adaptive capacity. We maintain, as do others (Moorosi, 2014; Santamaría & Jean-Marie, 2014), that the work of leaders is to create constructive environments to engage in dialogue that induces dissonance in psychologically safe environments. In such spaces, referred to by Heifetz as "holding environments," micro-level engagement offers opportunities for "conversations and new definitions, acknowledging losses … discouraging defensive behavior, … and exposing mistakes rather than hiding them" (Eichholz, 2014, p. 32). Thus, this chapter will champion micro-activism, offering insight into the nuances adaptive leaders may expect to encounter when orchestrating dialogue. It will outline action learning as an effective structure for the empathic and reflective dialogue we argue is essential for progress. And it will reposition our differences as duality in order to celebrate and progress, rather than denigrate and impede, the diversity that empowers a society to thrive.

DOI: 10.4324/9781003099109-9

We argue that dualities of values and beliefs are present within individuals as well as in the collective. Large-scale activism often results in collective polarization, leaving individuals to commit to sides rather than wrestling with and accepting the duality inside themselves. In contrast, acting on collective duality surfaces the inherent ideological contradictions that are in each of us, a discovery that involves micro-moments of self-awareness, small-scale and careful induction of cognitive dissonance in ways that reframe opposition—polarization—into the opportunities afforded by duality. In short, this chapter will champion micro-activism as a construct to mitigate polarization by presenting a celebrated alternative—cognitive duality—and with this a renewed capacity for positive social change.

Cognitive Duality

With the recognition that our growth as individuals and the growth of society relies on the cognitive conflict that accompanies change, adaptive leaders hold immensely powerful tools for micro-activist work. Consistent small-scale, inclusive actions allow adaptive leaders to carefully take themselves and their communities to the productive edge of dissonance and discomfort without falling over. In this context, strategies to find common ground release negative tension to enable what we term cognitive duality, a self-awareness of the ideological contradictions we hold in ourselves. Through cognitive duality, we establish a capacity that includes acceptance of the other and their associated ideas in tandem with our own—because we have recognized such dualities within ourselves. Experiencing cognitive duality is personal; its promotion must recognize the vulnerable and disorienting nature of discovery through dissonance. Thus, cognitive duality occurs at the micro-level and through micro-inclusion.

Micro-Inclusion

Large-scale inclusion is exclusive. Ironically, many of the inclusive practices that are professed and put into place exclude individuals who do not conform to the collective rules of inclusion. Even language can create an exclusive barrier in an inclusive group, as we will point out below. Thus, we propose a micro approach and maintain that feelings of inclusion are dependent upon micro-moments, micro-connections between individuals where one experiences another's curiosity, empathy, and acceptance.

Micro-inclusion is preliminary to recognizing and accepting cognitive duality; both are prerequisites to micro-activism and, as we explain, to developing and maintaining adaptive capacity through conflict.

Conflict and Adaptive Capacity

Conflict is a necessary element of adaptive work. How a social system uses conflict productively is a measure of its adaptive capacity. Adaptive capacity uses conflict strategically to advantage learning, including "creating a state of disequilibrium before it is created by external conditions, [avoiding the] complacency that can arise [during] a long period of equilibrium" (Eichholz, 2014, p. 20). Adaptive learning is central to adaptive capacity; Heifetz clarifies that such learning is not about "answers or assured visions but of taking action to clarify values" (1994, p. 35). Heifetz (1994) describes low adaptive capacity as situations in which individuals ignore any "disparity between values and circumstances" (p. 35) and function as technical problem solvers, providing only one-dimensional solutions to complex problems. Heifetz (1994) asserts, "Low adaptive capacity may derive from lack of experience in conflict resolution, absence of shared orienting values, reluctance to endure short-term pain to obtain long-term benefit, or feeble bonds of identity and trust among the parties" (p. 121).

In the simplest of terms, Eichholz (2014) measures adaptive capacity through the degree of responsiveness and participation, which we interpret as intimately related micro-processes of activism and inclusion. He distinguishes varied types of conversations: those that are entrenched and inauthentic, reinforcing patterns of the past with those that open possibilities, in which "people feel the tension yet remain engaged in the conversation" (2014, p. 108). See also Chapter 8. Tension caused by operationalizing reflective practice can control dissonance for the purpose of increasing productivity. Dissonance, however, can lead to social hostility between groups and individuals (Allen & Wergin, 2009; Kegan & Lahey, 2001). Argyris (1997) would argue that socially hostile tension often arises when individuals discover contradictions in their own thinking; Festinger (1957) notes the struggle to assuage the discomfort of these cognitive disparities. Such hostility is exacerbated through different approaches to learning, understandings of problems, and aptitudes for adapting to challenges (Baltes et al., 1999; Drago-Severson, 2009; Houchens & Keedy, 2009). In other words, coming to grips with our own, sometimes competing, dualities and those of others leads to social tension.

Stakeholders in systems with high adaptive capacity engage in authentic dialogue in response to environmental realities. This type of dialogue, and by extension adaptive capacity, is essential to micro-activism, where stakeholders are willing to examine differing values and belief systems through intentional micro-inclusion. Conflicts that emerge, when reframed and harnessed, become the source of energy and resolution and in doing so, a source of learning. We also assert, as do others, that adaptive capacity can be developed at multiple levels: within individuals and across a collective, or a system. As Coudel et al. (2011) explain, "The increasing complexity of objectives can only be addressed through increasing complexity of learning processes from individual learning to group learning, to organizational learning, and finally to societal learning" (p. 130).

In our view, activism is impeded by our collective inability to resolve conflict well, and by, as Heifetz (1994) points out, a reluctance to engage in the social tension and resulting cognitive dissonance needed to resolve ideological differences well. In micro-activism, conflict becomes an opportunity for an enhanced perspective about orienting values and one's dualities, necessary ingredients for developing adaptive capacity. We assert that our sense of identity, loyalties to one set or another of ideologies, are either discounted, affirmed, or modified through a well-orchestrated process.

We return here to the premise of our chapter, which is that polarized social tension becomes productive through cognitive duality. Essential components that reveal cognitive duality include managed cognitive dissonance supported by empathic disposition and strategic, adaptive learning. These actions are fueled by micro-inclusion and allow for positive significance on differing perspectives and values within and across individuals (duality), furthering a new collective purpose and framework for solving problems. Key, then, to activism is managing cognitive dissonance to forward a duality perspective.

Managing Cognitive Dissonance

Wheatley (2002) positions the conversations we have, in work, in life, and in love, as the "natural way ... humans think together" (p. 42), yet this seems a far cry from current communicative trends that weaponize words to fortify or exclude one ideology over another. Even in drafting this chapter, our original phrasing of "safe space" to describe psychologically safe environments incited raw emotions from one of us who was once excluded in an environment that claimed to be "safe." (See Chapter 8 for further discussion of safe space.) We found our own dialogue an apt illustration of the ways in which word choice influences how information is perceived and processed, including its potential to cause polarization. Language matters. In an era of misinformation and its super spreaders (i.e., social media, slanted news coverage), language can also be an excuse for distinctly missing the point, consciously and subconsciously sidelining important conversations, a classic case of what Heifetz et al. (2009) would term "work avoidance" of addressing complex social issues. Carefully managed, however, language that might otherwise be polarizing can subtly provoke an internal questioning process through dissonance that powers a journey through the loops of learning and adaptation.

Managing language to reframe dissonance into learning requires an understanding that polarized reaction and avoidance are, in part, a result of the bias, judgment, and ideological contradictions that exist within individuals. Psychological theorists provide that these "psychological processes operate outside of people's awareness" (Strack & Deutsch, 2015, p. 894), which "cause conflicts between incompatible judgments and behaviors" (p. 892). Strack and Deutsch further explain that our experiences are subjective and are filtered cognitively through "a specific elicitor ('I have a bad feeling about this chair')" [p. 895], driving our inferences and behavioral decisions. Most individuals "do not follow optimal rules for information aggregation. They rely on simple heuristics for updating their beliefs" (Bottom et al., 2002, p. 148), leading to judgment as a product of information updating, with the frequency of recall about an event associated with an increase in skewed judgment. Humans are incredibly adept at displaying confirmation bias and disregarding experiences that do not reinforce previously held beliefs and judgment; reinforcement is a natural function and outcome of cognitive processing.

Unfortunately, Bottom et al. (2002) also claim that judgment becomes more skewed within a larger group context. The more complex the context, the more likely judgments are based on bias, and the less likely the group will help to reform an individual's skewed perspective. Bias-to-judgment of one individual can propagate rapidly through the ranks, resulting in bias at scale, and reinnforcing contradictions (i.e., polarization, between two opposing groups or individuals).

These contradictions, though, also represent the zone of cognitive duality, where one becomes acquainted with inconsistencies and contradictions in one's own—and others'—belief systems. Frankish (2010) theorizes that we hold multiple dualities within us, one of which is a dual *processing* system. He argues that we process with two systems, one that is reactive, quick, and emotional. A second processing system is slower, more prone to rational thought. Important to adaptive work, however, is another line of theories related to dual "systems," which assert that we are able to hold dual, and often conflicting, beliefs and values simultaneously, often without knowing that we do so. Frankish (2010) points out that "it has been argued that a two-systems perspective can explain forms of irrationality involving mental conflict" (p. 10), thus confirming what others have suggested around duality, even if not termed in that exact manner. (See, for example, Kegan and Lahey [2009] and their discussion of competing commitments.)

The careful management we note above requires attention to stakeholders' cognitive processing, turning early signs of polarization into duality and, by extension, opportunities for learning. Duality then becomes a tool to orchestrate conflict, to recognize the benefits and reasoning of the other, and, drawing upon an inherent need for inclusion, surface shared values to capitalize upon that duality. To be clear, this is micro-level work, dependent upon micro-inclusion that is person-specific and that ultimately repositions socialized trends to capitalize upon group duality. This is micro-activism in action and is, we argue, dependent upon empathic disposition.

Empathic Disposition

Critical for adaptive leaders to understand is that the dispositions that drive behavior can change and that the experiences one constructs with others can serve to change one's disposition. Thus, when managing social tension, adaptive leaders must carefully attend to stakeholder disposition to disrupt and outsmart cognitive processes that may become polarizing (Hardesty, 2018; Weick, 1995). Hector et al. (2013), for example, discovered that the type of social tension we describe earlier is exacerbated by group members who are socially dominant. Sidanius et al. (2013) found that one's social dominance orientation affects their political conservatism, ideology of colorblindness, justification of suppression—precisely the type of polarized tension encountered in activist, adaptive work. Social dominance also relates to "individual differences in the preference for group-based hierarchy and inequality" (Sidanius et al., 2013, p. 313) and often manifests in neglectful attitudes toward others, resulting in systematized social suppression (Hector et al., 2013; Nordgren et al., 2011; Sidanius et al., 2013).

Whereas suppression is not the only source of social tension, the relationship of social dominance to the suppression of others, particularly during times of cognitive dissonance and polarization, cannot be overstated. Empathy, however, has the potential to mitigate social dominance (Nordgren, et al., 2011; Sidanius, et al., 2013; Zorza et al., 2013) and thus relieve social tension. Empathy is an ideological attitude (Hector et al., 2013; Sidanius et al., 2013) and significantly influences all types of social interactions (Nordgren, et al., 2011; Sidanius, et al., 2013; Zorza et al., 2013). As Wheatley (2002) emphasizes the strategic, social, and psychological need for conversation, it is also imperative to acknowledge that conversations taking place in heated environments carry the capacity for explosive as well as productive results. Intentionally utilizing the micro aspects of activism and inclusion opens the door for empathy to slowly shift the degree of reciprocal understanding and guard against dramatic moves into polarized thought.

Empathic Concern and Perspective

There exists a large body of research and theoretic discourse on the concept of empathy. Appropriate to this chapter, we examine the role an empathic disposition plays in a social setting between individuals as they examine their values and beliefs in managing social tension. For this purpose, we narrow our discussion to the basic constructs of empathic concern and empathic perspective-taking. Empathic concern is demonstrated through affective response to another individual's emotional experience. Empathic perspective-taking is the act of seeing something from another person's point of view (Nordgren et al., 2011; Sidanius et al., 2013). Interestingly, researchers have found that an individual's empathic disposition impacts an individual's social competence and social standing. Members of a social group are often granted a higher social status based on their level of empathic concern (Hardesty, 2018; Zorza et al., 2013) and can dictate the outcome of discussions geared to serve underrepresented individuals through empathic concern and empathic perspective-taking (Hardesty, 2018; Nellis, 2012; Sanger et al., 2012).

Further, empathy has been found to govern emotions during socially uncomfortable interactions and to moderate social suppression of others. Researchers determine that some individuals exhibit empathy gaps whereby the individual underestimates another's social pain during social exclusion (Nordgren et al., 2011), a low level of empathic concern. Nordgren et al. point out that empathy gaps can become "systematic" (p. 120) as an ideological configuration that falls on one side of a polarized social argument or the other. Recall our discussion that information updating serves as a cognitive process to affirm pre-existing ideologies, including bias and judgment. The degree of empathic concern and perspective-taking mitigates or exacerbates the systematization of ideology in a social setting; one's response to empathic attitudes can fortify the very stances that promote or impede dialogue and adaptive progress (Bloom, 2016). Empathic feelings extended only to individuals and groups with shared traits, background, or experience create a risk of exacerbating an exclusionary or concurrence-seeking environment (Johnson, 2015), whereas the presence of empathic perspective-taking and concern have the opposite effect, enhancing feelings of inclusion.

Thus, while the presence of empathic concern and perspective-taking are pivotal to an inclusive environment and the resolution of social tension, critically important to that process are reflective practices that push past immediate bias and predilection to sameness to an alternative way of thinking, reframing polarization into duality to set the stage for micro-activist and micro-inclusive work. Strategic management of empathy, then, requires an awareness of stakeholders' respective dispositions, ideological attitudes, and social positioning, what Hardesty (2018) terms disposition mapping.

Disposition Mapping

We've been referencing polarization as if it is a negative, inhibiting progress and we don't argue that point. At the same time, diversity is a critical component to progress and without diversity, polarization would not exist. The challenge is not to strive for an absence of polarization, but instead, as discussed earlier, a reframing of the concept in ways that draw on its power, rather than its detriment. In this chapter, we hold reframing as synonymous with what Argyris and Schön (1974, 1978, 1996) term "double-loop learning" and Nielsen's (1993a, 1993b) extension to "triple-loop learning." Discussed in detail below, what is important to understand at this juncture about double- and triple-loop learning is that these processes systematically and intentionally produce cognitive dissonance, which we have positioned as essential to micro-activism and Heifetz et al. (2009) argue is critical to adaptive work. Clearly a stressful process at best, leaders are challenged to maintain a level of dissonance at a rate that is tolerable, yet still productive toward goals. Heifetz et al. (2009) recommend diagnosing a system's political landscape as a matter of course in addressing an adaptive challenge, considering, as examples, stakeholders' relationship to the issue, their loyalties, and noblest values (p. 100). We offer a tool for setting the arrangement, disposition mapping, which provides a "roadmap for understanding socialization while conducting … sense-making opportunities" (Hardesty, 2018, p. 154).

Disposition mapping is a social learning construct assembled from many contributions from organizational learning, adult learning, and social justice scholars, as well as contributions from the field of psychology. Simply put, disposition mapping is "a construct for making the complex nature of human interaction less complex by conceiving personality patterns as predictable arrangements" (Hardesty, 2018, p. 154). Hardesty (2018) maintains that leaders should understand "… how individuals are positioned by others socially in … variable contexts" (p. 154). Pertinent to this chapter, disposition mapping includes empathic disposition, which we have claimed to be a key contributor to managing social tension and strategic social positioning.

Thornton (2006) examined disposition as the active nature of a person and studied how dispositions manifest themselves in complex social settings. She views dispositions as habits of mind, including "cognitive and affective attributes that filter one's knowledge, skills, and beliefs and impact the action one takes" (p. 62) in a social setting. Thornton states further that dispositions "are manifested within relationships as meaning-making occurs with others and they are evidenced through interactions in the form of discourse" (p. 62). Mischel and Shoda (1995) maintain that dispositions can be calculated through personality patterns of individuals across a variety of situations or by viewing personality patterns as a developmental process during social interactions. Recall, for example, our ability to predict that members of a social group are afforded social status based on their empathic disposition.

Position Theory

Social justice scholars and social psychology literature further illuminate the importance of status in social settings through position theory. Position theory examines how systematized dominance patterns and ideological attitudes grant or deny access to others (Camicia, 2015; Santamaría, 2014) and how the ways in which people find meaning from these experiences (Baines, 2014; Harré & Slocum, 2003; Harré et al., 2009) can entrench social conflict (Harré & Slocum, 2003). Recall our earlier discussion about social dominance and its relationship to systematized social suppression (Hector et al., 2013; Nordgren et al., 2011; Sidanius et al., 2013). Position theory addresses a propensity for entrenchment and social dominance through the discovery of positional storylines that can be reframed to achieve resolution (Harré & Slocum, 2003; Harré et al., 2009). Heifetz (1994) has discussed this notion as a strategy to drive adaptive change by capitalizing on the relationships between formal leaders and informal leaders—how they position each other socially and politically to leverage action or inaction toward social change.

Key to managing empathy and productive social tension, then, are (1) predictions of stakeholder behavior, including empathic concern and perspective-taking; (2) awareness of the role of social positioning within a group; and (3) understanding that, while predictable, disposition can still be developed through social interaction. These insights form the basis of disposition mapping.

Disposition mapping draws upon a leader's knowledge of the stakeholders they lead. Too, leaders must recognize their own disposition and how it may interact or influence others. Importantly, Allen and Wergin (2009) explain the need for leaders to adjust to stakeholders' "cognitive resources, motivational dispositions, [and] socialization strategies" in order to support their growth (p. 6). With a keen awareness of stakeholder dispositions, the predictability of personality trends allows leaders to position stakeholders in the best holding environments for collective activism to be realized, effectively arranging the reflective experience for a social change to be eventually realized. In doing so, leaders learn more about the respective dispositions of their stakeholders and the social positions that have been assigned to them by their peers, and even society. Careful grouping allows leaders to control the ebb and flow of social tension (Houchens & Keedy, 2009), thereby managing an intentional reflective process within that specific social dynamic (Hardesty, 2018). For example, an individual with an outlier ideology might be grouped with individuals who exhibit empathic dispositions. The deliberate presence of empathy in the group will allow the outlier member to feel heard, potentially raising the social status of those who exhibit empathy to the outlier, shifting the social dynamics from one of opposition to reflection and learning. Empathic disposition allows those with an aversion to the outlier ideology to engage in authentic dialogue, micro-inclusion, while developing the outlier's disposition through empathic concern and perspective-taking in a psychologically safe holding environment. In other words, disposition mapping enables the productive and purposeful use of cognitive dissonance through micro-inclusion, as we have argued, an essential element of micro-activism.

Disposition mapping, with particular attention to empathic disposition and social positioning, allows leaders to consider stakeholders' readiness to engage in a model known as action learning, a process that ultimately aligns stakeholder behaviors with the collective values and beliefs for organizational productivity (Hardesty, 2018), which we believe can also be an inherent process for activist pursuits. Action learning forwards a reflective practice that develops "instruments [to] enable common problem solving and close communications" (Cohen & Moffitt, 2013, p. 78). Coupled with disposition mapping, action learning uses micro-inclusion as a route to push polarization into duality and micro-activism.

Aligning Beliefs and Behaviors through Action Learning

We have argued that purposeful creation of social tension can increase capacity for activism, and indeed, Heifetz et al. (2009) maintain that progress cannot happen in the absence of conflict. As Heifetz (1994) asserts, "The leader as educator has to engage the parties in a process of inquiry that accounts for their fear or pain, if learning is to be productive" (p. 245). There is, however, a potential risk in orchestrating social conflict if it leads to a premature alignment of values and beliefs before the groundwork has taken place to help individuals identify contradictions in what they say they believe with how they behave and act (Allen & Wergin, 2009; Kegan & Lahey, 2001). The discomfort of dissonance commonly results in self-justification behaviors to protect oneself from the disruptive nature of change; thus illogically, the more convincing the argument, the greater the likelihood of resistance and perhaps an even more polarized position (Tavris & Aronson, 2020). Adaptive leaders must identify the opportunities of dissonance and orchestrate this dissonant energy to power a shift in thinking around new and perhaps radically disparate views. The cascading single-, double-, and triple-loops of action learning discussed below are critical to this evolution (see also Chapters 2 and 8). Contrary to grand gestures of activism, action learning embodies micro-inclusion and, as is true with all adaptive work, is dependent upon a strong holding environment, in this case, to allow stakeholders to process contrary information and find comfort in dualities.

Single- and Double-Loop Learning

Organizational scholars Argyris and Schön (1974, 1978, 1996) found that internal tension often arises when individuals discover contradictions in their own thinking. They offer a framework through which stakeholders engage in a reflective process to identify contradictions between what they state as their beliefs (espoused theories) and what is reflected in their behaviors and actions (theories-in-use). The learning that takes place through this type of reflection, termed double-loop learning, is distinct from single-loop learning that fails to consider one's internal sensemaking (Argyris & Schön, 1974, 1978, 1996). Single-loop learning falls in line with one aspect of Frankish's (2010) theory on dual processing systems. Recall that one of the ways we process information is reactive, quick, and emotional. This is typically how one might experience single-loop learning; we reinforce what we already know, or change behavior to align with the results, but without examining the underlying assumptions and structures that cause us to behave the way we do in the first place. Single-loop learning can be very effective for technical challenges.

On the other hand, double-loop learning addresses an individual's meaning-making system, the values that govern one's ideas and actions. In a process we term reframing, double-loop learning asks stakeholders to, at a minimum, surface assumptions around a given challenge and illuminate behavioral inconsistencies or contradictions (i.e., espoused theories versus theories-in-use). The desired outcome is better alignment between one's guiding principles, and beliefs and behaviors. Importantly to this chapter, however, is that, coupled with disposition mapping and micro-inclusion, such contradictions expose and explain the challenges Heifetz et al. (2009) associate with adaptive work: conflicting loyalties, values, and accompanying loss. Recognizing *and accepting* one's internal contradictions is a first step to cognitive duality and ultimately overcoming polarization. It is also preliminary to triple-loop learning.

Triple-Loop Learning

Nielsen (1993a, 1993b) introduced triple-loop learning as action learning in a larger social context. "In triple-loop action learning, actors go beyond questioning their own values and consider the values of the societal tradition system in which their actions are taking place" (Foldy & Creed, 1999, p. 213). Triple-loop learning generates "exchange mechanisms" to acquire new knowledge and develop social [adaptive] capacity for changes in practice to occur particularly in complex systems. Coudel et al. (2011) explain:

> In the case of more complex [adaptive] problems, for which existing strategies do not work, the actors need to define new ways of acting

to better interact and to define new values through double-loop learning. And in a situation of uncertainty, actors need to explore new possibilities. It may be necessary to use triple-loop learning to find new ways of thinking and therefore new ways of seeing problems and their solution. The increasing complexity of objectives can only be addressed through increasing complexity of learning processes from individual learning to group learning, to organizational learning, and finally to societal learning. (pp. 129–130)

Triple-loop learning reframes *collective* action, the values, beliefs, and contradictions within a system, or at an organizational level. We assert that it is at the systems level that grand gestures of activism trend toward fragmentation and polarization and it is through double- and triple-loop learning that leaders can guide, first individuals, and then groups to recognize and embrace duality to enable inclusion. To quote Greenwood (1998), this type of learning "is essential to the creation of desirable social worlds since their creation hinges on the redesign of social structures as well as human action" (p. 1050).

The Artful Adaptive Leader

These are the moments in time when adaptive leaders do their most stirring work and we argue it to be an art form. Adaptive leaders anticipate and orchestrate difficult situations before they occur naturally, to halt cognitive processes that reinforce an individual's retreat into polarization. Artful leaders know that the greatest challenges often arise from the unexpected, that which we never considered. They draw on empathic disposition and micro-inclusive practices to bridge the gap of understanding through celebration of duality.

In this chapter, we have called out two foundational practices of adaptive leadership—the holding environment and orchestrating conflict—in service of activism. We have chosen to position activism in its smallest form—micro activism—in recognition that large-scale movements exacerbate polarization and fail to take into account the individual nature of adaptive work, that of surfacing and positioning values and beliefs in service of larger goals. We argue that a duality of values, biases, and beliefs is present within individuals, as well as in the collective, and that acting upon collective duality is dependent upon surfacing inherent ideological contradictions that are in each of us. In doing so, we point out the opportunities afforded through action learning to reposition polarization toward duality—and the ability to celebrate the complex nature of our intellectual, emotional, and social selves.

The evolution of our ideas and how we as individuals adapt to changing stimuli are the critical components of adaptive leadership successes. Through the recognition of the prevalence of adaptive change and the cognitive dissonance that comes with every change, as well as opportunities to match and utilize the skills and experiences of all involved participants, adaptive leaders hold immensely powerful tools for activist work. Although there will always be a strong temptation to envision sweeping changes and use these tools to follow up with accompanying action, we believe that it is prudent and essential to maintain a balance between the large-scale activist goals and the small intentional actions that will help us to achieve them.

References

Allen, S. J., & Wergin, J. F. (2009). Leadership and adult development theories: Overviews and overlaps. *Leadership Review*, 9, 3–19.

Argyris, C. (1997). Learning and teaching: A theory of action perspective. *Journal of Management Education*, 21(1), 9–26.

Argyris, C., & Schön, D. A. (1974). *Theory in practice: Increasing professional effectiveness*. Jossey Bass.

Argyris, C., & Schön, D. A. (1978). *Organizational learning: A theory of action perspective*. Addison-Wesley.

Argyris, C., & Schön, D. A. (1996). *Organizational learning II: Theory method and practice*. Addison-Wesley.

Baines, A. M. (2014). *(Un)Learning disability: Recognizing and changing restrictive views of student ability*. Teachers College Press.

Baltes, P. B., Staudinger, U. M., & Lindenberg, U. (1999). Lifespan psychology: Theory and application to intellectual functioning. *Annual Review of Psychology*, 50, 471–507.

Bloom, P. (2016). *Against empathy: The case for rational compassion*. Random House.

Bottom, W. P., Ladha, K. & Miller, G. J. (2002). Propagation of individual bias through group judgment: Error in the treatment of asymmetrically informative signals. *Journal of Risk and Uncertainty*, 25, 147–163. 10.1023/A:1020643713354

Camicia, S. P. (2015). Positionality, recognition, and dialogue in democratic education. In Tillman, L. C. & Scheurich, J. J. (Eds.), *Handbook of research on educational leadership for equity and diversity* (pp. 166–175). Routledge.

Cohen, D. K., & Moffitt, S. L. (2013). The influence of practice on policy. In Mitchell, D. E., Crowson, R. L., & Shipps, D. (Eds.), *Shaping education policy: Power and process* (pp. 63–80). Routledge.

Coudel, E., Tonneau, J. P., & Rey-Valette, H. (2011). Diverse approaches to learning in rural and development studies: Review of the literature from the perspective of action learning. *Knowledge Management Research & Practice*, 9(2), 120–135.

Drago-Severson, E. (2009). *Leading adult learning: Supporting adult development in our schools*. Corwin.

Eichholz, J. C. (2014). *Adaptive capacity*. LID Editorial.

Festinger, L. (1957). *A theory of cognitive dissonance*. Stanford University Press.

Foldy, E. G., & Creed, W. D. (1999). Action learning, fragmentation, and the interaction of single-, double-, and triple-loop change: A case of gay and lesbian workplace advocacy. *The Journal of Applied Behavioral Science*, 35(2), 207–227.

Frankish, K. (2010). Dual-process and dual-system theories of reasoning. *Philosophy Compass*, 5(10), 914–926.

Greenwood, J. (1998). The role of reflection in single and double loop learning. *Journal of Advanced Nursing*, 27(5), 1048–1053.

Hardesty, J. M. (2018). *Participatory action research: An examination of equity for the underrepresented student during response to intervention implementation* (Doctoral dissertation, Washington State University).

Harré, R., & Slocum, N. (2003). Disputes as complex social events: On the uses of positioning theory. *Common Knowledge*, 9(1), 100–118.

Harré, R., Moghaddam, F. M., Cairnie, T. P., Rothbart, D., & Sabat, S. R. (2009). Recent advances in positioning theory. *Theory & Psychology*, 19(1), 5–31.

Hector, C., Zick, A., Haye, A., Gonzalez, R., Manzi, J., Kocik, C., & Bertl, M. (2013). On the relation between social class and prejudice: The role of education, income, and ideological attitudes. *European Journal of Social Psychology*, 43(4), 272–285.

Heifetz, R. A. (1994). *Leadership without easy answers*. Harvard University Press.

Heifetz, R. A., Heifetz, R., Grashow, A., & Linsky, M. (2009). *The practice of adaptive leadership: Tools and tactics for changing your organization and the world*. Harvard Business Press.

Houchens, G. W., & Keedy, J. L. (2009). Theories of practice: Understanding the practice of educational leadership. *Journal of Thought*, 44(3-4), 49–61.

Johnson, D. W. (2015). *Constructive controversy: Theory, research, practice*. Cambridge University Press.

Kegan, R., & Lahey, L. L. (2001, November). The real reason people won't change. *Harvard Business Review*, 79, 77–85.

Kegan, R., & Lahey, L. L. (2009). *Immunity to change: How to overcome it and unlock potential in yourself and your organization*. Harvard Business Press.

Mischel, W., & Shoda, Y. (1995). A cognitive-affective system theory of personality: reconceptualizing situations, dispositions, dynamics, and invariance in personality structure. *Psychological Review*, 102(2), 246.

Moorosi, P. (2013). Constructing a leader's identity through a leadership development programme: An intersectional analysis. *Educational Management Administration & Leadership*, 42(6), 792–807.

Nellis, L. M. (2012). Maximizing the effectiveness of building teams in response to intervention implementation. *Psychology in the Schools*, 49(3), 245–256.

Nielsen, R. P. (1993a). Varieties of postmodernism as moments in ethics action-learning. *Business Ethics Quarterly*, 3(3), 251–269.

Nielsen, R. P. (1993b). Woolman's "I am we" triple-loop action-learning: Origin and application in organization ethics. *Journal of Applied Behavioral Science*, 29(1), 117–138.

Nordgren, L. F., Banas, K., & MacDonald, G. (2011). Empathy gaps for social pain: Why people underestimate the pain of social suffering. *Journal of Personality and Social Psychology*, 100(1), 120–128.

Sanger, D., Friedli, C., Brunken, C., Snow, P., & Ritzman, M. (2012). Educator's year long reaction to the implementation of a response to interventions (RTI) model. *Journal of Ethnographic & Qualitative Research*, 7(2), 98–107.

Santamaría, L. J. (2014). Critical change for the greater good: Multicultural perceptions in educational leadership toward social justice and equity. *Educational Administration Quarterly*, 50(3), 347–391.

Santamaría, L. J. & Jean-Marie, G. (2014). Cross-cultural dimensions of applied, critical, and transformational leadership: Women principals advancing social justice and educational equity. *Cambridge Journal of Education*, 44(3), 333–360.

Sidanius, J., Kteily, N., Sheehy-Skeffington, J., Ho, A. K., Sibley, C., & Duriez, B. (2013). You're inferior and not worth our concern: The interface between empathy and social dominance orientation. *Journal of Personality*, 81(3), 313–323.

Strack, F., & Deutsch, R. (2015). The duality of everyday life: Dual-process and dual system models in social psychology. In M. Mikulincer, P. R. Shaver, E. Borgida, & J. A. Bargh (Eds.), *APA handbook of personality and social psychology, Volume 1: Attitudes and social cognition.* (pp. 891–927). American Psychological Association.

Tavris, C., & Aronson, E. (2020). *Mistakes were made (but not by me): Why we justify foolish beliefs, bad decisions, and hurtful acts.* Houghton Mifflin Harcourt.

Thornton, H. (2006). Dispositions in action: Do dispositions make a difference in practice?. *Teacher Education Quarterly*, 33(2), 53–68.

Weick, K. E. (1995). *Sensemaking in organizations* (Vol. 3). Sage.

Wheatley, M. J. (2002). Leadership in turbulent times is spiritual. *Frontiers of Health Services Management*, 18(4), 19.

Zorza, P. J., Marino, J., Lemus, S., & Mesas, A. A. (2013). Academic performance and social competence of adolescents: Predictions based on effortful control and empathy. *Spanish Journal of Psychology*, 16(87), 1–12.

10 Leading Through Crisis: The Adaptive Leadership of Jacinda Ardern

Deidre M. Le Fevre

Perhaps you know the Rt Hon. Jacinda Ardern as one of the world's youngest leaders of a country elected prime minister of Aotearoa New Zealand in 2017 at the age of 37. Maybe you know her as a woman who became a mother during her first year in office as prime minister. Perhaps you are familiar with her social media postings with a focus on "kindness." However you may know her, Ardern challenges some of the traditional expectations of what it means to be a world leader in current times. Significantly, her approach challenges traditional notions of leadership and reveals a powerful example of what is possible.

Ardern has global recognition for her capacity to respond effectively in times of crisis in ways that created widespread responsiveness, improvement, and societal change. In early 2019, Aotearoa New Zealand experienced a devastating terrorist attack on the Muslim community by a lone gunman. Fifty-one people died. Many others were seriously injured. Lives were devastated. The country was shattered. Less than 12 months later, the world faced the rapid emergence of a global COVID-19 pandemic. Prime Minister Ardern led Aotearoa New Zealand through these and other crises.

Ardern has a vast portfolio of responsibilities as prime minister; this chapter focuses specifically on how she has responded to two challenges—the 2019 terrorist attack and the COVID-19 pandemic. These events impacted the lives of many in significant and disturbing ways; they demanded powerful leadership to enable the responses that have been possible. This chapter analyzes Ardern's leadership in relation to her response to urgent and complex crises. This analysis of policy and media data explores how Ardern embodies key constructs and practices of adaptive leadership in the challenges she faces.

Adaptive Leadership in Times of Crisis

Across disciplines and sectors, there has been a tendency for leadership to be viewed in terms of an individual exerting influence and providing direction and solutions to problems. However, these traditional or heroic

DOI: 10.4324/9781003099109-10

notions of leadership underrepresent the reality of organizational life wherein influence is usually multidirectional in nature. Positional leaders are sustained by complex webs of support and expertise. Analyzing the adaptive leadership of Ardern, therefore, required exploring the collective activity and webs of expertise and influence that surround her leadership.

Acknowledging and Navigating Complexity

Leaders today face significant, complex, and ongoing problems which demand they lead in spaces where disagreement, uncertainty, and ambiguity often prevail. Heifetz and his colleagues refer to these sorts of problems as adaptive challenges (Heifetz et al., 2009; Heifetz & Linsky, 2017). Leaders work in complex systems where unpredictable and unforeseen consequences are inevitable and where problems often have no predictable or known solution. Possible solutions to adaptive challenges lie beyond current ways of operating and demand continual learning (Heifetz et al., 2019). Rather than being able to simply "fix" these problems, leaders need to navigate through complexity, work systemically, and face uncertainty while continually changing the way they and others think, feel, and act.

When Ardern was asked during her October 2020 campaign for reelection as prime minister of New Zealand what she had learned over the past three years in office she responded, "If there's one thing I learned over the last three years…it's what you do when the unexpected hits that counts" (Young, 2020, p. A3).

New Zealand was a nation that had not experienced terrorism in its modern history until March 15, 2019. The terrorist was in New Zealand from another country; he entered two different mosques in Christchurch (New Zealand's second-largest city by population) and started shooting people while they were praying. He livestreamed his attack on social media. Massive shock, horror, grief, pain, and uncertainty rocked Aotearoa New Zealand. The nation turned to the Prime Minister to see how she would respond. As Duff (2019) observed,

> In tumultuous times like these leadership is everything. How a head of state acts in the aftermath of such an event, how they frame it, is a kind of blueprint for the rest of the country—they decide to be either a guiding light or to create a bigger tear in the fabric that's been ripped. (p. 130)

From her first media appearance immediately following the attack, Ardern modeled the way in which she would lead the country in responding to the attack. Foremost, she responded as a human being, reaching out to others in grief. She hugged, wept, and connected human to human with the victims and their families. In her first address to Parliament following the attack, Ardern spoke directly to the families saying, "We cannot know your grief, but we can walk with you at every stage" (Ardern, 2019b, March 19, para 13).

The attack on the mosque was undertaken by an individual who was acting within a world of complex influences and impact. In the weeks and months that followed, Ardern continually communicated through her policy decisions and public media releases that the problems of racism, violence, and right-wing extremism are complex global problems that require a complex, multifaceted response and she took a systemic approach to the challenges faced. Her responses included taking action, creating influence, changing policy, and providing support. When asked what support the United States could provide New Zealand, Ardern's message was "sympathy and love for all Muslim Communities" (Ardern, 2019a, March 16, para 4). The morning following the attacks, Ardern announced there would be changes to New Zealand gun laws. Within a week, gun law reform was passed, banning all military-style semiautomatic weapons, assault rifles, and high-capacity magazines in New Zealand. The law took effect immediately.

Ardern chose to mute focus on the terrorist. In her address to Parliament, she said: "He is a terrorist. He is a criminal. He is an extremist. But he will, when I speak, be nameless" (Ardern, 2019b, March 19, para 44). She intentionally directed attention away from that specific terrorist, focusing instead on the victims and their families and the complex web of contributing influences and problematic societal beliefs that surrounded the event. Ardern immediately began making changes to address these more systemic enablers. For example, she took action on social media platforms that publish violent, hate-related materials. Ardern called for solidarity in confronting the presence of racism in our society, leading the nation in what Heifetz et al. (2009) term an "interpretation mind-shift" (p. 114), helping her constituents "see the issues *as systemic rather than personal* ... to look for the leverage points in the system ... as targets of attention to effect change" (p. 115, emphasis in original).

Acknowledging and navigating complexity was also a hallmark of the way Ardern responded to the COVID-19 challenge. Referring to the global COVID-19 situation, Prime Minister Ardern's Chief Science Advisor, Dame Juliet Gerrard, said, "Presenting the uncertain science and the evolving, ever-changing evidence base for COVID has not gone well [in other countries], but in New Zealand we have managed collectively to build enough trust that it has gone well" (Bruce, 2021, para 16). Gerrard suggests a number of reasons for this. The informal culture in New Zealand and nature of communication between herself as chief science advisor and Ardern was helpful. Rather than having multiple levels of bureaucracy between scientists and politicians, Ardern would call Gerrard daily and simply say "talk me through it." Ardern was not afraid of uncovering the complexity, uncertainty, constant ambiguity, and ever-changing information of the evolving situation. She was consistently transparent about the challenge the country faced in fighting the virus rather than attempting to create any illusion that the government had total control over the COVID-19 situation and that everything would be okay. Engaging stakeholders in understanding the challenge or conflict rather than simply trying to restore the illusion of order is a hallmark of adaptive leadership and an important step in mobilizing toward action.

Mobilizing New Zealanders and Influential Leaders Across International Sectors

Adaptive leadership involves mobilizing people, systems, and communities (Heifetz, 1994). This includes leveraging sometimes unusual networks of relationships and expertise to help problem-solve (Heifetz et al., 2009). Ardern's leadership focused on mobilizing others following the mosque attacks and during the COIVD-19 pandemic response.

After the mosque attacks, Ardern spoke of the victims and said "They were New Zealanders. They are us" (Ardern, 2019b, March 19, para 1). In doing so she mobilized New Zealanders to focus their attention and energy towards acting with empathy and compassion to the Muslim community rather than reacting with hatred and anger to the lone gunman (Duff, 2019). Refusing to use his name was one strategy. Another was that crowds across the country were encouraged to gather. Adults and young people wrote cards, laid flowers, and made signs: "we love you, we grieve with you, assalamu alaikum." Ardern met with survivors and families, communities, and young people and said, "There are lots of things that Governments can do to make sure people are free from violence and we will do those things" (Cooke, 2019, para 15). In her next sentence she moved the focus from the government to mobilize the young people in the school she was addressing saying "But it also means making a place where there is no environment for violence to flourish-where we don't let racism exist" (Cooke, 2019, para 16). Ardern encouraged the nation to respond with compassion while at the same time mobilizing leaders and policy makers to take action against violence. It was through compassion that Ardern was able to outline an aspiration—reducing violence—that a nation in mourning could fully embrace.

Ardern then turned her attention to the international community, mobilizing leaders at an almost unprecedented pace. She brought together leaders of 48 countries, the European Commission, international organizations, and eight major technology companies for what she termed the "Christchurch call." The call had a single goal: To eliminate terrorist and violent extremist content online. The call garnered considerable support and action, with Ardern reiterating that "we are dealing with a global problem, which requires a global response" (Ardern, 2020c, May 15, para 12).

In the days and months following the attack while Ardern worked with international leaders, New Zealanders were encouraged to not simply leave the government to take care of the situation; Ardern knew that, in an adaptive challenge, all stakeholders had an integral role to play in its resolution. Thus, during her speech at the memorial service, she said,

> And so to each of us as we go from here we have work to do, but do not leave the job of combatting hate to the government alone. We each hold the power, in our words and in our actions, in our daily acts of kindness. Let that be the legacy of the 15th of March. To be the nation we believe ourselves to be. (Ardern, 2019c, para 47)

Mobilizing people has also been central to Ardern's response to the COVID-19 pandemic. Early in the pandemic she spoke to the nation saying, "Like the rest of the world, we are facing the potential for devastating impacts from this virus. But, through decisive action, and through working together, we have a small window to get ahead of it" (Ardern, 2020a, para 3). Successfully confronting COVID-19 depended on getting five million people (the population of New Zealand) to be with her and to stay with her. Referring to the devastating death toll and overwhelmed health systems internationally Ardern said, "Together we must stop that happening, and we can" (Ardern, 2020a, para 12).

Urgent, sudden, difficult changes needed to be made by every New Zealander as the country quickly entered one of the most stringent nationwide lockdowns in the world. An analysis of Ardern's press conferences, broadcast daily at 1 p.m. for the nation, indicates she predominantly described how the country would respond, as "… a team of five million" and then she would explain the next strategy being employed.

Leveraging and connecting unexpected networks of expertise is a strategy Arden continued to employ throughout the pandemic. For example, in New Zealand those appearing in daily media were leading epidemiologists, mathematical data modeling experts, social anthropologists, business leaders, and politicians jointly giving press conferences. By expanding the landscape of expertise to be consulted, the scope of possible solutions increased. Ardern intentionally distributed the leadership required to confront the pandemic, drawing on stakeholders from multiple sectors in her efforts to mobilize the entire country. She knew that she, alone, would not be able to address such a complex and adaptive challenge.

Mobilizing people is central to Ardern's leadership—not just in times of crisis. In a speech to the United Nations General Assembly in 2019 she made this clear:

> We, the political leaders of the world, have been the authors of our own domestic politics and policies. Decisions have been our own, and we have lived with the consequences. But the world has changed. Over time we have become increasingly interdependent. We see more and more often domestic decisions that have global ramifications. Physical events have taught us that in obvious ways: oil spills that show no respect for maritime boundaries; nuclear accidents and testing, the impacts of which are never confined to the exact location in which they occur. But our interdependence, our connection, runs so much deeper than that, and experiences in recent years should lead us to question whether any of us ever truly operate in isolation anymore. (Ardern, 2019d, September 25, para 12)

Communicating with Clarity Amidst Uncertainty

Adaptive leadership involves being willing to be decisive in uncertain contexts and addressing adaptive challenges where there are no known solutions (Heifetz et al., 2009). Solutions to adaptive challenges require taking action and experimenting while developing necessary knowledge and understanding (Heifetz et al., 2009). Progress in addressing adaptive challenges requires more than existing approaches and expertise offer and requires new learning amidst uncertainty (Heifetz, 2010).

Drawing on deep knowledge of the issues and leading in a decisive way amidst uncertainty are hallmarks of Ardern's leadership. These are necessary components of adaptive leadership; so too is the use of evidence in that communication. For example, following the terrorist attack, Ardern took time to connect with and understand the situation faced by the survivors of the attack. She listened to them talk about what they had experienced and what they said they needed. As an adaptive leader, Ardern does not rely solely on the knowledge of others in making her decisions. Rather, she engages others in sharing their knowledge and expertise so that she can continually deepen her *own* knowledge and understanding, enabling her to make and communicate informed decisions.

Ardern's leadership throughout the COVID-19 pandemic crisis has been decisive and clear. She has not apologized for making decisions that are difficult for people but instead explained the reasoning for her decision and the science that backs it up. At times, when the science is not clear, Ardern is transparent in her communication about what she does and does not know. She consistently talks of how the landscape is constantly changing and that she is using the best science available, but that science still leaves many things unknown. In other words, Ardern has provided constant communication even when there are more questions than answers and has been transparent in naming the uncertainties that surround people's lives. This is atypical with leaders, particularly those in political positions where stakeholders seek stability in uncertain times.

Ardern has managed this balance of inspiring confidence while maintaining integrity. One of the ways she does this is by providing transparent structures that are stable guideposts within a context of uncertainty. These structures have given New Zealanders the opportunity to have confidence to maintain trust in Ardern and to follow her lead. For example, she laid out four alert levels in the initial response related to the state of COVID-19 in New Zealand, she explained what each of the levels would mean for everyone, and continually referred to them. With each shift to a different level of alert, Ardern would continually inform the nation of the implications of that level and the reasoning behind any changes to people's lives (Ardern, 2020a, March 23).

Ardern brought together a vast network of experts and advisors. These networks activate systems for gathering, analyzing, and conveying information related to COVID-19. However, these systems have sometimes failed and it is notable to Ardern's leadership that she is transparent about failings as well as about successes. Vulnerability is an important part of developing trust and showing or being open about one's vulnerability can increase trust in relationships, particularly relationships that encompass unequal power, such as with a senior political leader (Meyer et al., 2017). It is also the situation, as in all complex societies, that not everyone in New Zealand trusts science, or the government for that matter, and there are dissenting voices in relation to the Ardern's COVID-19 response. Ardern and her chief science advisor recognize that "tension and disagreement is the normal state of science" (Bruce, 2021, para 26). Ardern seeks to understand the reasons for dissent and to respond accordingly. For example, different views existed within New Zealand regarding the extent to which borders should remain closed to enable an elimination strategy of the virus. Some people have advocated strongly for maintaining closed borders, whereas others advocate the importance of opening up the border to allow business and tourism priorities to resume. Ardern continually acknowledges and navigates these tensions within a complex and rapidly changing environment in which she is willing to change direction when warranted by new evidence.

Ardern's depth of understanding of the evolving science of COVID-19 has been a key feature of her communication, where deep knowledge is essential to understanding the complexities of adaptive challenges. Gerrard notes that Ardern was incredibly keen to understand everything .... She's not someone who just takes a script and reads it out. She's someone who writes the script and interrogates it. She wanted all the details of what was going on, so I spent a lot of time explaining the science and she understood the science. That's why she was good at communicating it ... she's very good at synthesizing a lot of detailed information, so she was on top of it. (Bruce, 2021, para 19)

Leading from a Stance of Empathy, Compassion, and Kindness

Addressing adaptive challenges often generates a sense of loss for people (Heifetz et al., 2009). Effective leadership requires leaders to have the capacity to recognize and connect with the values, beliefs, and anxieties of those impacted by a challenge. Adaptive change "involves tough tradeoffs, and the uncertainty of ongoing, experimental trial and error" (Heifetz et al., 2009, p. 23). Thus it is essential that adaptive leaders help people navigate through periods of disturbance and upset.

World leaders are not typically characterized as empathic but are instead seen as assertive, providing direction, and making difficult decisions. Ardern is all of this—and she is also deeply empathetic. Following the Christchurch attack, Ardern hugged and listened to people who were grieving and in pain. Her compassionate actions were broadcast by global media, perhaps in many ways because they were so unexpected of a world leader. Her authentic and heartfelt response challenged assumptions that leaders need to be emotionless to retain authority and command respect.

Several months after the Christchurch attack, Ardern addressed the United Nations General Assembly, saying, "there is no changing a nation's history but we can choose how it defines us." She then said,

> ... in Aotearoa New Zealand, the people who lined up outside of mosques with flowers, the young people who gathered spontaneously in parks, and open spaces in a show of solidarity, the thousands who stopped in silence to acknowledge the call to prayer seven days later, and the Muslim community who showed only love in their grief ... these are the people who collectively decided that New Zealand would not be defined by an act of brutality and violence, but instead by compassion and empathy. (Ardern, 2019d, September 25, para 20)

Promoting kindness was a hallmark of Ardern's leadership even before these two crises. In a speech to the United Nations General Assembly (September 28, 2018, para 79) she said,

If I could distil it down into one concept that we are pursuing in New Zealand it is simple and it is this. Kindness. In the face of isolationism, protectionism, racism—the simple concept of looking outwardly and beyond ourselves, of kindness and collectivism, might just be as good a starting point as any.

Although New Zealanders have typically followed government guidelines to reduce the spread of COVID-19, not every New Zealander is a rule follower. Ardern continually navigates the tension between mounting pressure to utilize external compliance and punitive measures for those who break the rules and her belief that building trust and accepting that people will sometimes make mistakes is the best way forward. She does so with her customary transparency, regularly communicating this dilemma and the reasoning behind her actions to the general public through television interviews with traditional media, government press releases, and social media. For example, a possible breach of quarantine restrictions prompted a public debate regarding whether or not the police should be used as an enforcement agency, with legal ramifications for individuals who did not comply with government COVID-19 guidelines. Ardern maintained, "Nobody would benefit from 'pile-ons' if someone did break the rules, because it could make people less likely to get tested.... Any division when you're tackling something like this has a really negative effect" (Trevett, 2021, February 27, A9, para 57). Ardern believed that heightened punitive measures in the name of accountability would instead deter from people sharing accurate information with officials.

Arden has shown it is possible to be both empathetic and to take decisive action. Communicating through a range of modes, including social media videos from her couch at home late in the evening (Ardern, 2020a, March 25), she has acknowledged how disruptive the COVID-19 pandemic lockdown was for families, how harsh it has been for small businesses, and perhaps, most of all, how sad it is for families who were not able to be together for funerals of their lost loved ones. "I understand that self-isolation is a daunting prospect" (Ardern, 2020a, March 23, para 32), Ardern said. "If it feels hard right now it's because it is" (Ardern, 2020d, August 24, para 4). Moving out of lockdown caused more anxiety for some people than being in lockdown and Ardern publicly acknowledged the uncertainty, fear, and anxiety her citizens felt about an unknown future.

Naming and acknowledging losses that may be felt by others is an important part of adaptive leadership and a significant component to helping others "tolerate the discomfort they are experiencing" (Heifetz et al., 2009, p. 29). Ardern's actions reflect the practices of adaptive leadership to intentionally focus on connecting with the "values, beliefs, and anxieties" (Heifetz et al., 2009, p. 29) of the people who are being asked to change and experience the losses that may accompany change.

This type of leadership demands moving people out of their comfort zone and acknowledging what people are experiencing.

Developing Adaptive Leadership in Others

Ardern is viewed as a highly successful adaptive world leader who has led through challenging times. While it is important to remember that her work is situated in a specific context, it is likely that much can be learned from her leadership to support the learning and development of leaders elsewhere as they confront increasingly complex, learning-oriented challenges across different cultures and contexts. Conceptual constructs developed from empirical research can provide powerful insights into effective leadership practices and these, extrapolated from Ardern's leadership, are explored next.

Accept and Work with Uncertainty

Ardern's approach highlights the importance of accepting and working with uncertainty. Uncertainty is inherent in complex systems (Le Fevre et al., 2020) so accepting and working with ambiguity and helping others to do the same are important leadership skills (for a detailed discussion of complexity, see Chapter 1). Complex systems are dynamic. They change, grow, and learn through feedback loops; small events can have large and unpredictable effects and vice versa (Cochran-Smith et al., 2014). Adaptive leadership practices involve transparency, as Ardern exhibits, where whatever certainties exist are framed as processes so as to allow a reliable source of information and some level of control and stability amidst uncertain terrain. In this way, adaptive leaders are able to regulate at least some of the turbulence inherent in adaptive work—an essential function of the holding environment.

Take Time

While some of Ardern's responses needed to be immediate, she also took time to thoroughly diagnose challenges utilizing her networks of expertise throughout the process. Leaders often feel that they are in a reactive mode and there can be pressure to quickly jump to solutions even when working in a context of ambiguity, paradox, and uncertainty with no known solution. However, Heifetz and colleagues remind us of the need to "resist the pressure to do something, and spend more time diagnosing the problem" (Heifetz et al., 2009, p. 44). People who demonstrate adaptive expertise spend more time diagnosing the problem rather than jumping to conclusions about possible solutions, which are more likely to be a technical "quick fixes," providing temporary relief, but not lasting improvement.

Embrace Disagreement and Discomfort

It is human nature to gravitate towards a solution that will avoid disruption, distress, and disagreement in an organization, even if the "solution" has been tried before and is known to be ineffective (Heifetz et al., 2009). A key principle of adaptive leadership relates to orchestrating conflict, to lean into discomfort in order to make progress. Thus it is important that leaders be confident as they embrace disagreement (Robinson et al., 2014) and resulting discomfort. Ardern made difficult decisions. Some of her decisions upset people, generating debate and disagreement through differing points of view. However, adaptive challenges require learning and learning thrives on diversity. As Heifetz et al. (2009) point out, "Adaptive work involves orchestrating multiple and passionately held points of view. In an ideal world, people would not be threatened by the existence of contrasting points of view" (p. 122).

Distribute Leadership

Ardern draws heavily on distributed leadership and expertise. Effective leadership is more than any one person can achieve alone, especially in this era of complex, adaptive challenges. An awareness that the system in which a leader operates is inherently dynamic with interconnected webs of influence compels leaders to draw upon varied expertise and the diverse perspectives held by stakeholders (Spillane, 2006). Distributing leadership shifts the role of a stakeholder from passive recipient to one who is actively engaged, a key tenet of adaptive leadership (Heifetz et al., 2009). Distributed leadership widens the focus and responsibility away from the positional leader as sole actor within a social system and shares the work and responsibility with those who are most impacted.

Use Adaptive and Routine Expertise

Both adaptive and routine expertise contribute to leadership effectiveness. A common cause for failure in leadership is treating adaptive challenges as if they were simple problems that only require routine expertise when instead they require adaptive expertise (Le Fevre et al., 2020). Routine expertise can be applied to simple problems that can be resolved through the application of existing expertise, current structures, and procedures. However, routine expertise doesn't work for complex challenges which include adaptive components (Heifetz et al., 2009). Thus both adaptive and routine expertise are needed for effective leadership.

Ardern constantly drew on both adaptive and routine expertise. For example, routine expertise likely predominantly informed the way she initially responded to COVID-19, quickly establishing and announcing a system to provide immediate short-term financial support (government payments) during lockdown periods for people who had lost or significantly reduced their employment or business income. Adaptive expertise, however, was required when considering how to provide support for people and businesses expected to experience long-term financial repercussions of COVID-19. For instance, some young people had to leave school early to go to work to support their families who had lost income, thus forfeiting their own opportunity for an education and future job choices. Adaptive expertise in this scenario involves the ability to engage stakeholders from multiple sectors (e.g., education, local communities, business, political, and higher education) to consider the challenge from multiple angles, creating a strong holding environment in which it is safe and productive to rethink traditional pathways and to consider alternative resources and support for young New Zealanders during unpredictable times.

Importantly, adaptive leaders are able to discern when to draw upon routine and/or adaptive expertise, knowing when each is needed.

Navigate Perceptions of Risk

Leading in times of risk and uncertainty creates what is sometimes viewed as resistance. As Heifetz (2010) notes, "Adaptive work generates resistance in people because adaptation requires us to let go of certain elements of our past ways of working or living, which means to experience loss" (pp. 74–75). However, what might appear to be resistance to change may in fact be that people have perceptions of risk that get in the way of being able to change (Twyford & Le Fevre, 2019). Perceptions of risk occur when a person has a sense that they have something of value to lose (Marris, 1986). This might be one's sense of safety, as in warding off terrorism, or independence due to lockdowns in response to a public health crisis. It can also occur in less obvious ways, such as the loss of one's sense of autonomy, or competence, as a result of change. Whereas people generally like to remain in their comfort zone, adaptive challenges, by their very nature, demand some level of disequilibrium among stakeholders (Heifetz et al., 2009) and adaptive leaders must navigate that discomfort and the different perceptions of risk that people might hold. Ardern was deliberate in establishing her holding environment, using compassion and transparency to manage the environment, seeking to understand the perceptions of risk people might have and helping people to "tolerate the discomfort they [were] experiencing" (Heifetz et al., 2009, p. 29).

Develop Relational Trust

A common default mode among stakeholders is to hold those in positions of authority responsible for problems with the expectation that they fix them. Adaptive challenges, however, need more than authority. They require a coordinated response to problem-solving that mobilizes people to action and a willingness among stakeholders to consider personal sacrifice, or loss, for the greater good. That willingness does not occur without trust in those who are asking for sacrifice.

Ardern's reluctance to use punitive measures to gain societal buy-in for COVID-19 pandemic lockdown measures is an example of a coordinated response that also developed relational trust. Relational trust is created through compassion, expertise, respect, and integrity (Bryk & Schneider, 2002). Ardern publicly valued and practiced compassion and kindness, utilized vast networks of expertise to complement her own, operated with transparency so as to respect the needs of her citizens to have information to understand the changes taking place in their lives, and demonstrated the integrity of her actions by modeling what she promoted. These might, in fact, be the most critical lessons of her leadership.

In the ongoing challenges of the complex global society in which we live and leaders lead, the touchstones of Ardern's courage, compassion, and clarity in Aotearoa New Zealand offer lessons that reach beyond its shores. However, in keeping with the essential premise of adaptive leadership, when considering the leadership approaches and strategies that Arden encompassed during these two crises it is important not to slip into viewing this as a "heroic narrative" about one person and her influence. Effective leadership happens within a web of influence and support and through a belief in humanity itself. To quote the words of The Rt Hon. Jacinda Ardern,

> … in an increasingly uncertain world it is more important than ever that we remember the core values on which the UN was built. That all people are equal. That everyone is entitled to have their dignity and human rights respected. That we must strive to promote social progress and better standards of life in larger freedom. And we must consistently hold ourselves to account on each. (Ardern, 2018, September 28, paras 66–70)

While adaptive leadership demands more than any one person can do alone, Ardern's actions demonstrate the power of a strong leader who is unafraid of facing the complexity, uncertainty, and difficulties inherent in addressing adaptive challenges. This analysis of Ardern's leadership highlights how mobilizing others, communicating in a knowledgeable and transparent way that is informed by evidence, and holding a strong stance of empathy, compassion, and kindness can contribute to a unique picture of leadership that has the capacity to create change for improvement in times of crisis.

References

Ardern, J. (2018, September 28). New Zealand National Statement to the United Nations General Assembly. https://www.beehive.govt.nz/speech/new-zealand-national-statement-unitednations-general-assembly

Ardern, J. (2019a, March 16). Christchurch terror attack: Ardern asks Trump to provide "sympathy and love for Muslim communities". *New Zealand Herald*. https://www.nzherald.co.nz/nz/christchurch-mosque-shootings-prime-minister-jacindaarderns-message-to-donald-trump/27JJVOB6BC26YTHUPGY-OIF4KHM/

Ardern, J. (2019b, March 19). Address to Parliament, Wellington. https://www.beehive.govt.nz/release/pm-house-statement-christchurch-mosques-terrorattack

Ardern, J. (2019c, March 29). Prime Minister's speech at the national remembrance service. New Zealand Government release, Wellington, New Zealand. https://www.beehive.govt.nz/release/prime-minister%E2%80%99s-speech-nationalremembrance-service

Ardern, J. (2019d, September 25). New Zealand National Statement to the United Nations General Assembly. https://www.beehive.govt.nz/speech/new-zealand-national-statementunited-nations-general-assembly-2019

Ardern, J. (2020a, March 23). COVID-19 Alert Level increased. New Zealand Government release, wellington, New Zealand. https://www.beehive.govt.nz/speech/prime-minister-covid-19-alert-level-increased

Ardern, J. (2020b March 25). Evening everyone. Thought I'd jump online and answer a few questions as... [Video]. www.facebook.com/watch/live/?v=147109069954329&ref=watch_permalink. (accessed 14April2021)

Ardern, J. (2020c, May 15). Christchurch call makes significant progress. New Zealand Government release, Wellington, New Zealand. https://www.beehive.govt.nz/release/christchurch-call-makes-significant-progress

Ardern, J. (2020d, August 24). TV New Zealand broadcast. https://www.tvnz.co.nz/onenews/new-zealand/jacinda-ardern-praises-nzs-efforts-against-covid-19-resurgence despite-frankly-terrible-year

Bruce, G. (2021, February 20). Testing her hunches. *New Zealand Herald*, Canvas 6–7. https://www.nzherald.co.nz/lifestyle/juliet-gerrard-the-chief-science-advisor-in-the-earof-the-prime-minister/LML4COK3RK7CQME5DOCEXKOEQQ/

Bryk, A., & Schneider, B. (2002). *Trust in schools: A core resource for improvement*. Russell Sage Foundation.

Cochran-Smith, M., Ell, F., Ludlow, L., Grudnoff, L., & Aitken, G. (2014). The challenge and promise of complexity theory for teacher education research. *Teachers College Record*, 116.

Cooke, H. (2019, March 20). Prime Minister Jacinda Ardern asks Cashmere High students not to 'dwell' on attacker. *Stuff*. https://www.stuff.co.nz/national/christchurchshooting/111422844/prime-minister-jacinda-ardern-asks-cashmere-high-students-not-to dwell-on-attacker

Duff, M. (2019). *Jacinda Ardern*. Allen & Unwin.

Heifetz, R. A. (1994). *Leadership without easy answers*. Harvard University Press.

Heifetz, R. A. (2010, Spring). Adaptive work. *The Journal Kansas Leadership Center*, 72–77.

Heifetz, R., Grashow, A., & Linsky, M. (2009). *The practice of adaptive leadership: Tools and tactics for changing your organization and the world.* Harvard Business Press.

Heifetz, R. A., & Linsky, M. (2017). *Leadership on the line, with a new preface: Staying alive through the dangers of change.* Harvard Business Press.

Le Fevre, D. M., Timperley, H., Twyford, K., & Ell, F. (2020). *Leading powerful professional learning: Responding to complexity with adaptive expertise.* Corwin.

Marris, P. (1986). *Loss and change* (Rev. ed.). Routledge & Kegan Paul.

Meyer, F., Le Fevre, D. M., & Robinson, V. M. J. (2017). How leaders communicate their vulnerability: Implications for trust building. *International Journal of Educational Management*, *31*(2), 221–235. doi:10.1108/IJEM-11-2015-0150

Robinson, V. M. J., Sinnema, C. E. L., &. Le Fevre, D. (2014). From persuasion to learning: An intervention to improve leaders' response to disagreement. *Leadership and Policy in Schools*, *13*(3), 260–296. doi:10.1080/15700763.2014.922997

Spillane, J. P. (2006). *Distributed leadership*. Jossey Bass.

Trevett, C. (2021). "Covid is constantly on my mind": Jacinda Ardern looks back. *New Zealand Herald*, A8. https://www.nzherald.co.nz/nz/covid-19-coronavirus-prime-minister-jacindaarderns-year-of-pandemic-and-hope-for-alert-level zero/6WOGKFILOWA22ISC5RI62BKY7I/

Twyford, K., & Le Fevre, D. (2019). Leadership, uncertainty and risk: How leaders influence teachers. *Journal of Professional Capital and Community*, *4*(4), 309–324.

Young, A. (2020, October 12). Leaders sprint to the finish. *The New Zealand Herald*. (p. A3).

Part III
Adaptive Leadership Across Cultures

11 Adaptive Leadership in the Chinese Context: Can Adaptive Leadership be Applied in China?

Mohammed Raei

China has the world's largest population and second-largest economy (World Population Review, n.d., a, b). Additionally, China will have one billion urban residents by 2030 (McKinsey Global Institute, 2009). China has a rich history and is one of the oldest cultures; "China has a written history of over 4000 years" (Fu et al., 2007, p. 880). The Great Wall of China and other cultural artifacts attest to its rich history. China is experiencing massive urbanization, possesses a vast manufacturing scale, and increasing local consumption is starting to drive the economy (Towson & Woetzel, 2013). Nonetheless, it faces many challenges; its rapid economic growth in the last 30 years is decelerating (International Monetary Fund, 2016). Moreover, it is the world's largest emitter of greenhouse gases (Union of Concerned Scientists, n.d). It is also the country in which the 2020 COVID-19 epidemic originated.

Cultural and organizational dimensions are indivisibly linked in China (Hutchings & Weir, 2005). Moreover, the influence of Chinese culture extends beyond the borders of mainland China to Hong Kong, Taiwan, and Singapore. Furthermore, China is a diverse country with over 50 ethnic minorities. However, for the purposes of this chapter, I have limited the focus to mainland China and its dominant Han culture.

Given China's stature on the world stage, and the challenges it faces, the examination of the applicability of adaptive leadership concepts in the Chinese context is a significant and timely contribution. In this conceptual chapter, I first examine Chinese cultural concepts. Second, I explicate Chinese paternalistic leadership. Third, I overview adaptive leadership. Fourth, I analyze the compatibility of adaptive leadership with the different facets of Chinese culture. Finally, I provide concluding remarks.

DOI: 10.4324/9781003099109-11

Chinese Cultural Concepts

Confucianism

The founder of Confucianism is Confucius (551-497 BC). Confucianism has wielded an enormous impact on Chinese history (Fu et al., 2007). Confucian philosophy can be described as

> an open system that is founded on the basis of a humanist concern for people and the moral idealism of self-cultivation of individuals as the leader(s) or the led ... it involved a critique of the Daoist, the Maoist, and the legalist models that have implications on how [one] could develop contemporary global leadership among nations. (Cheng, 2011, p. 648)

Confucianism is an influential system of social, moral, and political principles governing virtually every facet of Chinese life since the Han era (206 BC-AD 220; Wang et al., 2005). Confucius instructed his disciples to practice more moralities. Among them, benevolence (jen) is the most imperative morality an individual should possess (Lin et al., 2012). Confucianism teaches virtue, order, and harmony. There are countless proverbs attributed to Confucius that Chinese people often quote and to which they try to aspire. The best-known leaders in China are said to be modeled after the Confucian approach (Gallo, 2011).

Confucianism focuses on five cardinal role relations: The emperor and his subjects, a father and his son, a husband and wife, younger and older brothers, and between friends. All these relationships involve a set of defined roles and mutual obligations (Wang et al., 2005). According to Li (2000), there is little doubt that Confucianism has oppressed women; Confucianism scholars upheld the idea that the masculine principle is superior to the feminine principle: "Therefore, between the husband and the wife, the husband is superior and the wife is inferior" (Li, 2000, p. 188). Li adds that Confucianism has to "change its behaviors and attitudes towards women" (p. 192). Despite the dissimilarity between feminism (which emphasizes equality between the sexes) and Confucianism, Li suggests that both have a similar way of thinking about ethics and that the Confucian concept of benevolence (jen) can lead to better conciliation of the two.

Guanxi in a Confucian Culture

Guanxi can be defined as "relationships that are based on mutual dependence" (De Mente, 2011, p. 147). In China, social networks permeate business activity despite the advent of modernization, industrialization, and globalization; "China has a business culture based on strong family networks, or guanxi connections, underpinned by strong *Confucian* [emphasis added] ethics" (Hutchings & Weir, 2005, p. 143). "Social networks are established on alliances built on common grounds [*sic*] and constitute bonds of allegiance to a common, mutual, or complementary set of interests or goals" (Lewis, 2005, p. 20). A Chinese person with a problem, personal or organizational, turns to his relationship network for help (Hutchings & Weir, 2005). There is a very strong belief that people with guanxi will give and receive favors over an extended period of time (Gallo, 2011). De Mente proclaims: "The essence of Chinese culture, still today, is based on guanxi" (2011, p. 147).

In China's highly bureaucratic organizations, guanxi acts as an enabler of transactions; "guanxi involves a series of activities carried out by the parties concerned within their network and frequently involves gift giving and favors" (Ramasamy et al., 2006, p. 132). In Chinese organizations where resources are controlled through hierarchy by a few individuals, guanxi becomes essential in nurturing business relationships and survival (Ramasamy et al., 2006). Whereas guanxi can overcome some of the rigid barriers in Chinese organizations, it is not all positive; there are legitimate concerns about the ethics associated with conducting business using guanxi (Yen et al., 2011).

Guanxi is transferable; "if A has guanxi with B and B is a friend of C, then B can introduce or recommend A to C or vice versa" (Luo, 1997, p. 44). Additionally, guanxi is reciprocal, utilitarian, personal, and intangible.

The concept of guanxi is similar to the concept of wasta in the Middle East, however, there are some differences. Wasta carries negative connotations (Hutchings & Weir, 2005); guanxi does not. Guanxi is also similar to the Russian concept of blat and the Brazilian concept of Jeitinho (Zhang et al., 2015).

Taoism

Lao-Tse (604-531 BC) founded Taoism. Similar to Confucianism, the philosophy of Taoism (Tao) is an essential thinking system in the Chinese civilization. It exerts great influence over Chinese culture. Taoism proclaims that the Tao *cannot be explicated* because it is part of everything; it is a process *and* a principle (Heider, 1985). It translates to English as the "the way" (Watts, 2010, p. 11). To have Tao is to recognize the perpetual interaction of Yin-Yang, the principle of opposites (McElhatton & Jackson, 2012).

Yin-Yang

Yin-Yang represent the reconciliation of opposites (For a discussion of balancing the opposites in the context of Native American culture, see Chapter 14); "Taoism [sic] made the idea of Yin–Yang popular to express ideas of balancing" (Ma & Tsui, 2015, p. 19). Yin-Yang is symbolized with two overlapping forms that express a whole circle. One form is black, representing the Yin, the feminine principle. The other form is white, Yang, the masculine principle. Both forms have a dot of the opposite color signifying that the feminine contains the masculine and the masculine contains the feminine. Yin and Yang can be described as the "starting point of the universe" (Bai & Roberts, 2011, p. 726). The Yin-Yang relationships between individuals are not static, they are in a continuous state of flux; "they wax and wane in inverse proportions" (De Mente, 2011, p. 19).

Wu Wei

Wu Wei means not forcing or not doing (Watts, 2010); a Wu Wei leader will provide followers with what is needed to get the job done but will not micromanage them with specific instructions. Gallo (2011) equates Wu Wei leadership with laissez-faire, or abdication of leadership. It assumes that interventions can be harsh or harmful and thus need to be minimized (Heider, 1985). Wu Wei means that leader interventions are a last resort. The leader does not need to intervene frequently; they know that there is a natural order and that events will follow that order (Heider, 1985). Wu Wei is also misunderstood. Gerstner (2011) writes: "Wu Wei is commonly translated as non-action. Although the concept is easily confused with in-action, which is passive and often ineffective, Wu Wei is rather a very responsive, supportive, and enabling mode of action, allowing sustainable accomplishment" (p. 676). He suggests that non-action is the opposite of top-down management.

Mianzi

The Chinese word for face is mianzi. Protecting face is an important facet of Chinese culture. Communism dismantled the prior extended Chinese structures of lineage and clan and even deeply affected relationships at the principal level of the family. The concept of family, however, endured as the core of the Chinese cultural model. Mianzi, or face, in China, is a system that symbolically extends the model of the family to a larger nexus of social relationships providing "a central cultural mechanism for informal conflict resolution in Chinese society when and where circumstances of such conflict might potentially be like a fuse to a powder keg" (Lewis, 2005, p. 17). The Chinese concept of mianzi is broken down into four basic categories: (1) Building a good reputation by avoiding errors and making prudent decisions; (2) Giving face to others through respect and compliments; (3) Receiving face from others who treat you respectfully and compliment you; and (4) Losing face through public knowledge of your failures (De Mente, 2011).

In China, losing face is socially comparable to the "physical mutilation of one's eye, nose, or mouth" (Luo, 1997, p. 45). Having someone lose face not only deprecates their status and reputation but also designates an absence of trust (Wang et al., 2005). For example, even if an employee does not have subordinates, the employee may be given the title "manager" to afford face (Gallo, 2011). To uphold face means to stay trustworthy and to honor commitments in social interactions (Wang et al., 2005).

Saving another's face has top priority in Eastern cultures. For example, a subordinate might refrain from pointing out to his superior that he is wrong, not because he does not want to help solve a problem, but because affording face is more important than problem-solving (Schein, 2010). In China, "Open contradiction to superiors in [the] presence of others is a taboo because it is considered as a threat to the superiors' face" (Lin, 2008, p. 309). In other words, "public disagreement is a face losing act" (Gao, 1998, p. 180). The Chinese tend to use an unforceful style of communication in social interactions. They articulate intentions in an indirect manner and allow room for private negotiations (Gao, 1998). The Chinese believe that self-control and self-restraint are the tactics of choice for dealing with conflict (Gao, 1998). Nonetheless, direct discussion may not necessarily insult social face; "confirming the face of the other protagonist may reduce concerns and promote direct, effective discussion of differences… people can accept strong negative evaluations of their position, provided they believe their personal face is confirmed" (Tjosvold & Sun, 2000, p. 259).

Chinese Paternalistic Leadership

The traditional form of leadership in China is paternalistic leadership. It is linked with Confucianism and its emphasis on maintaining harmony. According to Aycan (as cited in Chen et al., 2011), paternalistic leadership is a multidimensional construct; it consists of three dimensions—benevolence, authoritarianism, and morality. Benevolence implies that a leader displays concern for subordinates' personal and familial well-being. Authoritarianism refers to a leader's use of authority and control over subordinates and expecting unchallenged obedience from them. Morality indicates that a leader exhibits superior moral character and integrity by behaving altruistically and leading by example (Chen et al., 2011). Paternalistic leaders provide safety and care for their employees: "Not unlike the father in a family, management is believed to exercise its power within the constraint of protecting and improving the lives of its employees, which relieves considerable tension on the part of employees" (Pellegrini & Scandura, 2008, p. 569).

Paternalistic leadership differs from transformational leadership (Bass, 1985; Bass & Avolio, 1994), as it does not include the concepts of delegation, empowerment, or creating a vision. Moreover, paternalistic leadership values one-way communication in which leaders decide, and followers are expected to listen and follow orders (Chen et al., 2011). Because it is based on Confucian values, it assumes the need for leader action, instead of inaction.

Employees use "voice" to "express their dissatisfaction directly to management or to some other authority to which management is subordinate or through general protest addressed to anyone who care to listen" (Hirschman, 1970, p. 4). The different dimensions of paternalistic leadership can have different effects on employee voice behavior and how they bring up issues and problems to their superiors. The morality and benevolence dimensions of paternalistic leadership can lead to an increase in employee voice behavior. However, the authoritarian dimension can also be detrimental to employee voice (Zhang et al., 2015).

The Adaptive Leadership Framework

Heifetz (1994) makes a distinction between adaptive challenges and technical problems. Technical problems have an existing solution. Thus, they do not require much learning to solve them; often, one can hire an expert to apply the required solution. Adaptive problems have no existing solution and require an exploration of the nature of the problem and the creation of the solution. Moreover, they require engagement with the various stakeholders and factions in an organization, what Heifetz (1994) terms giving the work back.

Heifetz et al. (2009) define an adaptive challenge as "the gap between the values people stand for (that constitute thriving) and the reality that they face" (p. 301). In other words, it is the lack of capacity to concretize those values in their context. The complexity of adaptive challenges does not stem from their technical aspects; they are based on social complexity.

Adaptive leadership fuels learning by asking tough questions and by re-framing people's expectations; adaptive leadership requires "learning to address conflicts in the beliefs, and values people hold" (Heifetz, 1994, p. 22). This kind of learning is hard and can be accompanied by a variety of negative feelings including a sense of loss and distress (Heifetz, 1994). Because of these adverse feelings, individuals may resist change and engage in adaptive work avoidance. Typically, this means a focus on technical solutions, faulting the authority figure for the problem, and blaming others outside the group.

In adaptive leadership, the leader creates interventions to generate movement on adaptive challenges, which can generate distress. Therefore, the leader has to maintain the distress within an endurable zone; if the distress is too high, there might be repercussions for the leader. On the other hand, if the distress level is too low there is inaction on the challenge. Heifetz employed a pressure cooker metaphor to describe this pattern: When the pressure is too high, the leader reduces the heat so that the pressure cooker will not explode. When things are not moving forward, the leader increases the heat.

The environment in which adaptive work takes place is called a holding environment. This is a place to hold the distress of adaptive work and do the collective adaptive work of examining values and assumptions, a place where the conflicts are safely worked through. Reinforcing the holding environment provides safety and structure for people to discuss particular values, assumptions, and perspectives and to generate potential solutions. The conflicts in adaptive leadership are conflicts around values and interpretation of reality.

The tactics that a leader can use to create movement on an adaptive issue will depend on whether they possess authority or lack it (Heifetz, 1994). When they have authority, the intervention strategies include asking tough questions (that people might not be comfortable answering) or questions that might reframe the situation. Moreover, a leader can orchestrate conflict, challenge existing norms, and demonstrate the reality of external threats. To reduce the stress level in the holding environment, they can use their authority to take action. Conversely, when they do not take any action, the stress level is likely to rise.

In addition to leading with authority, one can lead without authority:

> When we speak of leadership without authority, we are referring to a very large set of stances, from the person operating from the margins of society even to the senior authority figure who leads beyond his pale of authority, challenging either his own constituents' expectations or engaging people across the boundary of his organization who would ordinarily or preferably pay him no mind (Heifetz, 1994, p. 186).

Adaptive work is risky because of the losses it creates. To reduce the dangers of adaptive work, a leader has to alternate between action and reflection:

> If you stay moving on the dance floor, all you will see will be the people dancing with you and around you. Swept up in the music, it may be a great party! But when you get on the balcony, you may see a very different picture (Heifetz et al., 2009, p. 7).

In addition to what was mentioned earlier, an adaptive leader can employ a large number of other interventions, such as taking action, making observations, and offering interpretations (Heifetz & Linsky, 2017). At the most basic level, a word or gesture can serve as an intervention (Parks, 2005). A leader can also use silence or inaction to reduce the distress (Heifetz et al., 2009).

Adaptive leadership uses a rich set of metaphors to describe various leader actions and states: Going to the balcony, being on the dance floor, pressure cooker, lowering the temperature, raising the heat, ripening issues (making them ready to be tackled), modern ballet, walking the razor's edge, listening to the song beneath the words (Heifetz, 1994), getting divorced with children (Heifetz & Linsky, 2017), and vegetable stew (Heifetz et al., 2009). Most of these metaphors are borrowed from the biological sciences, music, psychiatry, and from Heifetz and colleagues' personal backgrounds and practices; they represent experiences that are commonplace. However, a few of these metaphors can be critiqued as being elitist in nature, such as the modern ballet and dance floor metaphors that might not be experienced by someone who has lived in poverty without access to ballet or a ballroom with a balcony.

Adaptive leadership rests upon the following implicit assumptions:

- Because losses are inevitable, then conflict is a necessary condition for accepting or distributing the losses;
- People resist adaptive change because it is painful;
- Stakeholders have a minimum level of ability to take back some of the adaptive work;
- A leader with authority possesses enough expertise (a) to take up some of work that the followers cannot handle and (b) create technical solutions to reduce the level of distress in the system; and
- Adaptive change can be slow because (a) it is linked to the adaptive capacity of the followers; (b) changing habits, mindsets, and values can take time; and (c) it can take a long time to ripen some issues.

Adaptive Leadership and Paternalistic Leadership

Adaptive leadership and paternalistic leadership differ in many respects. First, paternalistic leadership values harmony and face-saving. Adaptive leadership, on the other hand, relies on conflict, distress, and enough disruption to create movement on adaptive issues. Second, paternalistic leadership assumes that a leader should have the answers and provide solutions to problems. Adaptive leadership, on the other hand, assumes that problems are complex and that the leader does not have most of the answers. Third, paternalistic leadership assumes the need for control and individuals acting within their roles. In contrast, adaptive leadership assumes that a leader will need to go beyond their formal authorization (Heifetz, 1994). Adaptive leadership starts from the position that a leader exerts influence through social interventions, not control. Fourth, paternalistic leadership focuses on the leader-follower dyad and the larger guanxi, whereas adaptive leadership is concerned with group and system-wide change. Fifth, there is no effectiveness evidence for paternalistic leadership in the West. However, adaptive leadership has been shown to work in India (Heifetz, 1994), Meiji's Japan (1868–1912), and the Levant of the 1920s (Williams, 2005), in addition to the West.

Compatibility of Adaptive Leadership with Chinese Culture

Although Western leadership practices are successful in the West, they might not have the same level of significance and applicability in the Chinese context and, in fact, need to be altered to work in China (Gallo, 2011). One of the strengths of adaptive leadership is that it allows for "the values of various cultures and organizations" (Heifetz, 1994, p. 26).

A leader coming from the Taoist tradition might have an advantage in using adaptive leadership when compared with a paternalistic Chinese leader; as mentioned earlier, following Wu Wei, a Taoist leader avoids unnecessary interventions and only intervenes when there is no other choice. The patience and the ability to hold steady before intervening echoes adaptive leadership's interventions where the leader waits for an issue to ripen, or waits to see the effect of an intervention. Nonetheless, adaptive leadership requires an interventionist stance because its goal is to create movement on adaptive challenges. It holds that people avoid adaptive work and that an intervention might be needed to dislodge them from their habits and mindsets.

Another Taoist concept compatible with adaptive leadership is Yin-Yang. I suggest that adaptive leadership uniquely represents that merging of the opposites. It integrates both reflection (going to the balcony) and action (being on the dance floor); intervening and waiting; lowering the heat and raising the heat, alternating between dealing with technical and adaptive issues, and exercising leadership with authority and leadership without authority. This compatibility with the Yin-Yang concept might not be directly apparent to the followers in China, however, it might have great utility in explicitly teaching adaptive leadership practices.

Adaptive leadership uses a holding environment to hold the distress of adaptive work. In the Chinese context, the holding environment will have to also serve as a cultural island (Schein, 2010). According to Schein (2010), cultural islands improve communication by suspending the rules of communication "so that the members of the group can explain their own experience and learn to calibrate the experiences of others" (p. 119). Cultural islands may make it acceptable to engage in conflict without affront to face and to engage in ways that will not disrupt the social order.

The holding environment will have to be stronger in China than it is in Western cultures. Even in Western cultures, when an individual without authority raises an adaptive issue

> the mechanisms for killing the messenger are varied and subtle depending on the culture, the organization, and the problem ....

First, a person or faction raises a difficult question that generates some distress by pointing to a potential conflict over values and purpose, norms and organizational relationships, power, or strategy. Second, in response, the disquieted members of the system will turn their gaze to a senior authority figure, expecting him to restore equilibrium. Finally, the authority figure, pressed by these expectations to reduce distress, feeling emotionally compelled to act, neutralizes or silences the "problem" faction, directly or indirectly. (Heifetz, 1994, p. 225)

Cultural islands might provide a certain level of protection for those who raise a difficult issue. Schein suggests the use of procedures and checklist as neutral cultural islands: "The subordinate is licensed to ask challenging questions of the more senior person if it is a checklist item without thereby threatening the senior person's face" (p. 398). To further adaptive work, these checklists and procedures can be used to ask questions about potential adaptive issues, without significantly increasing the level of distress in the system. They can also serve as the technical component of an adaptive solution. Thus, they might result in a reduction in distress in the social system.

A Chinese adaptive leader will have to contend with guanxi in their organization. Prioritizing relationship over effectiveness can be a major hindrance to adaptive work. Also, adaptive leadership is about bringing different stakeholders together in the interest of dealing with adaptive work. This will and requires that the leader gives equal value to individuals who are not part of their guanxi. This may mean the need to discuss the role of guanxi in the holding environment, perhaps leading to a loss of face. Hence the need for a very strong holding environment/cultural island, mentioned earlier, is critical. A leader might also be able to use guanxi to their advantage to further adaptive work. In the short term, the social capital in the guanxi might help absorb some of the pressure of adaptive work and add to the strength of the holding environment. The leader might also have informal authority through their guanxi that they can put to use. However, the use of guanxi might turn into a two-edged sword; in the long run, stakeholders might develop a dependency on guanxi, precluding the leader from putting additional adaptive issues on the table because the issues might affect their guanxi.

Adaptive leadership assumes followers have a minimum level of adaptive capacity to take back some of the adaptive work and gives back adaptive work at a rate followers can handle. In China, however, an adaptive leader might spend time developing the capacity to engage in adaptive work. In the Chinese context, the rate at which followers can handle adaptive work must adjust to meet the cultural expectations of the Chinese. For example, in adaptive leadership, a leader does not typically provide answers. In China, leaders might initially give more answers than they would in a

Western context, then as progress is made, give fewer answers and ask more questions; the rate at which the work is given back adjusts to cultural norms. As another example, an adaptive leader with authority purposely disorients people from their current roles. In China, this disorientation will have to take place at a slow rate. Disorienting from current roles might bring values and mindsets in question, resisted because it disrupts the expected hierarchy and natural order in Chinese organizations.

An adaptive leader uses a variety of interventions to create movement on adaptive problems. In the Chinese context, it might be prudent to start with low impact interventions, such as making an observation instead of asking a question. Asking questions suggests the expectation of an answer, which increases the possibility of losing face, or hiding problems to keep face. Making an observation, on the other hand, if worded carefully, might point to an adaptive issue while still saving face.

Adaptive leadership differs from more traditional forms of leadership in that it "is not about meeting or exceeding [one's] authorizers' expectations; it is about challenging some of those expectations, finding a way to disappoint people without pushing them completely over the edge" (Heifetz et al., 2009, p. 26). Heifetz (1994) has also claimed that "leadership is a normative concept because implicit in people's notions of leadership are images of a social contract" (p. 14). Chinese employees may resist efforts of empowerment in ways that follow Western schools of management. They consider a Western-educated leader who tries to challenge and empower them to be weak. They reason that a leader should be able to find the solution themself. Moreover, in China, a leader should not attempt to increase an employee's level of responsibility (Gallo, 2011). Employees in China expect a leader to act paternalistically with strong Confucian assumptions. There is no room for inaction on the part of the leader, or if there is, an adaptive leader in China might have to prove their competence first by taking action before slowly giving work back to the employees.

It is worth recalling that adaptive problems are different from regular work problems and the adaptive work that is given back to the followers and stakeholders is concerned with individual and organizational values and mindsets, not with mere technical problems. Moreover, with adaptive leadership, the leader is not providing the answer, not necessarily because they do not want to, but because the problem is complex and requires different consideration than one that is technical. One of these considerations is that the leader does not have the answer. A leader in the Chinese context will have to make this distinction clear. Kotter (1996) points out that leaders often under-communicate their vision; thus, leaders need to regularly and frequently communicate that an adaptive challenge is not a regular business problem for which they have the answer. However, China is a high-context culture (Korac-Kakabadse et al., 2001); in China, it is not the responsibility of the leader to spell out what they mean. Instead, it is the responsibility of the listener to discern the leader's intention from the context. It is also true that one can wrongly guess another's intention. One solution is to create a cultural island by using low-context language in which all communication takes place. Whereas this suggestion might seem linguistically imperialistic in that it imposes the language of one culture on another, this kind of intervention was successfully used by Hiroshi Mikitani, CEO of the Japanese company Rakuten who "felt that English had fewer power markers—words that specifically denote status and hierarchy—and could thereby facilitate problem-solving faster, without the restraints of the Japanese cultural norms that get played out in language" (Williams, 2015, pp. 111–112). The benefits of using English—or any other low context language—in the Chinese context can extend beyond reducing power markers to allow followers to bring adaptive challenges to the forefront, making communication clearer and more effective.

As mentioned earlier, in business settings, the Chinese communicate intentions in an indirect manner and allow room for private negotiations (Gao, 1998). While adaptive leadership advocates bring stakeholders to engage in adaptive work, a leader in China might instead hold these discussions privately. This might help reduce the chance that they might offend their face during a meeting where other stakeholders are present.

Heifetz (1994) points out that adaptive work avoidance will manifest itself differently by culture; "distinguishing work from work avoidance is no science. Each culture will have its own typical patterns of response to stress—work-producing as well as work-avoiding" (p. 39). Therefore, an adaptive leader in China will have to look for different signs of adaptive work avoidance than might be typical in the West.

Orienting Values

Engaging in adaptive work requires clarity around implicitly held values (Heifetz, 1994). Chinese culture tends to value relationships, harmony, and social order and Western cultures tend to value efficiency. Adaptive leaders, on the other hand, value adaptive work and believe that overcoming adaptive challenges cannot be achieved without some disruption of the social order. Can these values of harmony and disruption coexist? Heifetz (1994) writes, "a hierarchy [of orienting values] that would apply across cultures and organizational settings risks either being so general as to be impractical or so specific as to be culturally imperialistic in its application" (p. 21). Accordingly, if a discussion of orienting values were to take place in a typical Chinese organization, it might position relationships, harmony, and maintenance of social roles above participation, freedom, equality, justice, competence, or efficiency. In the United States, efficiency might be placed at the top of the pyramid. Argyris (1977) points out that often there is a discrepancy between the theories of action that organizations espouse and the one they use in practice (For a more detailed overview of espoused theories and theories in use, see Chapter 9). Any discussion of values and their prioritization would have to be in relation to the values that are used, not the ones espoused.

It is worth pointing out that not all Chinese organizations will have the same order of values. For example, some government-owned organizations might place efficiency at the bottom of the hierarchy. In contrast, a high-tech manufacturing company might place efficiency second to relationships. In any case, the specific order of values is not as important as the discussion itself. Adaptive leadership has an empirical quality; reality testing, sooner or later, will show whether a particular hierarchy is suitable or will need to be modified.

As mentioned previously, the authoritarian dimension of paternalistic leadership can be detrimental to employee voice behavior. As a result, problems may not be brought to the attention of the leader. However, the benevolence and morality dimensions are conducive for employee voice. Adaptive leadership looks for adaptive issues and encourages employees to surface problems. It may be possible for an adaptive leader to combine adaptive leadership with some level of targeted benevolence, where they show genuine care for their subordinates. This can add to the strength of the holding environment and reduce the distress in the system to allow for progress on adaptive work.

Some of the metaphors used in adaptive leadership can be considered universal because of their link with cooking and fermenting processes common to all cultures, as examples, ripening issues, lowering and raising the heat. Other metaphors can be criticized for being Western and might need modification for a non-Western audience. For example, the "divorced with children" metaphor is not a relatable metaphor in many parts of the world. A second example is the modern ballet metaphor. In order for adaptive leadership to work in China, an adaptive leader might have to create new metaphors that fit the culture.

Adaptive leadership brings different stakeholders together in a holding environment to work out differences over values and distribute losses. The largest challenge for implementing adaptive leadership in China is to distribute the losses without affront to face. As mentioned earlier, confirming the face of the other may decrease concerns and encourage direct discussion of differences; individuals can tolerate negative evaluation of their position if they think their personal face is confirmed (Tjosvold & Sun, 2000).

Conclusion

Every country faces adaptive challenges. What is interesting in the case of China is that despite its unparalleled economic growth in the last 40 years, it still has many problems, some of which can be solved with technical approaches. Others, however, are adaptive and reflect outmoded values, and require painful learning. Thus, I argue that adaptive leadership not only can be applied in China but that it *should* be applied in China and that the practices of adaptive leadership may well be essential for China's future thrivability. In this chapter, I explored the key concepts in Chinese culture and paternalistic leadership, grounded in Confucianism. After examining the compatibility of adaptive leadership with Chinese culture, I determined that application of adaptive leadership principles in China would need to be heavily modified to accommodate the need to protect face and avoid overt conflict. I suggested that holding environments in China will have to be stronger than those in Western cultures and that the pace of adaptive work might be slower. I also suggested that adaptive leadership might be combined with benevolence. Additionally, I postulated that guanxi, Wu Wei, and the concept of Yin-Yang might be used to facilitate adaptive change. Nonetheless, these prescriptions are tentative; adaptive leadership should be considered an experimental approach. In China, a great amount of experimentation would have to take place.

Ultimately, adaptive leadership, by its very nature, requires adaption by leaders and followers. As a leadership framework, I argue that it can be also be adapted to new contexts.

References

Argyris, C. (1977). Double loop learning in organizations. *Harvard Business Review*, 55(5), 115–125.

Bai, X., & Roberts, W. (2011). Taoism and its model of traits of successful leaders. *Journal of Management Development*. 10.1108/02621711111150236

Bass, B. M. (1985). *Leadership and performance beyond expectations*. Free Press.

Bass, B. M., & Avolio, B. J. (Eds.). (1994). *Improving organizational effectiveness: Through transformational leadership*. Sage.

Cheng, C. (2011). Confucian global leadership in Chinese tradition: Classical and contemporary. *Journal of Management Development*, 30(7/8), 647–662.

Chen, X., Eberly, M. B., Chiang, T., Farh, J., & Cheng, B. (2011). Affective trust in Chinese leaders: Linking paternalistic leadership to employee performance. *Journal of Management*, 40(3), 796–819. 10.1177/0149206311410604

De Mente, B. L. (2011). *Chinese mind: Understanding traditional Chinese beliefs and their influence on contemporary culture*. Tuttle Publishing.

Fu, P. P., Wu, R., & Yang, Y. (2007). Chinese culture and leadership. In J. S. Robert, J. House (Editor), F. C. Brodbeck, & R. J. House (Eds.), *Culture and leadership across the world: The GLOBE book of in-depth studies of 25 societies* (pp. 877–907). Lawrence Erlbaum Associates.

Gallo, F. T. (2011). *Business leadership in China: How to blend best Western practices with Chinese wisdom*. John Wiley & Sons (Asia) Pte. Ltd.

Gao, G. (1998). "Don't take my word for it."—understanding Chinese speaking practices. *International Journal of Intercultural Relations, 22*(2), 163–186. 10.1016/s0147-1767(98)00003-0

Gerstner, A. (2011). Leadership and organizational patterns in the Daodejing. *Journal of Management Development, 30*(7/8), 675–684. 10.1108/02621 711111150191

Heider, J. (1985). *The Tao of leadership: Lao Tzu's Tao te ching adapted for a new age.* Humanics New Age.

Heifetz, R. A. (1994). *Leadership without easy answers.* Harvard University Press.

Heifetz, R. A., & Linsky, M. (2017). *Leadership on the line, with a new preface: Staying alive through the dangers of change.* Harvard Business Press.

Heifetz, R. A., Grashow, A., & Linsky, M. (2009). *The practice of adaptive leadership: Tools and tactics for changing your organization and the world.* Harvard Business Press.

Hirschman, A. O. (1970). *Exit, voice, and loyalty: Responses to decline in firms, organizations, and states.* Harvard University Press.

Hutchings, K., & Weir, D. (2005). Guanxi and Wasta: A comparison. *Thunderbird International Business Review, 48*(1), 141–156. 10.1002/tie.20090

International Monetary Fund. (2016, January). Subdued demand, diminished prospects. http://www.imf.org/external/pubs/ft/weo/2016/update/01/pdf/0116.pdf

Korac-Kakabadse, N., Kouzmin, A., Korac-Kakabadse, A., & Savery, L. (2001). Low-and high-context communication patterns: towards mapping cross-cultural encounters. *Cross Cultural Management, 8*(2), 3–24. 10.11 08/13527600110797218

Kotter, J. P. (1996). *Leading change.* Harvard Business School Press.

Lewis, H. M. (2005). Golden face: Cultural reciprocity in the articulation of mainland Chinese social structure. *Thunderbird International Business Review, 48*(1), 9–23. 10.1002/tie.20082

Li, C. (2000). Confucianism and feminist concerns: Overcoming the Confucian "gender complex". *Journal of Chinese Philosophy, 27*(2), 187–199. 10.1111/0301-8121.00012

Lin, C. (2008). Demystifying the chameleonic nature of Chinese leadership. *Journal of Leadership & Organizational Studies, 14*(4), 303–321. 10.11 77/1548051808315552

Lin, L., Ho, Y., & Lin, W. E. (2012). Confucian and Taoist work values: An exploratory study of the Chinese transformational leadership behavior. *Journal of Business Ethics, 113*(1), 91–103. 10.1007/s10551-012-1284-8

Luo, Y. (1997). Guanxi: Principles, philosophies, and implications. *Human Systems Management, 16*(1), 43–51.

Ma, L., & Tsui, A. S. (2015). Traditional Chinese philosophies and contemporary leadership. *The Leadership Quarterly, 26*(1), 13–24. 10.1016/j.leaqua.2014.11.008

McElhatton, E., & Jackson, B. (2012). Paradox in harmony: Formulating a Chinese model of leadership. *Leadership, 8*(4), 441–461.

McKinsey Global Institute. (2009, February). Preparing for China's urban billion. http://www.mckinsey.com/global-themes/urbanization/preparing-for-chinas-urban-billion

Parks, S. D. (2005). *Leadership can be taught: A bold approach for a complex world*. Harvard Business Press.

Pellegrini, E. K., & Scandura, T. A. (2008). Paternalistic leadership: A review and agenda for future research. *Academy of Management Proceedings*, *34*(3), 566–593. 10.5465/ambpp.2007.26524291

Ramasamy, B., Goh, K., & Yeung, M. C. (2006). Is Guanxi (relationship) a bridge to knowledge transfer? *Journal of Business Research*, *59*(1), 130–139. 10.1016/j.jbusres.2005.04.001

Schein, E. (2010). *Organizational culture and leadership* (4th ed.). Jossey-Bass.

Tjosvold, D., & Sun, H. (2000). Social face in conflict: Effects of affronts to person and position in China. *Group Dynamics: Theory, Research, and Practice*, *4*(3), 259–271.

Towson, J. A., & Woetzel, J. R. (2013). *The 1 hour China book: Two Peking University professors explain all of China business in six short stories*. Towson Group LLC.

Union of Concerned Scientists. (n.d.). Each country's share of CO2 emissions. Retrieved June 1, 2021, from https://www.ucsusa.org/resources/each-countrys-share-co2-emissions

Wang, J., Wang, G. G., Ruona, W. E., & Rojewski, J. W. (2005). Confucian values and the implications for international HRD. *Human Resource Development International*, *8*(3), 311–326. 10.1080/13678860500143285

Watts, A. (2010). *What is Tao?* New World Library.

Williams, D. (2005). *Real leadership: Helping people and organizations face their toughest challenges*. Berrett-Koehler.

Williams, D. (2015). *Leadership for a fractured world: How to cross boundaries, build bridges, and lead change*. Berrett-Koehler Publishers, Inc.

World Population Review. (n.d.-a). GDP ranked by country 2020. Retrieved November 14, 2020, from https://worldpopulationreview.com/countries/countries-by-gdp

World Population Review. (n.d.-b). Total population by country 2020. Retrieved November 14, 2020, from https://worldpopulationreview.com/countries

Yen, D. A., Barnes, B. R., & Wang, C. L. (2011). The measurement of guanxi: Introducing the GRX scale. *Industrial Marketing Management*, *40*(1), 97–108. 10.1016/j.indmarman.2010.09.014

Zhang, X., Li, N., & Harris, T. B. (2015). Putting non-work ties to work: The case of guanxi in supervisor–subordinate relationships. *The Leadership Quarterly*, *26*(1), 37–54. 10.1016/j.leaqua.2014.04.008

Zhang, Y., Huai, M., & Xie, Y. (2015). Paternalistic leadership and employee voice in China: A dual process model. *The Leadership Quarterly*, *26*(1), 25–36. 10.1016/j.leaqua.2014.01.002

12 Kabuki Leadership: Cultivating Adaptive Leadership in a Hierarchical Collectivist Culture in Japan

Risako (Lisa) Watanabe and Ryosuke (Reo) Watanabe

Although Japan ranks third globally in gross domestic product (GDP; World Bank, 2019), its annual GDP growth has plummeted over the decade as it faced unprecedented adaptive challenges (Heifetz et al., 2009b) without clear solutions. The COVID-19 pandemic has added to the existing issues of global competition, technological innovations, and Japan's declining/aging population. Particularly, the latter causes diminishing labor and tax pools, difficulties in financing social security frameworks, and surging public expenditure on health care, nursing care, and pensions (Hong & Schneider, 2020).

In corporate Japan, executives feel an urgent need to transform their organizational culture in ways that embrace collaborative and adaptive leadership (PwC Consulting LLC., 2019). Such a shift would allow the industry to quickly find new solutions and thrive in uncertainty.

This chapter addresses how adaptive leadership has been practiced in a hierarchical collectivist culture in Japan and how a cultural shift toward more adaptive organizations is possible. Cultural change is an adaptive challenge that involves a change within people's minds as to how leadership and the challenge are defined (Heifetz et al., 2009b). Adaptive leadership has a significant impact on the strength and longevity of any organization (Heifetz, 1994), yet requires leaders to have commensurate maturity and a sufficiently developed organizational culture to overcome such adaptive challenges (Kegan & Lahey, 2009).

This chapter is divided into five sections. First, we describe Japanese culture and its relationship to leadership practices. Second, we explain adaptive leadership practices in *kabuki* (a classical Japanese theater). Third, we detail two cases of adaptive leadership practices in corporate Japan. Fourth, we profile our adaptive leadership development intervention for a fast-growing Japanese company. Finally, we conclude with implications for adaptive leadership development within a hierarchical collectivist culture.

DOI: 10.4324/9781003099109-12

Hierarchical Collectivist Culture in Japan

Visitors to Japan often experience a juxtaposition of tradition and technological innovation. Japan is one of the most technologically advanced economies in the world (Radu, 2020). However, a 2,000-year history of tradition and seniority represented through extensive honorific language still permeates the entire culture.

Japan has a collectivist culture with strong group emotions, high power distance, and loyalty to authority (Nahavandi, 2006). Its collectivism is not egalitarian, but highly hierarchical (Meyer, 2014), marked by a performance orientation (Nahavandi, 2006). House et al. (2002) proposed that a culture's differentiating characteristics could predict organizational practices and leadership behaviors. In short, the most acceptable and effective organizational practices and leadership behaviors and qualities in Japan are based on hierarchical collectivism, which puts importance on authority and self-sacrifice for the good of the group (Nahavandi, 2006).

Kabuki and its Uniqueness in Collaborative Improvisation

Kabuki is one of the major classical theater forms in Japan, dating back to the 17th century (Kodansha, n.d.a). With its blend of drama, music, and dance, kabuki is recognized as one of the world's greatest theatrical traditions (Kodansha, n.d.a). Since its inception, kabuki has adapted to the changing times (Kodansha, n.d.a) and, similar to how Heifetz et al. (2009a) describe leadership, is an "improvisational and experimental art" (p. 3), that fosters adaptation, embraces productive disequilibrium, and generates leadership. Heifetz et al. (2009b) define fostering adaptation as enabling an organization to thrive in a new or challenging environment. To embrace productive disequilibrium is described as generating enough distress among stakeholders to make progress, but not so excessively that the organization is incapacitated (Heifetz et al., 2009b). They explain generating leadership as the distribution of leadership responsibility and the mobilization of everyone for producing results (Heifetz et al., 2009a).

Kabuki Fosters Adaptation

Kabuki's cultivation of adaptation is seen in some actors' dissent to its inheritance system and the industry's trend itself (Kominz, 2006); the kabuki industry is still adapting. Its goal of advancing new creations along with classics results in the introduction of new kabuki productions—adaptations of storybooks, manga, works of Shakespeare, and classic Indian texts. These adaptations accentuate the basis of new creations as classic kabuki while reinforcing a kabuki tradition characterized by the introduction of new productions (Shochiku Co., Ltd., 2020).

Kabuki Embraces Disequilibrium

The kabuki industry held itself in a fruitful disequilibrium by "acting politically" (Heifetz et al., 2009a). During Japan's Tokugawa period (1603–1868 A.D.) of isolation from foreign contacts and oppressive government restrictions, Kabuki artists used "suggestion" to circumvent censorship and maximize entertainment (D'Etcheverry, 2011). During this period, one of the universal moral concepts, the Buddhist belief of *mujō* (impermanence), was integrated into the kabuki theater for plot turns, often exemplifying the collapse of a noble family or a mighty military head (Kodansha, n.d.a). The ways in which kabuki enlightens citizens about impermanence exemplifies adaptive leadership in its orientation to change (impermanence) and the role of non-positional leaders (those lacking formal authority) to embrace adaptation and disequilibrium in an ever-changing world (Heifetz, 1994).

Other elements of kabuki that enable an audience to embrace disequilibrium are pivot words with two meanings (kakekotoba), quick changes (hayagawari), and double casting, the same actor playing more than one character in a given play (D'Etcheverry, 2011). All three elements invite the audience to see an actor as multiple and often contradicting personae. These too align with the role informal authority may play in adaptive work and how adaptive leadership requires us to engage in multiple interpretations and enhance our complexity.

Kabuki as a Leadership Generator

Finally, kabuki epitomizes the mobilization of all stakeholders, one of the cornerstones of adaptive leadership (Heifetz et al., 2009a). Most remarkable regarding kabuki performance is that the music is composed and performed collectively and collaboratively (Kodansha, n.d.b). Unlike conductors in Western operas, the actors and musicians in kabuki take turns playing the role of conductor, unfolding naturally. The singers and players of shamisen, the three-stringed traditional Japanese instrument, are in charge of their parts. The stakeholder groups of the percussion and offstage music, consult with other roles in the production, such as the head of the association of percussionists, actors, and directors of the performance, to add their music to the theatrical piece. Like adaptive leadership, this collaborative improvisation process is perfected through practice and carried out on stage. Kabuki also mobilizes people (Heifetz et al., 2009a) in more subtle ways. The audience becomes another stakeholder group as they participate in performances through the use of *kakegoe* (set phrases cried out by attendees at particular points in the performance) and sensory conventions, such as allusion, requiring active audience participation (D'Etcheverry, 2011).

Thus, the distinctiveness of kabuki is that it promotes adaptiveness, maintains productive disequilibrium, and exercises collaborative leadership within a hierarchical collectivist culture while adapting itself to the needs of modernity, all of which are critical in the art of adaptive leadership.

Adaptive Leadership in Hierarchical Collectivist Corporate Japan

This section describes two corporate examples of adaptive leadership enacted in the hierarchical collectivist culture in Japan. The first example comes from Toyota Motor Corporation, a global manufacturer run by one family on a hereditary system, where *kaizen* (Imai, 1986) is one of the key principles of the production system. *Kaizen* is defined as a search for continuous improvement and a philosophy dedicated to maximum quality, waste elimination, and improved efficiency in equipment and work procedures (Toyota UK, 2013).

Kaizen activities are embedded in the daily work of the employees, even at the lowest level of Toyota. For example, since 1951, the company has been asking its employees (approximately 74,000) to reflect weekly and propose *kaizen* ideas. These range from minute improvements in daily workflows or production lines to corporate-wide initiatives. If an employee submits five ideas, the supervisor will give that employee between ¥500 and ¥30,000 ($4 and $250) the following week depending on the idea proposed. Ideas worthy of consideration at the highest level move up the chain of command. All ideas receive some renumeration, even those not classified as extraordinary, encouraging all employees to participate. This top-initiated but bottom-up weekly activity has led to numerous improvements and innovations for the company. It creates safe spaces for critical thinking, gives the work back to the staff, and encourages employees to speak out about what doesn't work, all of which exemplify adaptive leadership practices (Heifetz et al., 2009b).

A second example is the Amoeba Management methodology developed by Kazuo Inamori, the former president and chairman of Kyocera Corporation (Kyocera Corporation, 2020). Amoeba Management begins by dividing an organization into smaller units named *amoebas*. One leader is designated for each amoeba, who takes responsibility for drafting plans and goals for the unit based on corporate-wide philosophy and goals. Within this structure, each employee plays a leading role to achieve the unit goals while pursuing the corporate philosophy. This management-by-all approach is widely accepted in Japan. More than 700 companies, including Kyocera, KDDI, and Japan Airlines implemented this strategy with significant successes reported. As an example, Inamori directly led the successful turnaround of Japan Airlines in two years with Amoeba Management, from one of Japan's biggest bankruptcies in 2010 to the world's second-largest public offering in 2012 (Layne, 2012). This revival, enabled by the collaboration of all employees, is an example of generating leadership throughout the organization.

We can extract common threads from these two corporate cases and kabuki. Both corporations exercised elements of adaptive leadership in a hierarchical collectivist culture. Toyota was consistently committed to innovation, developed a business philosophy called *kaizen* to improve its business continuously, and remains an adaptive leader in the industry. Kyocera created the Amoeba methodology and still has an immense influence on the innovation of other corporate entities globally. The authors call this type of leadership model in which adaptive leadership is practiced within a hierarchical collectivist culture, "kabuki leadership." We now present a case study in which we tested our model of kabuki leadership in Japan.

A Case of An Adaptive Leadership Intervention in Japan

This is a case study of a fast-growing accounting firm in Japan and a leadership development program to develop an adaptive organizational culture. The company offered its top 15 executives, including the founder and CEO, a 5-month intervention using the adaptive leadership framework (Heifetz, 1994) and the immunity-to-change (ITC) process based on adult developmental theory (Kegan & Lahey, 2009). We utilized pre- and post-intervention assessments to evaluate a potential shift in two areas: Participants' stage of adult development and views on organizational culture. The primary instruments for this study were the Subject-Object Interview (SOI; Lahey et al., 1988) and the Culture Evaluation Tool (McCauley et al., 2008).

Background

The accounting firm in which this study took place has grown steadily since its inception in 2007 and, at the time of this study, was ranked among the top 30 accounting firms in Japan. It enjoys a solid reputation as a group of trusted business advisors to over 2,400 clients across a wide range of industries.

This firm has also faced serious challenges. Accounting services had become increasingly commoditized, and the pricing competition had reduced the firm's growth and profitability. As well, with growing pressure on compliance and demands for high-level client services, many employees experienced burnout, resulting in high turnover. Nevertheless, because of steady growth over the previous decade, the management lacked a sense of urgency.

Furthermore, there was a growing gap between espoused and enacted corporate values (H. Takahashi, personal communication, January 15,

2021). The CEO publicly committed to embracing diverse opinions and the growth and well-being of all associated stakeholders: Employees, clients, and the accounting industry in Japan. He introduced flexible working arrangements and created a website for accountant-hopefuls that offered career advice. His leadership style tended to be command-and-control in order to generate fast outcomes, which created dependency among the employees on these directives, and siloed communication.

Realizing the long-term impact of his leadership style and the contradictions of his actions in relation to the firm's values, the CEO felt the firm should shift from a hierarchical leadership culture to one that was more collaborative and process-oriented. He also recognized that what amounted to an organizational culture transformation would require his employees, especially the leaders, to cultivate a more complex mindset (Kegan et al., 2016). The authors noted the firm could be closer to his goal by promoting adaptiveness, maintaining productive disequilibrium, and exercising collaborative leadership, the pillars of kabuki leadership.

Theoretical Frameworks for Organizational Culture Transformation

Two theoretical frameworks were employed in this intervention: Adaptive leadership and adult development. Adaptive leadership encompasses an iterative process of observing and interpreting patterns before taking action (Heifetz et al., 2009b). Heifetz et al. (2009b) call this "getting off the dance floor and on the balcony" (p. 32).

Critical to addressing the complexities of adaptive challenges is a mindset able to recognize and make meaning of that complexity. Adult development theory offers a foundation for understanding this capacity (Kegan & Lahey, 2009) and, by extension, adaptive leadership. Kegan's (1994) theory of constructive adult development posits that adults move through successive developmental stages, each stage representing a qualitative evolution in mental complexity (McCauley et al., 2006). Kegan describes these stages as instrumental, socialized, self-authoring, and self-transforming. Because the majority of adults fall between a socialized and self-transforming mindset, this study focused its data collection on those three stages (see Table 12.1).

Kegan et al. (2016) emphasized that organizations should focus on supporting employees to transform their meaning-making systems to deal with organizational culture transformation. Thus, it is critical to drive both individual and organizational development as interdependent goals at the organizational level.

Adult development theory has been applied to the evolution of organizations (Torbert, 2004), with McCauley et al. (2008) proposing that organizations develop along a similar trajectory as Kegan's individual framing: From a dependent to an independent to an interdependent

Table 12.1 Three Adult Development Minds

Adult Meaning Stages	Description
Socialized Mind (3rd stage)	Can subordinate its desire to that of others. Loyal to the community with which it identifies. Importance of external validation. 59% of adults are believed to be in this stage.
Self-authoring Mind (4th stage)	Self-guided, self-motivated, and self-evaluative. Can mediate conflicts. Importance of internal validation. 34% of adults are at this stage.
Self-transforming Mind (5th stage)	Self-reflective regarding the limitations of internal authority. Collective and variable authority. Less likely to see the world as dichotomies or polarities. Dialectic. The percentage of adults in this stage is thought to be less than 7%.

Note: Created by the authors of this chapter referencing Kegan and Lahey (2009).

leadership culture. In a dependent leadership culture, people with positional authority are responsible for leadership, and there is an emphasis on a command-and-control approach, with deference to authority. This is similar to the socialized mind form where individuals exhibit dependence upon external authority. In an independent leadership culture, leadership emerges where needed, based on knowledge and expertise. This culture may emphasize decentralized decision making, with a high regard for individual initiative and responsibility; in Kegan's developmental framing, these individuals would be classified as self-authored. In an interdependent leadership culture, leadership is a collaborative activity of mutual inquiry and learning, in which people proactively use dialogue and horizontal networks, valuing diversity, inclusion, and learning (For details on networks, see Chapter 1). This culture enables working cross-organizationally for synergies. Kabuki creation, with its collaborative nature and use of dialogue, appears to be based on an interdependent leadership culture. The latter leadership culture includes and transcends the prior leadership culture and is more complex. Research indicates organizations with an interdependent leadership culture are better able to adapt to rapid changes (Drath et al., 2010). McCauley et al. (2006, 2008) argue that an interdependent organizational culture corresponds closely with the self-transforming mind form. Figure 12.1 illustrates these cross-theory comparisons, adapted and modified from McCauley et al. (2006, 2008).

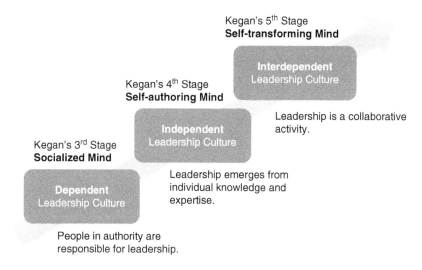

Figure 12.1 Stage Comparison of Individual Adult Development and Leadership Culture.

Note: Created by the authors of this chapter referencing McCauley et al. (2006, 2008).

Research Method

In 2019, the CEO of the accounting firm consulted with the authors to develop a leadership training program to embody its values: "We are all different and all wonderful, and we would like to move hand-in-hand and grow with you." His goal was to change the organizational culture from a hierarchical one to one that was adaptive, more developed, and inclusive.

Notably, the intervention that comprised this case study would be the first documented corporate attempt to develop an adaptive culture in Japan. The research team used Heifetz et al's (2009b) conception of an adaptive organizational culture, which includes: Authenticity and openness, shared responsibility, independent judgment, leadership capacity throughout the organization, and institutionalized reflection and continuous learning. The initial intervention was designed as an in-person 5-month leadership training based on adaptive leadership for the top 15 executives, including the CEO. From the kabuki leadership perspective, the CEO's participation was crucial not only for his own growth by perceiving his direct reports as colleagues, but also for the role modeling effect for his direct reports and the disequilibrium it might create in the training because of his dual role as CEO and fellow participant, enabling others to see his multiple personae. Due to the 2020 global pandemic, the study was redesigned to enable virtual delivery. As well, the original plan to offer two 1.5-day workshops in Tokyo at the start and end of the program was adjusted to comprise six 3-hour workshops over five months. This adjustment ensured more frequent gatherings due to the virtual nature of the training.

Another consideration related to the virtual intervention during the pandemic was the assumption that participants could not accommodate any excessive psychological stresses. Therefore, the ITC process (Kegan & Lahey, 2009) was chosen as a primary intervention strategy.

Immunity to Change

ITC offers a specific workflow to uncover invisible beliefs that prevent a desired change to take place. The ITC arc begins with a participant's identification of an "improvement goal," actions/inactions that counter that goal, the "hidden competing commitments" that rationalize the unproductive actions/inactions, and the "big assumption" that drives the hidden commitment and the counterproductive behaviors. Participants uncover a "map" of their behaviors that points to an "immune system" that is holding status quo behaviors in place. Subsequently, participants design and implement "tests" of their "big assumptions" to first understand if their assumptions are correct and, if so, they design experiments that will eventually help them overcome the immunities that prevent them from taking the actions they desire for themselves (Kegan & Lahey, 2009). This process often involves a level of discomfort, as it exposes and often questions strongly held beliefs (Kegan & Lahey, 2009) that can date back to childhood. The ITC exercise itself requires participants to be on the balcony, see themselves as systems—an essential characteristic of adaptive leaders (Heifetz et al., 2009) and, through that discomfort potentially expand their mental complexity (Helsing et al., 2013).

ITC and the adaptive leadership process of observing, interpreting, and intervening have common characteristics. First and as noted earlier, the ITC process of getting on the balcony and collecting data about the self is a key observation practice of adaptive leaders. Second, identifying "hidden competing commitments" that rationalize unproductive behavior and unconscious beliefs in ITC requires the interpretations adaptive leaders must make, in this case identifying and interpreting behavioral patterns. Finally, the design and implementation of experiments to test one's assumptions resembles intervention practices in adaptive leadership called "experiments" (Heifetz et al., 2009a), which intend to make progress on adaptive challenges (Heifetz et al., 2009b).

Process. For maximum learning, the participants were divided into four groups of three to four people. Each group had weekly group coaching meetings, designed to help participants share and reflect on their experiments, what they learned about themselves through the words and actions of those involved in the experiments, and their plan for the following week, all done collectively and collaboratively as in kabuki performances. As researchers, we believe people learn through collaborative inquiry and reflection. By observing other participants' reflections and analyses of their experiments, each participant might find similar dynamics in their own case. This mirroring dynamic could—and did—provide different interpretations of their cases. Moreover, the participants were asked to take turns becoming the weekly facilitator for their group, similar to kabuki in which musicians take turns playing the role of the conductor, to mobilize the system by exercising the functions of authority.

Holding Environment

An important component to the intervention was the development of a holding environment (Heifetz et al., 2009b) to support psychological safety among the participants and to maintain the disequilibrium at a productive level (For details on the holding environment, see Chapter 11). In the initial meeting, we asked participants to list rules which helped foster psychological safety during the program, along with a commitment to follow these "norms" and expectations of each other. The norms included: Maintain confidentiality, listen to others open-mindedly, participate physically and mentally, and celebrate small steps of change and success. The researchers also began each meeting with check-ins to share their intention for the work and concluded with check-outs to summarize reflections from the training session.

Furthermore, the researchers maintained a strong presence throughout the process. Virtual individual consultations were offered twice a month. The first four small group sessions were observed and supported. Weekly meetings were held with the CEO to make program adjustments according to his feedback.

Agile Methodology

The training took place from August to December 2020 and incorporated agile development methodology, a process that accelerates the progress of human growth and organizational culture change (De Smet et al., 2018). This time frame allowed for three cycles of a month-long agile cycle (Figure 12.2). Each cycle included one large-group workshop and four weekly small group meetings. As part of the intervention design, the authors changed the members in each small group and the theme of the ITC process every month to resemble *mujō* (impermanence or change) integrated in kabuki and promote adaptation as well as to enhance fellowship. Moreover, the authors created multiple group work opportunities with different group members during the workshops similar to quick change (hayagawari) in kabuki to simulate fluidity.

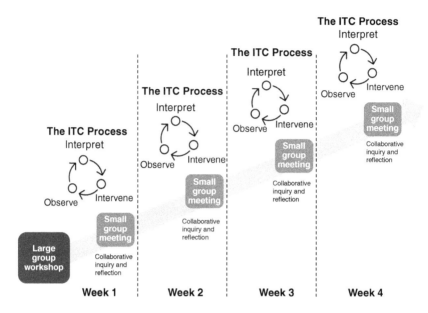

Figure 12.2 One Agile Cycle of the Leadership Development Intervention.

The first agile cycle centered on individual improvement goals to develop a reflective mindset and explore hidden biases. Participants were asked to recognize the adaptive and technical aspects of their personal challenge. The second cycle targeted organizational improvement goals. Each group chose and analyzed the adaptive aspects of one organizational improvement goal. Then, each group member made their own experimentations to overcome the adaptive challenges inherent in the organizational improvement goals and worked on them individually. The third cycle dealt with the organizational improvement goal of collaboration and moving beyond siloed practices. This cycle asked all participants to collaboratively work on experiments related to the goal within the cross-silo group or with other stakeholders not engaged in the training process depending on their goals. They shared their experiences and learnings regarding their big assumptions from the experiments with others within their small group and advised each other on how they might have done things differently. They also shared their learnings in the subsequent workshop with members from other small groups.

Data Collection

Pre- and post-intervention assessments were conducted: (1) the SOI (Lahey et al., 1988) to assess the participants' stages of adult development and (2) the Culture Evaluation Tool (McCauley et al., 2008), a survey to explore the participants' views on the organization's leadership culture.

Subject-Object Interview

The SOI is a 90-minute, one-on-one, semi-clinical, semi-structured interview that measures the interviewee's developmental stage related to mental complexity as defined by Kegan (1994). A certified interviewer asks participants about their recent experiences of "anger," "success," "sadness," "change," and so on. Two certified evaluators independently assess a transcript of the interview to determine that individual's developmental level, collaborating to confirm the accuracy of the evaluation. The SOI assigns a level of adult development out of 21 possible scores that corresponds to Kegan's developmental levels (explained earlier), including an assessment of how individuals may be transitioning from one level to another. The SOI is a time-consuming method (Helsing & Howell, 2013) with significant validity and reliability; it is widely used in leadership research (McCauley et al., 2006). Evaluators go through extensive training and testing to become certified to administer and score the SOI. The SOI was conducted virtually for all participants, pre- and post-intervention, and the post-intervention SOI was done a few weeks after the final agile cycle.

Culture Evaluation Tool

The Culture Evaluation Tool (McCauley et al., 2008) was developed to assess a respondent's perspective on whether they view the organization's leadership culture to be dependent, independent, or interdependent. The tool consists of ten sets of three statements. Respondents are asked to divide ten points among the three statements to show the degree to which these statements apply to their organization. The authors chose this instrument as an evaluation tool because its results clarify subtle shifts in organizational culture transformation. It also corresponds well with adult developmental theory and applies the theory to the organizational context.

Results and Data Analysis

The CEO's Journey

TOTAL Group has 250 staff members, 11 branches, and four nationwide affiliates. Takahashi, the CEO, was facing an adaptive challenge to grow the firm sustainably. Early on, he described himself as a "critic" and admitted, "My leadership style was highly centralized, and I believed that if I did not give directions, everything on the ground would be halted ...

Especially, before the pandemic, I believed that if I controlled everything, things would work out." At the onset of the pandemic, however, he came to see that his staff members "were there to help him" and wanted "all to be more actively involved with the business." The first goal of this intervention was to see if there could be a shift in the mindset of any of the executives and impact on the overall corporate culture.

A qualitative shift in Takahashi's mindset was evidenced in numerous comments in the post-program SOI. For example, when he talked about several members in the organization, he pointed out he could now understand that "they had their agendas and positions … because I could see myself from the 'balcony.'" This new perspective led him to learn to "wait for my subordinates more carefully and courteously." He shared that he sensed more of his subordinates were capable of balcony views. He also indicated that he felt more comfort delegating important jobs to his direct reports, as he noted, "people need a certain level of experience…even experience of failure." His mindset shifted from being the "critic" and "expert" problem-solver to being the one who can celebrate the growth of those around him. In other words, Takahashi realized he could not or did not need to solve every problem and that organizational capacity is built by giving the work back to the people. This is a key practice of adaptive leadership.

Organizational Change and Journeys of the Executives

The pre- and post-program SOIs showed notable shifts in the executives' mindsets. One significant finding was that through the ITC process, the executives came to understand and respect each other more deeply. Many realized they needed to intentionally sustain the effort to change themselves and the organization and that the ITC experiments helped initiate change, such as being adaptive enough to break down silos for collaboration. Additionally, an emerging pattern of language use was noted. For example, interviewees used terms such as "balcony," "adaptive challenge," "experiments," "big assumptions," "immunity," "adult developmental stages," and "leadership culture." Shared language strengthens the holding environment (Heifetz et al., 2009b), and the executives began to see common ground among themselves. Moreover, their new language enabled behavioral change. One executive said, "I allowed myself to behave differently by using the term 'experiment.'"

In addition to the aforementioned qualitative shift, a quantitative shift occurred: 7 out of 15 (47%) participants' developmental stages became more complex by the end of the intervention. Although 6 out of 15 demonstrated a construct closer to the self-authoring mind than the socialized mind before the program, 8 out of 15 were doing so after the program. Overall, many leaders experienced a widened perspective and a mindset shift, noted by the researchers, the participants, and in the data.

All-Company Business Plan Explanatory Conference

One of the learning outcomes was the first online execution of the annual All-Company Business Plan Explanatory Conference in October 2020. The goal of the conference was for the 250 staff members in attendance to discuss the theme: To help each other interdepartmentally while building a community. Co-designed by an executive planning committee and the researchers, the event began with the CEO's remarks regarding the theme, followed by management updates. Whereas previous conferences only involved executive presentations, the organizers planned the engagement of all attendees, as the goal for the company was to mobilize non-positional leaders to embrace productive disequilibrium and create a new "production" to foster adaptation as in kabuki.

Participants were divided into groups of eight, comprised of those in similar positions across the organization to enable candid, cross-departmental dialogue. The groups discussed the theme and presented one-minute idea summaries to the entire company. These presentations were designed to be adaptations for everyone: For young staff members lacking formal authority to take turns playing the role of the conductor as in kabuki, and for senior members with formal authority to experience the value of collaborative leadership.

The conference intended to promote a collaborative culture; all indications are that it was successful. One executive said, "We received many positive comments that the staff hoped we could continue these cross-departmental meetings." Another noted,

> It went really well. Some of us are already talking about doing Zoom gatherings with our favorite drinks. I was wondering how our leadership training could be rolled out to a company-wide initiative, but I now understand how it could be carried out.

The CEO was buoyant when he reported the "large experiment" succeeded. He declared, "There were some really helpful opinions. The executives are starting to face the same direction now and are evolving." A new company spirit was emerging.

Shifts in Perspectives on Leadership Culture

The Culture Evaluation Tool generated data to compare differences in the respondents' perspectives on leadership culture between the pre- and post-assessments. Table 12.2 shows the average number of points given to each statement by all respondents. The first statement in each triplet describes a dependent leadership culture, the second, an independent leadership culture, and the last, an interdependent leadership culture. The data in Table 12.2 indicate all three statements were endorsed to some degree in

Table 12.2 Leadership Culture Pre- and Post-assessment Comparison

No.	Theme/Question	Pretest (Aug. 2020) (n=15)	Posttest (Dec. 2020) (n=15)	Gap
1	**Decision Making**			
	Decisions are made by a few people at the top of the organization.	6.60	5.40	−1.20
	Decisions are made independently within businesses, functions, or groups.	1.53	2.67	1.13
	Decision making involves collaboration with people across multiple organizational boundaries.	1.87	1.93	0.07
2	**Source of Status**			
	What makes a person important is his or her position in the organization.	2.53	1.53	−1.00
	What makes a person important is his or her job performance and results.	3.60	3.67	0.07
	What makes a person important is the way he or she learns and changes with others.	3.87	4.80	0.93
3	**Measure of Success**			
	A person's success is judged by how well the person's boss thinks he or she is doing.	3.60	3.67	0.07
	A person's success is judged by how well he or she makes his or her individual performance goals.	2.60	3.27	0.67
	A person's success is judged by how well he or she helps the entire organization work together as an integrated whole.	3.80	3.07	−0.73
4	**Mistakes**			
	People do not talk about their mistakes because it might risk their future in the organization.	3.07	3.60	0.53
	People talk about their mistakes with people in their group because doing so helps improve the group's performance.	4.47	3.87	−0.60
	People talk about their mistakes with everyone as a way to help everyone do better throughout the organization.	2.47	2.53	0.07

(*Continued*)

Table 12.2 (Continued)

No.	Theme/Question	Pretest (Aug. 2020) (n=15)	Posttest (Dec. 2020) (n=15)	Gap
5	**Direction during Change**			
	During times of change, people take direction from above.	4.80	3.87	−0.93
	During times of change, individuals and groups create their own direction.	3.07	3.20	0.13
	During times of change, people use diverse perspectives to create new directions together.	2.13	2.93	0.80
6	**Values**			
	People value loyalty.	2.80	2.20	−0.60
	People value competitiveness.	3.67	3.87	0.20
	People value public truth-telling.	3.53	3.93	0.40
7	**Leader's Approach to Change**			
	Leaders are fairly conservative in their approach to change.	1.80	1.67	−0.13
	Leaders take significant risks for significant rewards.	2.67	2.20	−0.47
	Leaders practice continuous transformation to achieve long-term success.	5.53	6.13	0.60
8	**Responsibility for Learning**			
	The organization is responsible for identifying what people need to learn.	4.20	4.20	0.00
	People are responsible for their own learning.	3.67	3.80	0.13
	People take responsibility for one another's learning.	2.13	2.00	−0.13
9	**Executive Decisions**			
	Decisions made by senior leaders are typically reactive and tactical.	3.73	3.07	−0.67
	Decisions made by senior leaders proactively address needs in specific parts of the organization.	2.47	2.60	0.13
	Decision made by senior leaders create strategic synergies across the whole enterprise.	3.80	4.33	0.53
10	**Disagreements**			
	People want to keep the peace and not make disruptions.	5.27	5.80	0.53
	People openly disagree and argue about things they believe are important.	3.00	3.00	0.00

(*Continued*)

Table 12.2 (Continued)

No.	Theme/Question	Pretest (Aug. 2020) (n=15)	Posttest (Dec. 2020) (n=15)	Gap
	People take advantage of disagreements to solve complex challenges.	1.73	1.20	−0.53
	Leadership Cultures (Total Average)	Pretest	Posttest	Gap
	Dependent Leadership Culture	3.84	3.50	−0.34
	Independent Leadership Culture	3.07	3.21	0.14
	Interdependent Leadership Culture	3.09	3.29	0.20

Note: The Culture Evaluation Tool was designed by McCauley et al. (2008). Used with permission. Average number of points (out of 10) given to each statement. The first statement in each triplet signifies a leadership culture that is "dependent," the second shows one that is "independent," and the third represents one that is "interdependent."

the organization, but the perspectives regarding the organization's leadership culture shifted from dependent to independent or interdependent in the post-assessment, as evidenced in a 0.20 point increase in the average of the interdependent leadership culture and a 0.14 point increase in the average of the independent leadership culture, whereas a 0.34 point decrease in the average of the dependent leadership culture was noted.

The data in Figure 12.3 show the pre- and post-assessment comparison of the total average number of points given to statements indicating each leadership culture: The dependent, the independent, and the interdependent. The figure shows that the average numbers of the independent leadership culture in both the pre- and post-assessments were the smallest among the three leadership cultures, regardless of the general (not statistically significant) shifts from the dependent to the independent to the interdependent leadership culture. This might indicate the Japanese executives' hesitation regarding the independent leadership culture due to their embeddedness in hierarchical collectivism even though they might appreciate the value of Western individualism. Alternatively, it could indicate an evolving understanding of leadership within the organization. The trend line might be expected as belief systems begin to adjust. Overall, Figure 12.3 clearly visualizes the shift toward the independent and the interdependent leadership cultures.

Implications for Adaptive Leadership Development from a Japanese Case

This chapter concludes with a reflection on kabuki leadership development, namely, practicing adaptive leadership in a hierarchical collectivist

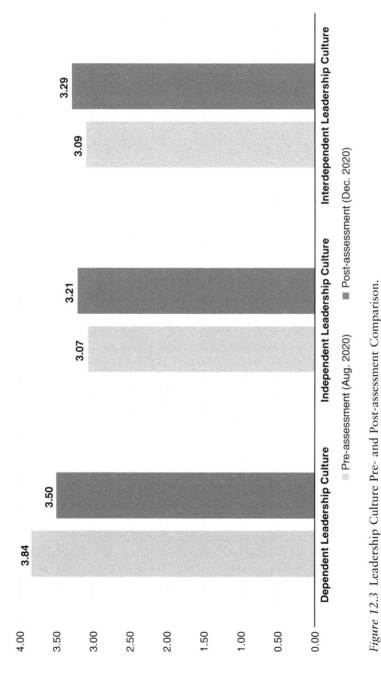

Figure 12.3 Leadership Culture Pre- and Post-assessment Comparison.

Note: Pre- and post-assessment comparison of the total average number of points given to statements indicating each leadership culture.

culture in a Japanese company. This improvisational art of leadership supports adaptation, adopts productive disequilibrium, and leverages collective leadership.

The differentiating characteristics of a culture predict organizational practices and leadership qualities most accepted and successful in that culture. Japan's hierarchical collectivist culture and typical information flow in a hierarchical chain of command in itself requires top-level leadership (e.g., the CEO) to initiate and rebuild a culture into one that is more adaptive.

In kabuki leadership, executives who participate in any program that intends to adjust an organization's culture and leadership practices must be authorized through that organization's formal authority. In this study, the CEO became a role model to his direct reports, showing commitment to the intervention, openness to collaboration, and vulnerability to motivate others to follow his lead. Modeling also strengthened the holding environment by building vertical bonds of trust in authority figures and lateral bonds of camaraderie (Heifetz et al., 2009b).

It is important to note that this process can cause disequilibrium for the CEO as well as for other executives, so special attention should be paid to orchestrate conflict carefully and foster open conversations (Heifetz et al., 2009b). Adaptive leadership practices are in and of themselves an adaptive challenge in Japanese culture—for the CEO as well as other members of the organization. The experiences in this intervention suggest the need for a special holding environment for the top authority in a system engaged in kabuki leadership, such as private executive coaching sessions and/or weekly check-ins as the culture is adapting. The need for psychological safety, however, is critical for adaptive work at all levels if a new cultural norm is to take hold. This was especially true during the pandemic crisis, where outside turbulence caused participants to already be challenged by disconnect, uncertainty, and distress. Formal authority must consider the external environment to be a key and uncontrollable component as they regulate the internal (and controllable) disequilibrium. As was shown in this study, the generation of group norms at the beginning of an intervention such as this, including confidentiality rules, can effectively authorize participants to share opinions freely in a hierarchical collectivist culture. These norms were supported by frequent access to individual consultations.

Small groupings for particularly intense and personal interventions, such as ITC, supported the participants in their shift to an experimental mindset (Heifetz et al., 2009b). These deliberate structures offered mutual support for productive disequilibrium, and, in a relatively short period of three months, the agile development process enabled a shift in the mind and behavioral change of executives. They became their own audience by "going to the balcony," reflecting deeply upon their beliefs and assumptions, and creating their own new storybook through experiments, like the theatergoers in kabuki who actively participate in the show with their imagination by dissecting the double meaning of kake-kotoba pivot words and double castings in the play. Additionally, taking turns as facilitators in their small group enhanced the adaptative capacity of executives leading collaborative work, similar to the artists who composed, conducted, and performed collaboratively in the music-making in kabuki.

Finally, this intervention utilized multiple tools and theories that worked to produce these positive results. These included theories related to adult development, practices of adaptive leadership, and specific process tools such as ITC. In concert, they enabled a more nuanced "balcony view" (Heifetz et al., 2009b).

This leadership development intervention adds to the growing body of knowledge around adaptive leadership and adult development in an international context by showing that a Western adaptive leadership framework could apply to an Eastern context, namely Japan, when advanced through strategic processes and applied instruments. This case study of adaptive leadership development in Japan produced evidence of a shift in the mindset of Japanese executives and their corporate culture. Practiced in a hierarchical collectivist culture, kabuki leadership enables the art of improvisation and experimentation of adaptive leadership and fosters adaptation, embraces productive disequilibrium, and promotes leadership generation (Heifetz et al., 2009a). Moreover, since this is a first-of-its-kind leadership development program in the Japanese context, we find that this type of kabuki leadership training merits further investigation.

References

De Smet, A., Lurie, M., & St. George, A. (2018). Leading agile transformation: The new capabilities leaders need to build 21st-century organizations. *McKinsey & Company*. https://www.mckinsey.com/business-functions/organization/our-insights/leading-agile-transformation-the-new-capabilities-leaders-need-to-build-21st-century-organizations

D'Etcheverry, C. (2011). Seducing the mind: (Edo) Kabuki and the ludic performance. *Early Modern Japan, 19*, 21–43.

Drath, W. H., Palus, C. J., & McGuire, J. B. (2010). Developing interdependent leadership. In E. V. Velsor & C. D. McCauley & M. N. Ruderman (Eds.), *The center for creative leadership handbook of leadership development* (pp. 405–428). Jossey-Bass.

Heifetz, R. A. (1994). *Leadership without easy answers*. Harvard University Press.

Heifetz, R. A., Grashow, A., & Linsky, M. (2009a). Leadership in a (permanent) crisis. *Harvard Business Review, 87*(7/8), 62–69. https://hbr.org/2009/07/leadership-in-a-permanent-crisis

Heifetz, R. A., Grashow, A., & Linsky, M. (2009b). *The practice of adaptive leadership: Tools and tactics for changing your organization and the world.* Harvard Business Press.

Helsing, D., & Howell, A. (2013). Understanding leadership from the inside out: Assessing leadership potential using constructive-developmental theory. *Journal of Management Inquiry, 23*(2), 186–204. 10.1177/10564926135 00717

Helsing, D., Kegan, R., & Lahey, L. L. (2013). *Supporting others development: Applying adult development theory to your role as leader and within your organization.* Minds at Work.

Hong, G. H., & Schneider, T. (2020). *Shrinkonomics: Lessons from Japan.* International Monetary Fund F&D. https://www.imf.org/external/pubs/ft/ fandd/2020/03/pdf/shrinkanomics-policy-lessons-from-japan-on-population-aging-schneider.pdf

House, R., Javidan, M., Hanges, P., & Dorfman, P. (2002). Understanding cultures and implicit leadership theories across the globe: An introduction to project GLOBE. *Journal of World Business, 37*(1), 3–10. 10.1016/S1090-951 6(01)00069-4

Imai, M. (1986). *Kaizen: The key to Japan's competitive success.* McGraw-Hill.

Kegan, R. (1994). *In over our heads: The mental demands of modern life.* Harvard University Press.

Kegan, R., & Lahey, L. L. (2009). *Immunity to change: How to overcome it and unlock potential in yourself and your organization.* Harvard Business Press.

Kegan, R., Lahey, L. L., Miller, M. L., Fleming, A., & Helsing, D. (2016). *An everyone culture: Becoming a deliberately developmental organization.* Harvard Business Press.

Kodansha. (n.d.a). Kabuki. In *Encyclopedia of Japan.* Retrieved December 26, 2020, from https://japanknowledge.com/library/en/

Kodansha. (n.d.b). Kabuki music. In *Encyclopedia of Japan.* Retrieved December 26, 2020, from https://japanknowledge.com/library/en/

Kominz, L. (2006). The new Sakata Tōjūrō's Grand Kabuki Show and the rebirth of Kamigata (Kansai) Kabuki. *Asian Theatre Journal, 23*(2), 396–400. 10.1353/atj.2006.0025

Kyocera Corporation. (2020). *What is amoeba management?* Official Website of Kazuo Inamori. https://global.kyocera.com/inamori/management/amoeba/

Lahey, L., Souvaine, E., Kegan, R., Goodman, R., & Felix, S. (1988). *A guide to the subject-object interview: Its administration and interpretation.* Harvard University, Graduate School of Education, Laboratory of Human Development.

Layne, N. (2012, September 9). Japan Airlines sets IPO at $8.5 billion in sign of strong demand. *Reuters.* https://www.reuters.com/article/us-japanairlines-ipo-price/japan-airlines-sets-ipo-at-8-5-billion-in-sign-of-strong-demand-idINBRE88907G20120910

McCauley, C. D., Drath, W. H., Palus, C. J., & O'Connor, P. M. G. (2006). The use of constructive-developmental theory to advance the understanding of leadership. *The Leadership Quarterly, 17*(6), 634–653. 10.1016/j.leaqua.2 006.10.006

McCauley, C. D., Palus, C. J., Drath, W. H., Hughes, R. L., McGuire, J. B., O'Connor, P. M. G., & Van Velsor, E. (2008). Interdependent leadership in organizations: Evidence from six case studies. *Research report no. 190*. Center for Creative Leadership

Meyer, E. (2014). *The culture map: Breaking through the invisible boundaries of global business*. Public Affairs.

Nahavandi, A. (2006). *The art and science of leadership*. Pearson/Prentice Hall.

PwC Consulting LLC. (2019). Global cultural survey. Managing culture change in Japanese organizations. Issue: April 2019. https://www.strategyand.pwc.com/jp/ja/global-culture-survey-jp-en/global-culture-survey-2018-japan-en.pdf

Radu, S. (2020, January 28). Top 10 countries for technological expertise, ranked by perception. U.S. News & World Report. https://www.usnews.com/news/best-countries/slideshows/top-10-countries-for-technological-expertise-ranked-by-perception

Shochiku Co., Ltd. (2020). *Kabuki endeavors "inheritance and creation."* https://www.shochiku.co.jp/play/kabuki/create/

Torbert, W. R. (2004). *Action inquiry: The secret of timely and transforming leadership*. Berrett-Koehler Publishers.

Toyota UK. (2013). The official blog of Toyota UK. *Kaizen - Toyota Production System guide*. https://blog.toyota.co.uk/kaizen-toyota-production-system

World Bank. (2019). *Data catalog. GDP ranking*. https://datacatalog.worldbank.org/dataset/gdp-ranking

13 Japanese Universities' Response to the Global Pandemic Crisis: Harnessing Collective Intelligence to Activate Adaptive and Collaborative Leadership Practices

Soyhan Egitim

In April 2020, the Japanese government declared a state of emergency due to the rapid spread of COVID-19. As a result, Japanese universities in the greater Tokyo area decided that all courses would be held online for the foreseeable future. This sudden shift to remote education posed a number of technical and logistical challenges in teaching and classroom management. Both teachers and students struggled to meet the demands of online classes. Under such unprecedented circumstances, leadership functions became critical within the normative hierarchical leader-follower dynamics of the Japanese education system (Aubrey et al., 2015; Lochland, 2012; Schenck, 2015). The global pandemic crisis highlighted disparities among stakeholder values and circumstances, a quintessentially adaptive challenge. The task of leadership was to close the values gap by forming a unified community for action, requiring ownership that is often best produced by those leading without authority (Heifetz & Linsky, 2017) and representing novel territory for Japanese leaders.

One of the key characteristics of Japanese organizations is that they prioritize the harmony of the group over individual expression. Members will conform to the norms and values of a group, making concessions to maintain harmony (Takano & Sogon, 2008). Hierarchy, homogeneity, and an emphasis on group needs over those of individuals are entrenched in Japanese organizational culture and practices, reflected in day-to-day operations (Sakikawa, 2012; Shani, 2019). When faced with adverse circumstances, members' strong commitment to the group's collective identity helps them unify around a need for action (Heifetz & Linsky, 2017). This collective awareness serves to activate the group's collective intelligence, which can then lead to adaptive and collaborative leadership practices (Aras & Ingley, 2017). This is what occurred during the global pandemic crisis.

Collective intelligence emphasizes collaboration, collective effort, and consensus in decision-making (Malone & Bernstein, 2015). When these

DOI: 10.4324/9781003099109-13

actions are cultivated by leaders, leader-follower relationships become more fluid, leading to higher levels of empathy, mutual understanding, and trust when the group faces adversity (Yukl & Mahsud, 2010). This chapter discusses the adversity faced by Japanese universities during the global pandemic of 2020 and how highly developed collective intelligence helped them to navigate these unprecedented circumstances. The chapter draws on the personal experiences of the author and faculty members from various Japanese universities. It explains the organizational learning across universities that came about through collective thinking, resulting in adaptive and collaborative responses to the crisis. A key contextual component relates to the organizational structure of Japanese higher education institutions and the role of day-to-day operations in maintaining collective values.

Organizational Structure of Japanese Academic Institutions

Although United States-originated civics education replaced Confucianism during the post-war reform era in Japan, deep-rooted characteristics of Confucian educational philosophy remain firmly in Japanese educational institutions (Paramore, 2016). Confucian norms emphasize power distance and clearly defined roles between superiors and subordinates (for a detailed discussion of Confucianism, see Chapter 11). This traditional organizational management system is fundamental to Japanese higher educational institutions (Aubrey et al., 2015; Lochland, 2012; Schenck, 2015). Their top-down management system assures decisions are made at the top and then communicated through a chain of command (Bebenroth & Kanai, 2011). The aim of this top-down approach is to prevent the distraction of employees and ensure that harmony is maintained.

Having said that, the higher education sector in Japan is operating in an increasingly complex global environment with constant pressure and demand for global competitiveness and excellence (Kitagawa & Oba, 2009; Rose & McKinley, 2018). Thus, universities are expected to operate in ways that are similar to profit-seeking organizations (Youngs, 2017).

Due to a dwindling number of domestic students, particularly in rural areas, many Japanese universities have started to bolster their international student recruitment while also creating new faculties and departments to attract students from diverse backgrounds (Inaba, 2020). As a result, universities have expanded their international faculty in recent years (Huang, 2018).

As the pace of globalization increases, academic leaders in Japan will be expected to continue to manage differences and unpredictability in increasingly diverse work and classroom environments, a function especially critical during a crisis situation. In this regard, the global pandemic provides a valuable contemporary perspective on how rapidly diversifying Japanese academic institutions have responded to the adversity of crisis.

The Effects of the Global Pandemic on Japanese Higher Education

2020 has been an unprecedented year for an increasingly interconnected and interdependent world. People were forced to change their ways of living and working across the globe. The pandemic took a toll on academic institutions around the world as they incurred billions of dollars of losses (Aristovnik et al., 2020; Wolinsky, 2020). Universities were forced to shift to virtual classes. By April 2020, 90% of the universities in Europe had moved their classes online (Wolinsky, 2020).

Japanese universities followed suit, shifting to virtual classes at the start of their new fiscal year in April. Some universities provided financial, technical, and logistical support to students to enhance participation in virtual classes and the Japanese government offered universities financial assistance to upgrade their broadband services and equipment to maintain access to education (Wolinsky, 2020).

Despite these efforts, the sudden shift to online education came with its fair share of challenges. One of the key challenges for educators and students was the lack of technical knowledge around online class management. Several studies reported that Japanese students showed a positive attitude towards certain aspects of online learning, such as computer-assisted language learning, but were unfamiliar with other essential digital technologies (McCarty et al., 2016). Teachers, accountable for student learning and by extension students' struggles with digital learning tools, firmly held onto their traditional teaching methods, refusing to experiment with new digital technology. Even when available, teachers were reluctant to incorporate contemporary educational methods into lesson plans (Sakamoto, 2012).

Japan has an exam-driven education system where student achievement is measured by their ability to pass tests (King, 2013; Machida, 2016; Steele & Zhang, 2017). The exam system is also evident in school curricula which are geared towards helping students achieve high test scores in entrance exams. Although this fairly inflexible system compromises teachers' ability to experiment with innovative teaching and learning methods, Japanese academic institutions successfully managed to adapt to virtual teaching and learning. Several months after the advent of the pandemic, a majority were holding their classes exclusively online. They managed to adapt to the rapidly changing circumstances quickly in spite of rigid bureaucracy and a societal reluctance to change. Their success warrants further discussion on the country's socio-cultural dynamics, specifically, the impact of collective intelligence in Japan's response to disasters.

Collective Intelligence in Response to Adversity

Traditionally, the Japanese prioritize group needs over those of individuals, which has helped manage the potentially devastating effects of past natural disasters and provided valuable lessons (Hibiya, 2013). Coming together in the face of disaster has contributed to a strong collective identity and may have led to accelerated adaptation to new circumstances (Graburn et al., 2008; Shani, 2019; Toyosaki & Eguchi, 2017). Some scholars believe that the Japanese collective identity activates a highly developed collective intelligence (Asaoka, 2018; McHugh et al., 2016). When leadership recognizes the need for a unified community, they tend to lead with strategic and specific use of their authority, such as the creation of holding environments in which collective intelligence can generate and adaptive change can take place (Heifetz & Linsky, 2017).

Wooley et al. (2010) confirmed the positive effects of collective intelligence on performance. In their study, individuals and groups with predetermined similar abilities were asked to carry out several tasks. The results indicated that group performance surpassed individuals and that this was due to an ability to utilize their intelligence collectively. Further, when intelligence is treated as a property of the group collective, response time and efficiency are improved; issues are tackled more effectively (McHugh et al., 2016).

One of the key attributes of groups driven by collective intelligence is that leader-follower relations become fluid when the need for adaptive change emerges (Kurvers et al., 2015). During this time, the primary role of formal leadership, those in positions of authority, is to provide individuals with a holding environment that can leverage individual knowledge and expertise (Heifetz & Linsky, 2017) toward collective intelligence. Because each individual has something unique to offer, Wooley et al. (2010) found that group members flexibly take on both leader and follower roles based on their areas of expertise.

The role of expertise in leadership in adverse circumstances was further studied by Kurvers et al. (2015), who argued that the quality of information an individual possesses helps them take on leadership when the group faces adversity. Japan's collectivist society, where in-group dynamics stem from a strong collective identity (Graburn et al., 2008; Shani, 2019; Toyosaki & Eguchi, 2017), appears to be a significant factor in Japanese people's response to crisis as they develop collective intelligence. According to Hibiya (2013), this collective identity that embraces conformity, commitment to groups norms, and mutual dependencies stems, in part, from high levels of empathy. In a crisis situation, an empathic collective is well situated to rapidly develop collective intelligence as a key strategy to an effective response.

Leading adaptive work can be both daunting and dangerous for leaders. Indeed, sometimes it is the very interaction with stakeholders that makes adaptive leadership dangerous (Heifetz et al., 2009). Japan's lessons in crisis management, however, show how attention to the collective and what might be considered unexpected action of those in authority can be so critical to successful resolution. When the Fukushima disaster occurred in 2011, Prime Minister Naoto Kan paid a visit to the crippled Fukushima nuclear power plant. Despite his background in applied physics, upon arriving at the nuclear site, he was not the one who made the critical decisions. Instead, he acted as a morale-boosting presence. The actual initiative takers were specialized nuclear engineers who had risked their lives to prevent the leakage of radioactive waste into the environment (Tabuchi, 2013). This leadership approach amid crisis is an example of a strategic interplay between expertise, empathy, and collective intelligence.

Collective intelligence is also embraced by Japanese corporations (Svyantek & Mahoney, 2014; Toyosaki & Eguchi, 2017; Wormer & Besthorn, 2010). Wormer and Besthorn (2010) noted that Japanese product quality, reliability, and competitive pricing are reflective of the collectivist and collaborative nature of organizational culture. Japanese organizations' adherence to collective norms extends beyond the workplace to influence on their employees' lives. Many offer numerous benefits to enhance the collective and collaborative spirit in their organizations, including financial aid for families, home mortgage sponsorship, and arranging recreational or social activities (Wormer & Besthorn, 2010). This strong support system feeds into employees' collective identity, building loyalty and a willingness to take responsibility when needed.

Adaptive work typically takes place in a holding environment, where trust is both established and enhanced through the work itself (Heifetz & Linsky, 2017). The first step in building trust is to give the work back to people so that leading becomes the responsibility of the group. In Japan, this is seen as a sign of respect for the group. Adaptive leadership practices become more apparent when Japanese organizations face adversity, when, as noted earlier, hierarchical leader-follower dynamics become more fluid as the need for group expertise, or collective intelligence, becomes more acute. In these situations, individuals from all levels are mobilized as a unified community for action, and the emphasis on collective identity results in an accelerated adaptation process (DeRue, 2011).

As noted earlier, hierarchical Japanese organizational structures stem from Confucian influences on Japanese society (Aubrey et al., 2015; Lochland, 2012; Schenck, 2015). Decisions are made by a singular body of power at the top and communicated to subordinate units, allowing for smooth operation while maintaining group harmony (Bebenroth & Kanai, 2011). Hierarchy also provides clearly defined roles for leaders and followers. With a cultural commitment to collective identity (Asaoka, 2018; Wormer & Besthorn, 2010), these clearly defined roles help organizations work towards achieving their objectives.

DeRue (2011) describes this strong commitment by all individuals to the group as a socially complex yet adaptive process in response to emergent threats from the external environment. However, a key challenge for leaders is to convince others of the need for change (Yukl & Mahsud, 2010). Often, people do not resist change but what they *stand to lose* as a result of that change (Heifetz et al., 2009). Thus, adaptive leaders focus on identifying essential elements that need to be preserved for the future (Heifetz et al., 2009). As a result, members become less hesitant to make sacrifices while also knowing the essential elements are preserved for the future (Heifetz et al., 2009). In Japanese culture, a commitment to group considers that these sacrifices, while perhaps no less significant to the individual than in other cultures, work toward the good of the collective.

Leadership as a Collaborative and Adaptive Process

Successful organizational leadership is fostered through employee support and engagement (Heifetz et al., 2009). When this type of leadership is present, members form an alliance of thought and emotion based on "dialogical" and "non-judgmental" interactions which result in "leaderful practice" (Raelin, 2016). The group responds to challenges as a collaborative unit that allows anyone to take leadership initiatives. Organizations driven by collective intelligence view leadership as the property of the collective and members of an organization do not hesitate to take initiatives for the success of the group (Kramer & Crespy, 2011; Raelin, 2016).

Building relationships between members of a group takes more than engaging in communicative interactions. Leaders need to emphasize empathy, mutual understanding, and trust between members, especially when encountering adversity (Heifetz & Linsky, 2017; Senge, 2017; Yukl & Mahsud, 2010). It is when members possess these qualities that they develop a shared understanding of complex problems, producing solutions not evident to individual team members (Heifetz & Linsky, 2017; Senge, 2017).

Collective intelligence also activates the capacity for adaptation in changing circumstances (McHugh et al., 2016; Wooley et al., 2010; Asaoka, 2018) through those leading with and without authority as they mobilize others toward adaptive change (Heifetz & Linsky, 2017). Typically, those leading without authority have been authorized by the collective. In these scenarios, leaders become co-learners around adaptive challenges and the direction is determined from members of the group. Thus, both vertical and horizontal interactions between members matter for the success of the group (Raelin, 2016).

Mobilizing the System with its Stakeholders

The unprecedented challenges brought by the global pandemic provided an opportunity to examine the link between collective intelligence and leadership practices in Japanese organizations. During the first few months of the global pandemic, Japanese universities were in the middle of their spring break, anxiously monitoring the situation and hoping that the country's efforts would help curb the spread of the virus in the greater Tokyo area. However, as the virus continued to spread, the Tokyo governor declared a state of emergency and subsequently universities in the region postponed the start of their spring semester.

As COVID-19 cases spiked nationwide, the state of emergency was extended. Noted earlier in this chapter, universities in the greater Tokyo area chose to shift to remote education, the making of which lacked technical and logistical means of providing quality online courses. Neither teachers nor students were prepared for the sudden change to the way lessons would be delivered. Prior to the pandemic, online video conferencing platforms such as Zoom and Webex were hardly known by academics and students in Japan. In fact, the majority of teachers were only accustomed to traditional tools, such as hard materials and chalkboard classroom spaces. This "new normal" required a major adaptive change as there were no past experiences to serve as a reference point. According to Heifetz and Linsky (2017), when a group faces adversity, members are required to take an "adaptive leap" into the unknown, which creates considerable uncertainty and risk. Uncertainty leads to fear on the part of followers; gaining the trust and commitment of followers becomes crucial for leaders as they initiate adaptive change (Heifetz et al., 2009).

In the midst of all this uncertainty and chaos, the commitment of faculty members to the collective values, mission, and objectives of the group fostered more fluid leader-follower relationships in Japanese academic institutions. Faculty members, regardless of their status, were provided with a holding environment to take initiative and guide other faculty members and staff based on their knowledge and expertise, leveraging individual talents and expertise to foster collective intelligence.

Prior to the pandemic, there had been no urgent need for teachers and students to experiment with online learning management platforms such as Manaba and Blackboard. Thus, both teachers and students experienced a great deal of anxiety about online teaching and learning. In this regard, the online learning experiences the author gained during his doctoral studies proved beneficial both for the faculty personnel and students. Thanks to the psychological safety created by the human life design faculty members, he stepped into various leadership roles and helped his colleagues navigate these unprecedented circumstances. One of the roles he assumed was to teach the faculty how to use the Manaba online learning management system through instructional YouTube videos. Viewed multiple times by faculty members and administrative personnel, these videos built collective intelligence across the faculty, at the same time generating unconditional support and trust.

This sudden structural adaptation also fostered collaboration between members. Other faculty members supported each other by sharing various online teaching methods, tools, and materials. Moreover, the dean shared the instructional videos with the other departments, fostering university-wide collaboration. The message of leadership in this crisis was that every member could lead and contribute.

In another university in Tokyo, a female non-Japanese contract lecturer took a major leadership role and provided both the tenured faculty and students with virtual training on how to utilize computer-assisted language learning effectively. Her success resulted in a request to compile her sessions into a training manual to share with other faculty members and administrative personnel. Once again, the leader-follower relations became fluid. All members could become initiators and help their organization navigate through the crisis.

In several other universities, tenured faculty members created communication channels between part-time and full-time teachers to ensure leadership was viewed as an adaptive and collaborative endeavor. This also helped overcome the language barrier for non-Japanese faculty members typically imposed by the strict bureaucracy of Japanese universities. Through these communication channels, English translations of important documents and materials were shared with non-Japanese faculty members. In addition, various teaching materials and techniques were shared through these communication channels between part-time, contract, and tenured faculty members. This adaptive and collaborative process helped to empower individuals and motivated them to take new initiatives, regardless of their position in their respective departments.

Faculty members and administrative personnel also had to prepare students for online learning, unfamiliar to many first-year students. Universities used their resources to provide students with technical, administrative, and logistical support. More than 100 Japanese universities were reported to have offered financial aid to their students ("Over 100 Colleges in Japan Aiding Students," 2020). Encouraged by financial aid, students were less hesitant to take an adaptive leap. Universities also encouraged faculty members, administrative personnel, and alumni to donate to their emergency support funds and by August of 2020, donations had exceeded 500 million Japanese Yen (Waseda University, 2020). As a result, Waseda University released a thank-you note on their homepage to show their appreciation to those who donated to the university's emergency assistance funds. This collective response helped students brace themselves for the logistical, and technical challenges that came with online education.

The first step of this successful collective response was diagnosis before action. The collective's emphasis on diagnosis is also a key attribute of adaptive leadership; engaging stakeholders in the process of diagnosing an adaptive challenge builds ownership around the challenge itself, motivating stakeholders to act (Heifetz et al., 2009). Collective intelligence enables comprehensive diagnoses, pulling all members of a collective into collaborative problem-solving.

Increasing the Systems' Capacity for Continuous Learning

Collective intelligence emerges from an intrinsic self-organization process that is based on the collective contributions of members to an organization (Massip-Bonet & Bastardas-Boada, 2013). Coordination is essential to stimulating interactions between a system's components and its agents, or members. Once coordination is established, the link between structure and function emerges (Crowston et al., 2006), allowing individuals to work together in a harmonic way towards their collective goals. But non-linear coordination can be challenging in hierarchical structures, such as Japanese higher educational institutions. A commitment to working together towards the same goal may be insufficient. As complex problems emerge, however, organizations may be forced to adapt prior norms to new circumstances such as the ones brought by the global pandemic.

In the case of Japanese higher educational institutions, the first step towards adaptation came with the utilization of the knowledge and experience possessed by their faculty, administrative personnel, and students. As different tasks were performed by different agents specialized in their respective roles, complex technical and logistical problems were solved without major setbacks. Surowiecki (2005) describes this process as "division of labor." When each agent works in a complementary manner towards the same objectives, uncertainty within a complex organizational structure and functions is reduced and rigid structures dissolve, even if temporarily, to accomplish the objective. This type of organizational adaptation requires a leadership model based on the continuous and collaborative engagement of all agents in the process (Kotter & Cohen, 2015). The shared values, beliefs, and objectives held by group members establish safety for interpersonal risk-taking (Salicru, 2017), enabling all members to take a leadership role in their respective areas of expertise. As a result, a clear division of labor is achieved (around expertise), uncertainties dissipate, and opportunities for organization-wide learning emerge (Heifetz & Linsky, 2017).

During the global pandemic, Japanese universities exhibited swift adaptation to the online teaching and learning environment. Organizational objectives were prioritized over individuals. The coordination of tasks, along with the establishment of psychological safety and the ensuing collective intelligence brought faculty members, administrative personnel, and students on board with the demands of remote teaching and learning; they embraced the challenge as a collective unit. Contributions from individuals were synthesized into a cohesive response to tackle technical and logistical challenges brought by an adaptive change process. This people-and goal-oriented leadership approach began with the recognition and diagnosis of an adaptive challenge, harnessed the knowledge and skills brought by individuals, and finally synthesized them into an adaptive response that triggered organizational learning.

Adaptive challenges require organizational learning, often prior to initiating action (Obolensky, 2010). In the example above, it was the response to the crisis that triggered organizational learning. The external environment can also play a crucial role in organizational learning (Argote, 2013). In this instance, during the first few months of the pandemic, many non-profit academic associations held workshops and provided practical training opportunities for teachers on how to teach classes both synchronously and asynchronously using various online learning management platforms. Individual faculty members then shared their new knowledge with others in their respective departments. These dynamic interactions created synergy and enhanced collaborative work between individuals.

The holding environment both enabled and fostered collective intelligence, allowing members to examine deeply-rooted assumptions and values about teaching and leading, and providing the opportunity for members to take on leadership roles in their respective areas of expertise. This dualistic approach of self-reflection while benefiting from the knowledge and expertise of others brought a dynamic and reciprocated learning experience for all members.

The semi-isolated and decentralized structure of Japanese universities also deserves to be mentioned here. Each college is considered responsible for their own development, and thus, did not shy away from exploring innovative solutions that would best suit their own needs; this was not a standardized response. Larger departments created task forces and online support desks to navigate through uncharted territories. Smaller faculties (colleges) used their resources to equip teachers with adequate technology to enhance the quality of online education. As faculties harnessed the diversity of ideas within their departments, connections with other departments helped the critical function of knowledge transfer (Fang et al., 2010) across institutions. This dynamic model boosted intra- and inter-institution learning, which accelerated adaptation to the new circumstances.

Most Japanese higher education institutions have a rigid bureaucracy with day-to-day operations still depending on paper-based processes. However, in addressing a crisis that calls for adaptive change, Japanese organizational success cannot be overstated. Adaptive change requires awareness and adjustment in organizational values, attitudes, behavior, and approaches (Heifetz et al., 2009), often following periods of uncertainty and discomfort (Burke, 2017; Kotter & Cohen, 2015; Salicru, 2017). The discomfort associated with adaptive challenges can circumvent successful resolution. In the case of Japanese higher educational institutions, discomfort was mitigated and progress made through collective intelligence, fostered by collaborative thinking, learning, and mobilization towards the collective mission and objectives. The interdependence of adaptive leadership, collaborative leadership, and collective intelligence in the context of Japanese higher education institutions were critical linkages to enable a dynamic and efficient collective adjustment to the new pandemic era.

Conclusion

This chapter attempted to shed light on the role of collective intelligence in the emergence of adaptive and collaborative leadership with a focus on Japanese universities' response to the global pandemic crisis. As a nation, Japan has always dealt with natural disasters. Their commitment to deep-rooted Confucian values allows Japanese stakeholders to utilize collective intelligence to address major catastrophic events. This chapter illustrated how, in the event of adversity, collective intelligence appeared to foster adaptive and collaborative leadership practices. The ways in which Japanese universities responded to the crisis brought by the global pandemic demonstrate how collective intelligence can be utilized to promote adaptive and collaborative leadership. Leadership recognized the adaptive challenges, utilized a propensity toward collective intelligence to harness the knowledge and skills of individuals, which then triggered organizational learning. The swift adaptation of Japanese universities in dealing with a major crisis sets an interesting precedent for other organizations around the world.

References

Aras, G., & Ingley, C. (2017). *Corporate behavior and sustainability: Doing well by being good*. Routledge.

Argote, L. (2013). *Organizational learning*. Springer.

Aristovnik, A., Keržič, D., Ravšelj, D., Tomaževič, N., & Umek, L. (2020). Impacts of the COVID-19 pandemic on life of higher education students: A global perspective. *Sustainability, 12*(20), 10.20944/preprints202008.0246.v1

Asaoka, D. (2018). Collective intelligence or group thinking? Group decision-making under the Japanese company act. *Corporate Board: Roles, Duties and Decisions, 14*(2), 27–37.

Aubrey, S., Colpitts, B., Nowlan, A., (2015). Barriers to English communication in Confucian culture heritage countries: A focus on Japan. *Kwansei Gakuen Repository, 18*, 3–10.

Bebenroth. R. & Kanai. T. (2011). *Challenges of human resource management in Japan*. Routledge.

Burke, W. W. (2017). *Organization change: Theory and practice* (5th ed.). SAGE Publications

Crowston, K., Rubleske, J., & Howison, J. (2006). Coordination theory: A ten-year retrospective. In P. Zhang & D. Galletta (Eds.), *Human-computer interaction and management information systems: Foundations* (pp. 120–138). Sharpe, Armonk.

DeRue, S. D. (2011). Adaptive leadership theory: Leading and following as a complex adaptive process. *Research in Organizational Behavior*, *31*, 125–150.

Fang, C., Lee, J., & Schilling, M. A. (2010). Balancing exploration and exploitation through structural design: The isolation of subgroups and organizational learning. *Organization Science*, 21, 625–642.

Graburn, N. H., Ertl, J., & Tierney, R. K. (2008). *Multiculturalism in the new Japan: Crossing the boundaries within*. Berghahn Books.

Heifetz, R. A., Grashow, A., & Linsky, M. (2009). *The practice of adaptive leadership: Tools and tactics for changing your organization and the world*. Harvard Business Press.

Heifetz, R., & Linsky, M. (2017). *Leadership on the line, with a new preface: Staying alive through the dangers of change*. Harvard Business Press.

Hibiya, T. (2013). Comparison between the Occidental and Japanese mentality and way of thinking: Lessons learned from the 3.11 disaster. *Proceedings of Asian Pacific Conference on System Engineering*, *2013*, 1–9.

Huang, F. (2018). Foreign faculty at Japanese universities: Profiles and motivations. *Higher Education Quarterly*, *72*(3), 237–249. 10.1111/hequ.12167

Inaba, Y. (2020). Higher education in a depopulating society: Survival strategies of Japanese universities. *Research in Comparative and International Education*, *15*(2), 136–157. 10.1177/1745499920910581

King, J. (2013). *Silence in the second language classroom*. Palgrave MacMillan.

Kitagawa, F., & Oba, J. (2009). Managing differentiation of higher education system in Japan: Connecting excellence and diversity. *Higher Education*, *59*, 507–524.

Kotter. P. J. & Cohen. S. D. (2015). *The heart of change: Real-life stories of how people change their organizations*. Harvard Business Review Press.

Kramer, W. M., & Crespy, A. D. (2011). Communicating collaborative leadership. *The Leadership Quarterly*, *(22)*, 1024–1037.

Kurvers, R. H., Wolf, M., Naguib, M., & Krause, J. (2015). Self-organized flexible leadership promotes collective intelligence in human groups. *Royal Society Open Science*, *2*(12), 150–222. 10.1098/rsos.150222

Lochland, W. P. (2012). Moving beyond communicative language teaching: A situated pedagogy for Japanese EFL classrooms. *TESOL Journal*, *2*(4), 261–273.

Loucky, J. P. & Ware, J. L. (2016). *Flipped instruction methods and digital technologies in the language learning classroom*. IGI Global.

Machida, T. (2016). Japanese elementary school teachers and English language anxiety. *TESOL Journal*, *7*(1), 40–66.

Malone, W. T., & Bernstein, S. M. (2015). *Handbook of collective intelligence*. MIT press.

Massip-Bonet, A., & Bastardas-Boada, A. (2013). *Complexity perspectives on language, communication and society*. Springer.

Matsuda A. (2011). 'Not everyone can be a star': Students' and teachers' beliefs about English teaching in Japan. In P. Sergeant (Eds), *English in Japan in the Era of Globalization* (pp. 38–59). Palgrave Macmillan.

McHugh, K. A., Yammarino, F. J., Dionne, S. D., Serban, A., Sayama, H., & Chatterjee, S. (2016). Collective decision making, leadership, and collective intelligence: Tests with agent-based simulations and a Field study. *The Leadership Quarterly*, *27*(2), 218–241. 10.1016/j.leaqua.2016.01.001

McCarty, S., Obari, H., & Sato, T. (2016). *Implementing mobile language learning technologies in Japan*. Springer.

Nishino, T. (2011). Japanese high school teachers' beliefs and practices regarding communicative language teaching. *JALT Journal*, *33*(2), 131–155.

Obolensky, N. (2010). *Complex adaptive leadership: Embracing paradox and uncertainty*. Gower Publishing Ltd.

Over 100 colleges in Japan aiding students financially in virus crisis. (2020, May 8). *The Japan Times*. https://www.japantimes.co.jp/news/2020/05/08/national/japan-colleges-aid-students-coronavirus/

Paramore, K. (2016). *Japanese Confucianism: A cultural history*. Cambridge University Press.

Raelin, A. J. (2016). Imagine there are no leaders: Reframing leadership as collaborative agency. *Leadership*, *12*(2), 131–158.

Rose, H., & McKinley, J. (2018). Japan's English-medium instruction initiatives and the globalization of higher education. *Higher Education*, *75*, 111–129.

Salicru, S. (2017). *Leadership results: How to create adaptive leaders and high-performing organizations for an uncertain world*. John Wiley & Sons, Incorporated.

Sakamoto, M. (2012). Moving towards effective English language teaching in Japan: Issues and challenges. *Journal of Multilingual and Multicultural Development*, *33*(40), 409–420.

Sakikawa, T. (2012). *Transforming Japanese workplaces*. Springer.

Transforming management practices in Japanese workplaces. (n.d.). Transforming Japanese workplaces. 10.1057/9781137268860.0005

Sawa, T. (2019, January 18). The global decline of Japanese universities. *The Japan Times*. https://www.japantimes.co.jp/opinion/2019/01/18/commentary/japan-commentary/global-decline-japanese-universities/

Schenck, D. A. (2015). Improving education in Confucian countries through analysis of organizational challenges, leadership, and responsibilities. *Journal of International Education and Leadership*, *5*(1), 1–13.

Senge, P. M. (2017). The leaders' new work: Building learning organizations. *Leadership Perspectives*, 51–67. 10.4324/9781315250601-6

Shani, G. (2019). Consuming the Nihonjinron. *Nations and Nationalism*, *25*(1), 1119–1121.

Steele, D. & Zhang, R. (2017). Enhancement of teacher training: Key to improvement of English education in Japan. *Procedia-Social and Behavioral Sciences*, *217*, 16–25.

Surowiecki, J. (2005). *The wisdom of crowds*. Anchor Books.

Svyantek, J. D., & Mahoney, T. K. (2014). *Organizational processes and received wisdom*. Information Age Publishing ltd.

Tabuchi, H. (2013, July 9). Masao Yoshida, nuclear engineer and chief at Fukushima plant, dies at 58. *The New York Times*. https://www.nytimes.com/2013/07/10/world/asia/masao-yoshida-nuclear-engineer-and-chief-at-fukushima-plant-dies-at-58.html#:~:text=TOKYO%20%E2%80%94%20Masao%20Yoshida%2C%20a%20nuclear,He%20was%2058.

Takano, Y., & Sogon, S. (2008). Are Japanese more collectivist than Americans? *Journal of Cross-cultural Psychology. 39*(3), 237–250.

Toyosaki, S., & Eguchi, S. (2017). *Intercultural communication in Japan: Theorizing, homogenizing discourse*. Routledge.

Waseda University. (2020, August 6). *Thank you note for your donations to help our students suffering from the COVID-19 pandemic*. https://kifu.waseda.jp/english/donationkind/w_supporters-covid19

Wolinsky, H. (2020). Mobile students, remote education, free-fall economics: Campus life in 2020. *Science & Society, EMBO Reports, 21*(9), 1–5.

Wooley, A. W., Chabris, F. C., Pentland, A., Hashimi, N., & Malone, W. T. (2010). Evidence for a collective intelligence factor in the performance of human groups. *Sciencexpress, 330*, 686–688.

Wormer, V. K., & Besthorn, H. F. (2010). *Human behavior and social environment: Groups, communities and organizations*. Oxford University Press.

Youngs, H. (2017). A critical exploration of collaborative and distributed leadership in higher education: Developing an alternative ontology through leadership-as-practice. *Journal of Higher Education Policy and Management, 39*(2), 140–154.

Yukl, G., & Mahsud, R. (2010). Why flexible and adaptive leadership is essential. *Consulting Psychology Journal: Practice and Research, 62*(2), 81–93. 10.1037/a0019835

14 Democratic Indigenous Adaptive Leadership (DIAL): An American Indian Women Leadership Model

Shannon Kenny and
Four Arrows aka Don Trent Jacobs

In 1992, Rigoberta Menchú, a 33-year-old Maya Quiché Indian, won the Nobel Peace Prize for her work on behalf of Guatemala's Indian peoples. After witnessing the torture and murder of her parents, she rallied mothers and daughters throughout the country to see justice and egalitarianism. As a result of her efforts, the United Nations declared 1993 the International Year for Indigenous Populations. Her story is one of many similar stories relating to how contemporary Indigenous women throughout the world are leading their communities to help them adapt and ultimately thrive in challenging environments. In this chapter, Shannon Kenny tells her own adaptive leadership story from her Choctaw heritage perspective. She connects her story to some of the ways traditional Indigenous women participate in "adaptive leadership" put forth by Four Arrows, an Oglala Lakota-based Sun Dancer and scholar.

Four Arrows: I refer to the Indigenous Woman's model for adaptive leadership as "Democratic Indigenous Adaptive Leadership" (DIAL). My idea for the DIAL mnemonic is for us to begin to "dial" in to our original worldview and how adaptive leadership can help us all survive the many current crises facing us today. Indigenous women leaders have long served to guide and nurture their communities. Their creative and courageous ability to adapt to new conditions and renew community was recognized and respected by everyone (Medicine & Albers, 1983). Shannon's entrepreneurial work reflects such adaptive leadership. It exemplifies a common Indigenous worldview precept often expressed by the Lakota: *Okiciya makiyokip na lyuteya, cuke wayokap, mitakuye oyasin*, which translates to "Help each other acclimate and adjust, because the truth is, we are all related."

Shannon: I am a granddaughter, daughter, sister, mother, aunt, historian, and technology startup founder. I created my company, Prontopia, because I see an urgent need to value our common humanity as the focal point for developing the technology the world needs today. It is ironic that modern society has become so distanced from the importance of inclusive communities so necessary to human survival. And so, I set out to create

DOI: 10.4324/9781003099109-14

ways to provide flexible, affordable help for those who need it the most. Today we have great need among our Elders across the globe for community help. The social and communal support networks that used to provide them with well-being, respect, and dignity in aging have progressively disappeared, as demographically their needs for help are exponentially increasing. Our starting point at Prontopia for understanding how to build tech- and people-powered solutions was to utilize the most essential and powerful tool humanity has: the stories of us. We started by listening with open hearts and minds. Leaving assumptions or biases aside, we heard stories from among voices that are less heard, yet are essential to city and community well-being.

In Indigenous culture, storytelling and listening are the starting point for problem-solving, especially in an intergenerational context. As I was growing up, my Choctaw grandmother, Ruth Bereznak, and my Choctaw-Haida mother, Carolyn Kenny, used storytelling to guide me, and to help me find my own voice. Through these experiences, I learned that the best way to find power in one's voice is to learn how to listen because language, especially that of our Elders, is sacred. Oral traditions convey meaning that for centuries has been instrumental to human survival.

Native stories inherently illustrate the interconnectedness of all things and in doing so they generate empathy and human understanding. As Four Arrows notes, Native worldviews consider humanity as a part of nature, as opposed to Western ideas of the primacy of humankind. Stories can transport us across time and space. The stories my mom and grandmother told me during their lifetimes endure today. They help me to maintain my "intimate relationship with the land" (Kenny, 2012, p. 3), and this intimate relationship with the land powerfully includes their spirits. Growing up here in Santa Barbara, California my mom would tell me the Chumash stories of the Rainbow Bridge and that the spirits of our ancestors, across all waters ranging from the Chumash to the Haida territories, embrace us with the smell of the sea, and of sweetgrass, to signal they are here with us. In her book, *Living Indigenous Leadership,* my mom evokes this story and comments, "One day, I, too will arrive on the scent of sweetgrass through the morning windowpanes to greet my loved ones with the morning light" (Kenny, 2012, p. xiii). Her storytelling has helped me to survive the pain of grief at her loss and to continue to experience her presence in the scent of sweetgrass, the moonrise over the sea, and a hummingbird fluttering its wings.

Stories help us to survive and thrive. In feminist Native traditions, they are the catalysts for collaboration and community action. They are the foundation upon which the DIAL principles are woven. In my experience with growing a tech startup company, we began with respecting our origin stories, deriving from a multitude of voices, because beginnings are important. This has created a corporate culture that values story-telling and listening as powerful practices for achieving our goals to-gether.

For the rest of the chapter, we briefly address seven principles Indigenous women foster as they relate to DIAL. These include freedom, balance, spirituality, peacemaking, social/ecological justice, economic power, and creativity.

Freedom

Four Arrows: For Indigenous people, freedom and justice refer to a way of life rather than to a set of laws. American Indian women were con-fident, self-directed, and truly free in ways that might still seem ambi-tious in many contemporary Western societies. In 1632, the Dominican missionary, Gabriel Sagard, complained about the amount of freedom Wyandott women enjoyed and about how they, as their own bosses, used this time to feast, party, and gamble (Sagard, 1939). DIAL shares this commitment to freedom. Although sometimes frustrating to those in need of more structure and specificity, DIAL intentionally avoids po-licies, rules, and procedures that might stifle other voices. The story of how the Lakota women allow men their voice when making their own decisions about the value of an action is but one example. Like tradi-tional First Nations' women, the DIAL community illuminates strong, independent, nurturing voices that demand to be heard. When issues emerge, space is made to give everyone the freedom to speak. Ultimately, consensus is about everyone understanding one another, even if dis-agreement on particulars occurs. As one might imagine, this is what might be expected from a model based on women's nurturing ways.

Shannon: Concepts of freedom in Western society based on in-dividualism and determinism are hard to compare to Native worldviews because we view the world in a holistic framework that is not binary. We are not taking actions tied to freedom versus defined limitations because when you view yourself as an interconnected part of nature your actions are adaptive and synchronous with the needs of the communal or eco-logical context around you. Now, putting a Western worldview hat on, and translating across cultures, I feel that this Indigenous concept of what we otherwise call "freedom" today is liberating.

As Four Arrows mentions, this can be frustrating for those who expect "structure and specificity," but from a holistic Native worldview, nature is a complex dynamic system that is ever-evolving, and our human ex-periences are a part of this system. So, conceptions of freedom and justice are therefore oriented around our recognition of how our actions as individuals are connected to nature. We recognize Mother Earth as our first "embodied concept of leadership," and traditions such as the seven generations guide ideas of justice from a systems framework that is not rooted in a specific time or place (Kenny, 2012).

Balance

Four Arrows: Another principle of leadership practiced by Indigenous women relates to seeking and restoring balance. The ability of Indigenous women to maintain balance and complementary relationships may explain why most Indigenous cultures were matrilineal and why "all the real authority" resided in the women (Parker, 1916, p. 55). Patriarchal systems of domination tend to focus more on power struggles between individuals. This is why European men set out to change things with their anti-women hegemony. Women were never seen as inferior until the Europeans came to our shores and colonization's influence, policy, and reservation government brought forth their beliefs in male superiority.

Indigenous women used their authority in ways that gave balance to male and female energies, to human and nonhuman life forms, and to work and play activities. Even today Indigenous women activists around the world engage the most crucial issues of our time without compromising the vision of balancing vital relationships. With DIAL, political power can never be self-serving. It reflects transparency, honesty, and caring for others. It prioritizes future generations. It balances political power with the kind of genuine humility that keeps the focus on the community rather than on personal gain.

Such a focus on balance and complementarity between *apparent* opposites that Indigenous women practiced may also have helped with honoring diversity in all of its forms, even in the face of European attitudes toward sexual identity. Europeans did not understand distinctions between their sex-role stereotypes. They did not like First Nation's gendering of tasks and were critical of the powerful role women had in governance, especially when they saw judges, male or female, carry corn-pounders and wear skirts (Mann, 2008). Judicial affairs so entirely belonged to women that any woodlands man who wished to become a jurist or a negotiator first had to be "made a woman" in order to be qualified for the job. This meant learning how to pound corn and other tasks generally of the woman's expertise.

The natural balance between solar and lunar energies, and among male and female energies in complex but symbiotic relationships, is shaped by what individual landscapes have in common. Variety depends on the particular life entity. This natural balance is reflected in the relationships between men and women in the majority of Indigenous cultures. Women traditionally played a central role. They were seen as life-givers and caretakers of life. They were honored for their wisdom and vision: "In Aboriginal teachings, passed on through the oral histories of Aboriginal people from generation to generation, men and women were equal in power and each had autonomy within their personal lives" (Aboriginal Justice Implementation Commission, 1999, para 4).

Shannon: In *Living Indigenous Leadership,* my mom raises the point that, in general, Native cultures did not have a word for feminism. I feel the influence of this as a startup entrepreneur today because I am in an industry that lacks balance between the feminine and the masculine qualities of leadership that nature has shown are essential. There is a great opportunity in the startup world to tap into the power of this Native viewpoint and establish corporate environments representative of the complementary attributes of both feminine and masculine leadership. Describing leadership traits as feminine or masculine (e.g., rather than women do X, men do Y) creates a conceptual fluidity that allows men to summon feminine leadership attributes, and vice versa, according to the situational context, as Four Arrows' examples of Native men performing feminine tasks illustrates. Nature shows us that maintaining balance requires a constant iterative process of recalibration.

Spirituality

Four Arrows: Indigenous spirituality is about a sacred realization that everything is related and that there is great significance in the "other" (Jacobs, 2002). Spirituality is essential for DIAL. It allows for emphasis on process and a commitment to restoring harmony. It understands the humanness of cognitive dissonance so that it is not rationalized or denied, but rather it is resolved through a respectful talking out process. It honors the role of women in creating and maintaining harmony. It requires all leaders to practice DIAL, remember Mother Earth, and the feminine and lunar aspects so vital a part of creation. DIAL's openness to integrating spirituality into its program manifests itself in numerous ways. In higher education, its focus is curriculum. In corporations, the focus is on the product "doing no harm." It includes seeing sentience in other-than-human life forms, including trees, rivers, birds, and insects. DIAL recognizes that COVID-19, climate change, and extinction rates are the result of forgetting what the Lakota say when they pray with the words, *Okiciya makiyokipi na lyuteya, cuke wayokapi, mitakuye oyasin* (Help each other acclimate and adjust, because the truth is, we are all related.) Until we learn with DIAL to refer to "natural resources" as our "relatives" and truly mean it, we will continue with a colonization leadership taking us to the brink of extinction.

Shannon: My grandmother and mom showed me that spirituality is the feeling that in every thought, action, and deed we are a part of something bigger than ourselves. This is the heart of experiencing our interconnectedness. Of course, this is ultimately tied to meaning for us during life on earth as humans. This is a core concept behind how we create solutions for generating a sufficient "supply" of people helping people at Prontopia. We are disrupting existing transactional notions about labor tied strictly to economic market value to reorient them in alignment with community value. This enables workers to feel their work has a meaningful impact and a sense of connection to an output that is greater than the sum of its parts. We see the potential for this to change the feedback loop and create a more sustainable (balanced) labor market.

Peacemaking and Social/Ecological Justice

Four Arrows: Transformational leadership theory rather than re-tributive, hierarchical, adversarial, punitive, or codified assumptions guide action in traditional Native cultures, and once again women have led the way throughout Indigenous history. For example, the founding of the Iroquois League was guided by a woman known as "the Peace Queen." Without her involvement, the great peace movement that led to this council (and to the U.S. constitution) would not have occurred. She worked tirelessly to help create "The Great Law of Peace," and she provided the ultimate solution to difficult problems blocking ratification of the new constitution (Mann & Fields, 1997). Today, Indigenous women worldwide are taking on leadership roles in their communities to assert peace and are crucial to DIAL work.

Shannon: All of the examples listed above beautifully illustrate the fact that Native leadership is unbound. We are all leaders. Indigenous beliefs recognize that we all inherently have our own unique strengths that we can use for the benefit of the community and the greater good. Throughout my journey as founder of Prontopia, I am honored and full of wonder at how this plays out across our diverse team. We are all working toward a common goal. With this core value guiding us, conflict resolution involves all voices. We respect each other, and respect this place while working to resolve inevitable conflicts that exist in this ever-changing world. It is an opportunity for growth, and not something to be feared.

Peacemaking and social/ecological justice are not optional activities that are undertaken when circumstances get to an unsustainable or dangerous tipping point; they are intrinsic to holistic worldviews that seek to constantly restore a state of harmony. The driving motivations behind this are of course tied to a recognition that we must look to nature as our guide. Respect for Elders plays a key role in peacemaking and social/ecological justice. My mom liked to proudly quote a poem by my daughter Isabella when she writes of nature, "Without you, we wouldn't be here." She loved this line of the poem because it comforted her that the seven generations hence will be okay. Isabella's reverence for nature is tied to reverence for our Elders because when they die, they are a part of the natural world around us. There is thus an embodiment to activities related to peacemaking and social justice.

Economic Power

Four Arrows: Lionel Robbins offered a popular definition for economics as a "science which studies human behavior as a relationship between ends and scarce means that have alternative uses" (as cited in Stigler, 1984, p. 301). Before their oppression, Indigenous worldviews led to economic decisions that emphasized deep appreciation for resource scarcity, yet without the competitive associations regarding use of those resources. Authoritarian systems were not needed to assure wise and equitable use of resources. Such non-competitive philosophies came from the feminine understanding of the world. They understood accountability in terms of restoring healthy relationships. As a result, they guided barter and minimized warfare between tribes for thousands of years.

Shannon: Native women have traditionally played essential roles in maintaining accountability in their communities. There are some very interesting trends emerging today related to startup performance in general that indicate that startups with at least one woman founder perform better (Kenny, 2012). One of the key metrics in support of this is accountability, as well as the fact that women are intrinsically motivated to solve social problems through entrepreneurial solutions (Fatemi, 2019). Ironically, this intrinsic motivation produces more profitable companies than founders with an extrinsic motivation such as pure financial gain (Fatemi, 2019).

Our mission statement validating the economics of what we are building at Prontopia is as follows:

> Prontopia is a dynamic system of sustainable networks, working from within local communities to cultivate labor market growth and global local economic vitality. We believe large scale social change is accomplished through face-to-face interactions. Human relatedness is the essence of our product's value. We view the rise of the gig economy as potential for economic renewal that supports workers who feel autonomous, personally invested, and connected to their work. (Prontopia, n.d.)

Native perspectives on economic power are beautiful to me because they are oriented toward abundance and generosity. The market-based economic system in contemporary Western society has become dangerously detached from the ecological system of value in Native societies. To survive and thrive we must take care of this land. We belong to the land; the land does not belong to us.

Four Arrow's point above that feminine economic priorities focus on maintaining equitable access to resources, which often requires the action of constantly working to restore healthy relationships, is at the core of the model of Prontopia. I was surprised when I initially presented my business plan and was told that the social impact elements were a risk that might be perceived as detracting from financial profit. In fact, our model has produced the exact contrary: We have saved money as compared to traditional marketplace platform models because we cultivate community and human connectedness and this intrinsically helps us to deploy resources in the form of both human and financial capital most efficiently. I am excited about the opportunity to pioneer this model as a new way to develop sustainable economic "growth."

Creativity

Four Arrows: DIAL is always ready for creative thinking that supports the nurturing model. The efforts correspond to how Indigenous women around the world manage to cultivate healthful foods, even developing natural pesticides and fertilizers, in spite of being denied land ownership in many countries. In her acceptance speech for the Prize for Women's Creativity in Rural Life, Marta Benavides emphasized this important creative contribution when she said,

> It is women, especially Indigenous women, who maintain traditional knowledge for food, and medicinal plants, as well as traditional methods to preserve seeds, for planting, for natural control of insects and plagues. They have safeguarded biodiversity. Without doubt, rural women's work and creativity, make a great contribution to the family's economy, thus to the Gross Domestic Product, to food security, to the caring of biodiversity, to the quality of life of rural families and communities and understood conservation. (Benavides, 2003, p. 74)

Shannon: I have cherished memories of my mom's professional collaborations with anthropologist Ellen Dissanayake, author of *Homo Aestheticus: Where Art Comes from and Why* (1995), in which Dissanayake chronicles how art is essential to human adaptation and survival. Natives value seeing beauty in nature. This is an imperative that intersects with the other areas of DIAL because seeing beauty in nature is an act of immersing ourselves in the harmony all around us. Native rituals and traditions evoke creativity through the arts—chanting, drumming, masks, jewelry— and bring us together in transcendent experiences of beauty that reveal the sources of creativity in nature. Through creativity, we overcome the pain of suffering and loss by continuing to beautify the world together, because this helps to keep the Earth in balance.

Concluding Thoughts

Shannon: Transformative change that reconnects human society to the land, and in doing so acknowledges our interconnectedness, is essential to our survival today. Implementing feminine Indigenous leadership models into educational and corporate contexts will drive holistic solutions to the systemic problems we face today. The "living between two worlds"— Native and Western—I experience as a technology startup founder is exhilarating because I see opportunities all around us to change the feedback loop. Technology today has gone too far in disconnecting us from the land, and from each other. We have time-hallowed stories that show us a path toward creating sustainable technology solutions that restore nature, and within nature, humanity, as the focus. In doing so we honor our Elders, and the seven generations to come.

Four Arrows: While respect and support for sovereignty for Indigenous Nations and women must involve peaceful resistance to efforts in opposition to such support, we can also work to operationalize DIAL in our communities and workplaces. As an educator, I call for higher education to do more to decolonize and practice counter-hegemonic democracy as many educators have advocated for decades (Altbach et al., 1999). At this moment in history, DIAL must find its way into hearts and minds of caring, courageous humans in all walks of life. With it, perhaps we can bring forth a concept of "leadership" that Indigenous women have been modeling for tens of thousands of years. It is a matter of survival (Four Arrows, 2016).

References

Aboriginal Justice Implementation Commission (1999). http://www.ajic.mb.ca/volumel/chapter13.html

Altbach, P. G., Berdahl, R. O., & Gunport, P. J. (1999). *American higher education in the twenty-first century: Social, political, and economic challenges.* John Hopkins Press.

Benavides, M. (2003). *In celebration of women's creativity in rural life.* Retrieved February 22, 2005, from http://www.humiliationstudies.org/news/archives/000337.html

Dissanayake, Ellen. (1995). *Homo Aestheticus. Where art comes from and why.* University of Washington Press.

Four Arrows (2016). *Point of departure: Returning to our more authentic worldview for education and survival.* Information Age Publishing.

Jacobs, D. (2002). The red road: The Indigenous worldview as a prerequisite for effective character education. *Paths of Learning, 9,* 6–9.

Fatemi, Falon. (2019). "The value of investing in female founders." *Forbes.* https://www.forbes.com/sites/falonfatemi/2019/03/29/the-value-of-investing-in-female-founders/?sh=15e991f35ee4

Kenny, Carolyn. (2012) *Living indigenous leadership: Native narratives on building strong communities.* University of British Columbia Press.

Mann, B. A. (2008). Where are your women? Missing in action. In Four Arrows (Don Trent Jacobs) (Ed.), *Unlearning the language of conquest: Scholars expose anti-Indianism in America* (pp. 120–133). University of Texas Press.

Mann, B. A. & Fields, J. L. (1997). A sign in the sky: Dating the league of the Haudenosaunee. *American Indian Culture and Research Journal*, 21(2), 105–163.

Medicine, B., & Albers, P. (1983). *The hidden half: Studies of Plains Indian women*. University Press of America.

Parker, A. C. (1916). *The constitution of the five nations*. The University of the State of New York.

Prontopia (n.d.). http://www.prontopia.com

Sagard, G. (1939). *The long journey to the country of the Hurons*. (G. M. Wrong, ed. & H. H. Langton, Trans.). The Champlain Society. (Original work published 1632), p. 101.

Stigler, G. J. (1984). Economics: The imperial science? *Scandinavian Journal of Economics*, 86(3), 301–313.

15 The Adaptive Leader as a Mentor—A Practice from Brazil

Magda C. Kaspary and Rita Michel

This chapter presents Be-a-Mentor, a leadership program created in Brazil in 2016 that develops leaders through mentoring and the principles of adaptive leadership (Heifetz et al., 2009). These principles disrupt traditional leadership paradigms and frame mentoring as a useful leadership model. Adaptive leadership expands leadership possibilities in an organizational era that prioritizes networks over hierarchy (Latour, 2005), collaboration over competition (Palmer, 2000), and holistic over mechanistic processes (Capra, 1996).

How to Read this Chapter

The authors invite readers into a three-fold experience. The first experience relates to the Brazilian ways of understanding and practicing adaptive leadership through the authors' own communication and cultural styles. The second experience is the bolding of key concepts for easier visual identification for possible deeper reflection. Using italics, the authors bridge and emphasize important ideas, simulating a dialogue with their readers. In the third experience, and perhaps the most important, the authors extend an invitation to their readers to *pause* and reflect on how *being a leader* with adaptive awareness—more than "doing" leadership activities—might offer greater social impact.

In conjunction with the three-fold experience, this chapter is organized in three sections: the leadership context in Brazil, leaders-as-mentors and the practice of adaptive leadership, and a description of the framework and modules used in the Be-a-Mentor program. The following key terms are used in specific ways in this chapter:

- Leaders as Individuals in Positions of Influence (IPIs): Leadership is more than a job or a role and is independent of supervisory responsibility. A leader through influence can be "anyone who takes responsibility for *finding potential* in people and processes, and the courage to develop that potential" (Brown, 2018, p. 22).
- Leader-as-Mentor: A leader-as-mentor commits to being a facilitator

DOI: 10.4324/9781003099109-15

of learning processes involving other individuals, or mentees. They create new possibilities by holding generative conversations to share knowledge, experiences, and personal visions. The concept of leader-as-mentor is anchored in a stance of constant *openness to learning*. According to Echeverría (2010), when designing "conversations for possible actions" (p. 239), one builds a space for innovation and the expansion of possibilities.

- Mentee: In this chapter, mentee refers to an individual who seeks to enhance their knowledge, expertise, and effectiveness by partnering with someone with personal experience in the focus area of the mentoring process.

The Leadership Context in Brazil

Specific economic, historical, political, and cultural events have influenced Brazilian leadership practices in the last century. Some of these events are global whereas others are influenced by the nation's intrinsic cultural dynamics. The local historical-political *context* still influences leadership practices in the country. Brazil was a colony of Portugal until 1822 and still to this day the motto of the national flag reads Order and Progress (*Ordem e Progresso*), a clear heritage from the positivist mindset during the time of the Proclamation of the Republic of Brazil (which occurred in 1889). The first democratically held presidential election did not take place until 1989. These facts show that Brazil is a young democracy; the practices of leadership are still embedded in a hierarchical culture seen in Brazil's organizations and institutions, both private and public.

Meyer (2014) offers *intercultural lenses* to better understand Brazilian culture, especially in the *context* of the workplace. A preference for indirect communication, avoiding confrontation, and hierarchical learning are important factors in this culture, influencing not only internal but also external organizational systems and foreign relations. The leadership capacity and performance of leaders of multinational organizations with subsidiaries in Brazil are greatly impacted by these *cultural characteristics*.

From a global lens, as one of the five BRICS economies (Brazil, Russia, India, China, and South Africa), Brazil's reaction to the Volatile, Uncertain, Complex, and Ambiguous (VUCA) world (Kraaijenbrink, 2018) was to accelerate professionalization and technology (Mari, 2020). The global movement of total quality management, which became prominent in the latter part of the 20th century, represents an important influence on how professionalization and leadership have been transformed in Brazil. Quality circles, teamwork, and process improvement methods required leadership development across the country, lessening the hierarchical model to a more participatory approach.

Adaptive leadership practice has the potential to expand the capacity of IPIs, leaders, and organizations through its emphasis on *context* (Heifetz et al., 2009). *Context* is a core concept of Brazilian culture and is therefore an important consideration when examining how to better lead teams and deal with organizational challenges. Attention and intention towards *context* bring the possibility of expanding frames of reference, which in turn improves leadership. The next section introduces the leaders-as-mentor program and the connection to adaptive leadership.

Leaders-as-Mentors and the Practice of Adaptive Leadership

Leaders-as-mentors are leaders who commit to the learning processes of other individuals. This section presents how adaptive leadership (Heifetz et al., 2009) principles and practices serve to nurture the process of becoming a leader-as-mentor, where leaders learn to deploy mentoring competencies for themselves and others. Becoming a leader-as-mentor involves a considerable degree of *awareness-of-self*, including intra and interpersonal impact. Table 15.1 highlights important aspects of adaptive leadership and the corresponding Be-a-Mentor competencies and concepts developed during the program.

A leader-as-mentor presupposes a broader performance than supporting and guiding the discovery of solutions to technical challenges. For a leader-as-mentor, it is imperative to work in a *non-hierarchical* way (see Chapter 7 for a non-hierarchical perspective based on rhizomic principles), *intertwining objective and subjective perspectives*, aligned with a mindset that emphasizes an individual's growth and performance. The technical capacity of a leader-as-mentor requires leaders to identify their expertise (strengths, skills, experience) and to translate that expertise to their environments, mentees, and organizations. On the other hand, a leader's adaptive capacity is tied to the idea that both a leader-as-mentor and their mentees may face challenges that require changing their own mindsets. The interplay between one's self and one's environment is one of continuous movement. In this sense, life and work can be an adaptive leadership *laboratory* (Heifetz et al., 2009) where opportunities are available for expanding one's adaptive capacity for personal growth.

When expanding the adaptive capacity of a leader-as-mentor, it is critical that the leader utilizes two *recursive processes*: (1) accessing their stored knowledge and acquired expertise for a given situation, while at the same time (2) having the willingness to update that expertise to the situation at hand. Ultimately, this is a process of the leader-as-mentor honoring their own and others' values, beliefs, and competencies.

The principles and practices of adaptive leadership create the *holding environments* for the leader-as-mentor program and constitute a model

Table 15.1 Adaptive Leadership, Leader-as-Mentor Competencies, and Supporting Concepts

Adaptive Leadership Aspects (Heifetz et al., 2009)	Leader-as-Mentor Key Competencies	Supporting Concepts in the Be-a-Mentor Program
Self as a System: Identities, tuning, and triggers	**Presence:** The capacity of being in action while having the awareness of one's actions and surroundings, and the impact on one's self and others	• Theory U (Scharmer, 2009) • Presence (Senge et al., 2008) • Man's Search for Meaning (Frankl et al., 2014) • The 7 Habits of Highly Effective People (Covey, 1999)
Systems Intervener: Going to the balcony, process of observing > interpreting > intervening	**Conversations for Learning:** The capacity to sustain and develop a dialogue, sharing perspectives, and addressing performance	• Ontología del Lenguaje (Echeverría, 2010) • The Tree of Knowledge (Maturana & Varela, 2008) • The Fifth Discipline (Senge, 2006)
Partnerships: Identifying and prioritizing loyalties (both spoken and unspoken)	**Emotional Intelligence:** The capability to recognize one's own emotions and those of others and to manage emotions to adapt to different environments	• Conscious Business (Kofman, 2014) • Emotional Intelligence (Goleman, 1999) • Metamanagement (Kofman et al., 2004)
Tuning: Developing a state to understand and connect beyond what is said, being able to feel and see dynamics that seem invisible in a given situation	**Generative Learning:** The capacity to listen deeply, seek to understand beyond the message, and engage in cocreation with one's audience	• Four Levels of Listening (Scharmer, 2009) • Coaching – A arte de Soprar Brasas (Wolk, 2008) • The 7 Habits of Highly Effective People (Covey, 1999)
Bandwidth: Enhanced repertoire of approaches to lead situations while learning different managerial styles	**Learning Agility:** The capacity to continuously learn from different sources and modalities	• Learning Agility (Amato & Molokhia, 2016) • Knowledge Creation (Nonaka, 2008) • Immunity to Change (Kegan & Lahey, 2009)
Roles: The expected attributions —assigned or volunteered,	**Compassion:** The capacity to understand the distinction between	• Against Empathy (Bloom, 2018) • Metamanagement (Kofman et al., 2004)

(Continued)

Table 15.1 (Continued)

Adaptive Leadership Aspects (Heifetz et al., 2009)	Leader-as-Mentor Key Competencies	Supporting Concepts in the Be-a-Mentor Program
explicit or implicit, formal or informal— that a leader faces in specific contexts	empathy and compassion, and learning how to be present in different situations	• The Biology of Belief (Lipton, 2016)

on how to lead. In this context, the central focus of leadership is to generate reflection, possibilities, analyses, perspectives, and learning that are continually being (re)integrated into one's performance. Adaptive leadership is a model that invites observers to question themselves, to step back from a situation without losing their own presence (on the balcony), and to relinquish previously preconceived ideas and judgments to launch themselves into the best possible action(s) for everyone involved. In summary, the recursive nature of adaptive leadership is based on three key processes: (1) observation from the balcony of events and patterns, (2) interpretation of what is being *observed through multiple hypotheses*, and (3) design of possible interventions to be shared with others.

The recursive nature of adaptive leadership is at risk when a leader believes they have a solution to the challenges they observe. It is at this precise moment that adaptive capacity ideally manifests itself and positively alters outcomes and solutions. For this to occur, it is necessary for a leader to have previously developed an awareness of their own *blind spots* and those of any team(s) they lead. Awareness of blind spots can be developed by "engaging above and below the neck" (Heifetz et al., 2009), which allows leaders to move from a place where they tend to operate automatically to one more grounded in authenticity (for an expanded reflection on authenticity, see Chapter 5). When leaders-as-mentors find themselves at a crossroads, the practices of adaptive leadership—with a strong connection between one's personal purpose and values—are powerful tools.

Finally, embracing *strategic inquiry* as an everyday practice is a practical tool for leaders-as-mentors: What actions and methods have already been tried? What other strategies can provide leaders, IPIs, mentees, teams, and organizations the sustained presence, attention, and inspiration to develop further? What if by expanding leadership from a technical-only capacity to including adaptive practices organizations and societies are transformed?

Be-a-Mentor Program—Adaptive Leadership in Action

This section describes a specific mentoring development program in Brazil, called Be-a-Mentor, which was implemented in 2016 to develop the mentoring capacity for IPIs and formal organizational leaders. The concepts presented earlier in Table 15.1 are "worked" during the entire Be-a-Mentor program. "Worked" means intentional inner and group exploration sustained by the program facilitator. The key competencies and concepts are discussed in a systemic way (holistic, contextual) in juxtaposition to a systematic way (sequential, predictable), considering that systemic is a prominent characteristic of the Brazilian culture.

The Be-a-Mentor program *design* emerged from decades of work observing Brazilian organizations and countless hours of work with local and global leaders and their teams addressing organizational challenges. The program represents an alternative to traditional leadership training programs that lose their effectiveness over time by not giving particular attention to the building and strengthening of leadership *relationships* and the constant learning necessary to be effective leaders (Hijfte, 2020). The program is aligned with the 70-20-10 learning model developed by the Center for Creative Leadership (2020); this model asserts that 70% of learning stems from the challenges that individuals face daily, whereas 20% of learning results from the exchange of experiences and interactions between people. Only 10% comes from formal classroom training. Using a *reflective* model, Be-a-Mentor draws on lived experiences as the basis for discovering one's leadership identity, capacity, and potential and involves an awareness of and willingness to embrace the process of self-development. The Be-a-Mentor program involves three phases: entering, emerging, and rising.

Phase 1: Entering

Be-a-Mentor uses an approach capable of accelerating sustainable leadership development—a co-creation process—throughout the entire program. Applicants (IPIs, leaders, and/or organizations) interested in Be-a-Mentor certification start by engaging in self-reflection and generative dialogue about the program's theoretical and practical principles, concepts, and experiential model. Applicants commit to experimenting with concepts, followed by individual and/or group reflections that culminate in a process of cognitive and emotional transformation, also referred to as *transformational learning*. Even before starting the actual program, participants learn that only through keen observation, interpretation based on well-designed hypotheses, and the construction of assertive interventions will they be effective mentors. The Be-a-Mentor entering process encompasses discovery, reflection, commitment, and a willingness to embrace change—which participants sometimes refer to as "the work before the work." This contextual expression emphasizes that getting prepared is real work so that more work can be done.

Phase 2: Emerging

Be-a-Mentor is based on the concepts of heutagogy (Hase & Kenyon, 2013), which assumes that people have the potential to continuously learn in real-time through their interactions with their environment. Heutagogy, the study of self-determined learning, may be viewed as a natural progression from earlier educational methodologies—in particular from capability development—and may well provide the optimal approach to learning in the 21st century (Hase & Kenyon, 2000).

Be-a-Mentor promotes creative experiences in which people *learn how to learn*, work and build meaning with others, and make use of their skills, both in their personal and professional spheres, experiences that align with heutagogy. This approach extends beyond providing solutions to problems and instead aims to make people feel *solid*—ready and capable to confront the adaptive challenges faced by their organizations. Be-a-Mentor requires its participants to take active roles in the co-creation of their own development and holds them equally responsible for group learning. This learning approach is best reflected in the following passage:

> The only man who is educated is the man who has learned how to adapt and change; the man who has realized that no knowledge is secure, that only the process of seeking knowledge gives a basis for security. Changingness, reliance on process rather than upon static knowledge, is the only thing that makes any sense as a goal for education in the modern world. (Rogers, 1969, p. 104)

Be-a-Mentor is anchored in the broader theory of *ontology* (from the Greek *study of being*), that having a common nature is inherent in each person. Understanding what ontology means for the purposes of Be-a-Mentor does not presuppose a metaphysical perspective but rather is based upon what it means to be human. In other words, the interpretations we make reference both the characteristics that we share as human beings and those that give us a particular way of being.

Echeverría (2010) offers a perspective on how to understand ontology. When one says, "this apple is red," an assumption is being made that as a human being, one can determine the color of an apple. All actions, everything that is said or written, presuppose a judgment about what, as human beings, is possible to explain. Therefore, every time an individual acts or says something, they are manifesting a certain interpretation of what it means to be human and, therefore, an ontology, the given meaning to an object. The basic postulates of ontological language

(Echeverría, 2010) convey that humans are linguistic beings, and that language is the key to understanding human phenomena. These postulates are:

1   We interpret human beings as linguistic beings.
2   We interpret language as generative.
3   We interpret that human beings create themselves in and through language.

Generally speaking, humans find it difficult to establish a dialogue with someone who thinks differently than they do, as seen in the "logic" of wars and political divides throughout history. The popular saying attributed to Talmudic origin, explains that "we don't see things as they are: we see things as we are" (Kofman et al., 2004, p. 108). One's worldview is conditioned to one's "mental model" which Senge (2006) defines as deeply ingrained internal images about the external world, images that limit a better understanding of different ways of thinking and acting: "Mental models determine not only how one understands the world, but also how they act" (p. 201). New learning modalities, like Be-a-Mentor, make it possible for leaders to broaden their worldviews and, thus, increase leaders' capacities for action. However, if the repertoire of possible leadership tools only contains technically-related tools, the opportunity for deeper learning by reviewing one's assumptions, models, and values does not emerge. Echeverría (2010) calls this deeper learning *transformational learning*.

   This second phase of the program, emerging, takes participants through six modules that transmit the methodology of becoming a mentor in an experiential learning setting and subsequent application through supervised practice. Both settings are closely related to the principles of heutagogy and encompass principles of adaptive leadership. The modules are described below, with explicit links to key practices of adaptive leadership and the Be-a-Mentor competencies.

Module I: See Yourself as a System

Being human precedes the roles of leaders and mentors; hence, the importance of "being" is not only connected to what an individual knows, but also to how an individual shares this knowledge. Being a leader-as-mentor is a personal experience. No two leaders are exactly alike, just as no two humans are identical. Although the Be-a-Mentor methodology is delivered in the same way to all participants, each cohort is unique and considers the distinctiveness of individuals.

   Module I begins with self-knowledge. To become a leader-as-mentor, one must be aware of what is known and unknown about one's self. *Awareness-of-self*—the capacity to understand what is happening inside oneself while other things are happening outside of oneself—is an important differentiator for a leader-as-mentor. This learning module is focused on self-awareness and presence (Senge et al., 2008, Scharmer, 2009), using strengths inventories and exercises about beliefs, values, and learning styles. Based on these resources, participants start understanding that they are complex systems interconnected to other systems and practice "going on the balcony" (Heifetz et al., 2009, p. 182) to reflect on their identities and perspectives.

Module II: Contextualized Knowledge—Generating Multiple Interpretations

The path to transformational learning requires mapping the characteristics and peculiarities of a given scenario, as well as creating a responsive environment. In order to do this, a leader-as-mentor needs to create contexts for conversations and interactions based on *trust* and mutual respect. Leaders need to consciously work on developing greater adaptive responses, which in turn are conducive to creating conditions for permanent change within their organizations. Module II uses reflection as a primary tool to better understand knowledge management, learning agility, and personal presence.

During Module II, Be-a-Mentor guides participants to learn from the unique historical, economic, cultural, and social contexts of their own lives, careers, and worlds. The exercises help participants to create awareness of their own bandwidth (repertoire of adaptive approaches) by developing skills to deal with ambiguity (Heifetz et al., 2009) and expand their capacity to continuously learn and navigate change (for an in-depth discussion of adaptive capacity, see Chapter 8).

Module III: Cultivating Skills and Meta-Skills—Staying Connected to Your Purposes

Every job or task requires specific knowledge that will be useful in technical or adaptive challenges, or possibly both, at the same time. Leaders-as-mentors apply their knowledge and skills to create a work environment that favors an openness toward learning and sharing. Such skills presuppose identifying and developing leaders' internal resources, discovering their own blind spots, and analyzing their previously unquestioned beliefs. As stated by Maturana and Varela (2008),

> Reflection is a process of knowing how we know [something], an act of returning to ourselves, the only opportunity we have to discover our blindness and recognize that the certainties and knowledge of others are, respectively, as distressing and as tenuous as ours. (p. 30)

Module III is dedicated to supporting adaptive leaders-as-mentors to understand the dynamics of their "tuning" (Heifetz et al., 2009). All humans are born with reflective capacity, to learn and develop skills that uniquely distinguish humans as humans. The need for learning becomes evident when one views the gap between what one can do in the present moment and identifying where one's potential resides. The following critical processes support this gap analysis:

- Authentic assessment of the current level of not knowing (Broadwell, 1969) and potential for growth;
- Genuinely accepting and embracing the developmental journey;
- Willingness to detach from the tendency to project one's own limitations onto the external world; and
- Willingness to continually improve one's competencies.

Module IV: Intercultural Development—Generating Cultural Interpretations

A leader-as-mentor seeks to understand their own culture(s) and the culture(s) of others. Module IV helps participants to study the differences between mono, multi-, inter-, and cross-cultural approaches to leadership. Hofstede et al.'s (2017) cultural orientation supports the discovery of one's personal preferences and culture-of-origin preferences while providing leaders-as-mentors prompts for dialogue with their loyalties. Exercises based on the developmental model of intercultural sensitivity (Bennet, 1998), with an option of taking the Intercultural Development Inventory (IDI) assessment (Hammer, 2020), provide participants with tools to engage with mentees, colleagues, and communities from different cultural backgrounds. Module IV allows participants to be more effective in surfacing cultural norms that may be bound by personal loyalties: partnerships (internal or external), colleagues, and communities (local or global).

Module V: Conversational Tools—Inspire People

It is critically important that leaders communicate effectively and directly with others and support others in developing this same capacity. In this sense, Module V helps leaders-as-mentors transcend from a mechanistic to a holistic paradigm, recognizing the existence of relationships and the interdependence of various systems: individuals, teams, organizations, and societies.

In Module V, Be-a-Mentor participants are invited to reflect on their development as systems interveners and gain vital skills for conversations that are free of judgment. Argyris et al. (1987) call this "the ladder of inference." By understanding that the use of language is a form of action

(Echeverría, 2010), participants become conscious that their language can create realities. When we speak, we can influence reality and the future for ourselves and others. Leaders-as-mentors learn about their responsibility to create a narrative considering the current context, with observable data and facts to design effective actions and enable the de-construction of limiting beliefs.

Module VI: Process and Practice—Deploy Yourself

Module VI helps participants design their own mentoring process. First, they identify the roles they play in their professional settings and the areas of expertise in which they would like to mentor. They then combine all the learning from the previous modules and their own experiences with ideas on how to facilitate learning and expand thinking. It is a journey where a leader-as-mentor prepares to learn alongside their mentees, remaining open to reflect on the experiences of success and non-success shared by both. Be-a-Mentor helps participants reframe the non-successful experiences, commonly referred to as "failures," as "nested learning opportunities" and the practice of compassion. Once participants have completed the six modules of self-inquiry and initial design of their mentoring practice, they enter the third main phase of the Be-a-Mentor program, rising.

Phase 3: Rising

After attending and fully participating in the six modules, Be-a-Mentor participants plan and implement two pro bono mentoring practices before receiving their certification. They review what was learned during classroom instruction in order to create mentoring plans that incorporate areas of expertise, mentoring approaches, and preferred audiences. Participants are then required to recruit and mentor two mentees for at least 16 hours each. Participants—now mentors-to-be—generate reports to be discussed with the Be-a-Mentor program facilitator to process lessons learned. All this planning supports Be-a-Mentor participants to achieve the best performance in their future practice as leaders-as-mentors.

Mentoring and Adaptive Leadership—Key Learning Lessons

This section describes mentoring examples that are aligned with adaptive leadership and how mentoring is an effective method in developing one's adaptive leadership capacity. Included in these examples are reflections collected from Be-a-Mentor participants during and after the program.

Learning About Self

One Be-a-Mentor program participant expressed that they never stopped to reflect on their own leadership before, they thought leadership was about incorporating successful tools. The Be-a-Mentor program creates a holding environment for a state of "being" that puts one in a position to learn how to serve others while enhancing self-reflection. Maturana and Varela (2008) propose autopoiesis as a recursive organizational mode for living systems, that is, living systems can continuously recreate themselves. Heifetz et al. (2009) talk about "renewal of the heart and guts as well as the head" (p. 295) while thriving for growth and prosperity.

New Ways

A program participant stated: "I thought leadership was about having technical know-how like an expert; now my leadership is about supporting development." Adaptive change implies the creation of new scenarios and ways of thinking about the present and the future, following the idea that "a map is not the territory" (Korzybski, 1933, p. 58) but a space framed by one's beliefs and worldviews. A leader-as-mentor assesses reality and understands they have capacity and responsibility for leading development. Being a leader has to do with the ability to create new realities for oneself and for others (Senge et al., 2008).

Mentor and Mentee Relationship

Another participant of the program stated: "I am influencing my peers and organization to think of leadership as partnership, instead of command and control." The Be-a-Mentor program with adaptive leadership practices invites leaders to lead from a different place. Going to the balcony (Heifetz et al., 2009) is a strategy that invites a leader to see situations from a larger perspective. A leader-as-mentor spends a majority of their time on the balcony, supporting their mentees in discovery, design, reflection, and the exploration of possibilities.

The key concepts that are italicized throughout the chapter intend to offer a moment of pause and deeper reflection each time they are read. Figure 15.1 shows this was an intentional exercise to channel and mobilize an expanded leadership repertoire, that is, thinking beyond traditional models. The authors believe that these key concepts offer a deeper level of insight when visualized together.

Context—A Catalytic Concept

Context was intentionally cited in this chapter almost thirty times. As explained earlier, awareness of context is critical, especially in Brazilian

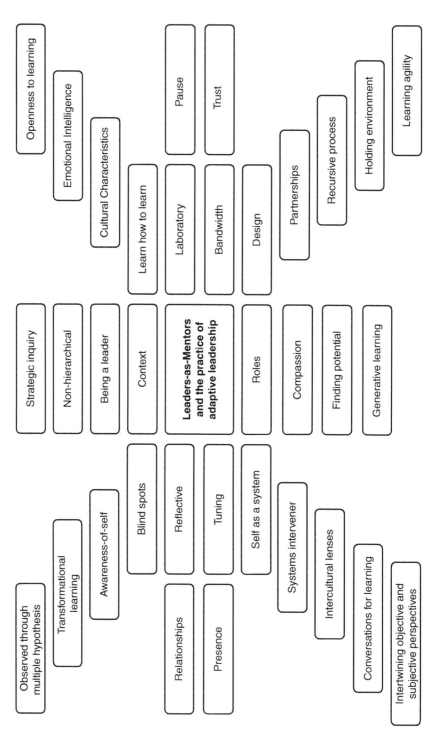

Figure 15.1 Key Concepts of Leaders-as-Mentors Program.

culture. Adaptive leadership requires—intrinsically—that a leader-as-mentor be able to cultivate honest attention to their own inner landscape (Palmer, 2007), as well as their mentees' contexts (Chapter 1 also presents context as a critical aspect of complexity leadership). Heifetz et al. (2009) directly address the importance of context in relationship to adaptive leadership for leaders and organizations:

- "To lead effectively, you also have to examine and take action towards yourself in the context of the challenge" (p. 6).
- "You need perspective on yourself as well as on the systemic context in which you operate" (p. 6).
- "What does *thriving* mean for organizations operating in any particular context?" (p. 14).

For this reason, a learning lesson at the core of mentoring and adaptive leadership is that both processes are relational, contextual, and incorporate one's previous knowledge along with continuous learning. Leaders-as-mentor and mentees grow as they co-create their own mentoring process. True leadership becomes more than an external action; it is an action from within, to promote desirable outcomes.

Final Reflections

The Be-a-Mentor program explains a learning experience that is transformational, with leadership skills and capacity anchored in adaptive leadership practices and tools. After many Be-a-Mentor cohorts, the authors witnessed that the processes inherent in leading through mentoring encompass an expansion of human potential. Adaptive leadership embraces this expansion through holistic, organic, and generative organizational processes. Adaptive leaders understand themselves as systems (identities, tuning, roles), so they are able to observe and interpret the systems they are leading, and design the interventions to build resilient teams, organizations, and cultures that *thrive* in continuous learning for sustained performance. Through its defined phases of entering, emerging (with its six modules), and rising, the Be-a-Mentor program provides a collaborative, systemic, and systematic approach for leaders as they take a courageous stance to transform people's lives and negotiate the challenges of our times.

References

Amato, M. A., & Molokhia, D. (2016). *How to cultivate learning agility.* Harvard Business Publishing. (December 6, 2018). https://www.harvardbusiness.org/insight/how-to-cultivate-learning-agility/.

Argyris, C., Putnam, R., & Smith, D. M. L. (1987). *Action science*. Jossey-Bass.

Bennet, M. J. (1998). *Basic concepts of intercultural communication: Selected readings*. Intercultural Press.

Bloom, P. (2018). *Against empathy: The case for rational compassion*. Vintage.

Broadwell, M. M. (1969). Teaching for learning. *Gospel Guardian*, 20(41), 1–3a. http://www.wordsfitlyspoken.org/gospel_guardian/v20/v20n41p1-3a.html.

Brown, B. (2018). *Dare to lead: Brave work. Tough conversations. Whole hearts*. Random House.

Capra, F. (1996). *The web of life: A new scientific understanding of living systems*. Doubleday.

Center for Creative Leadership. (2020). *The 70-20-10 rule for leadership development*. Center for Creative Leadership. http://www.ccl.org/.

Covey, S. (1999). *The 7 habits of highly effective people: Powerful lessons in personal change*. Simon & Schuster.

Echeverría, R. (2010). *Ontología del lenguaje*. Juan Carlos Saez Editor.

Frankl, V. E., Kushner, H. S., Winslade, W. J., Lasch, I., & Pisano, H. (2014). *Man's search for meaning*. Beacon Press.

Goleman, D. (1999). *Emotional intelligence: Why it can matter more than IQ*. Bantam Books.

Hammer, M. (2020). *Why consider using the intercultural development inventory® (IDI®)*. IDI Intercultural Development Inventory. https://idiinventory.com/wp-content/uploads/2019/08/Why-Consider-the-IDI-2019.pdf

Hase, S., & Kenyon, C. (2000). *From andragogy to heutagogy. Ulti-BASE In-Site*.

Hase, S., & Kenyon, C. (2013). *Self-determined learning: Heutagogy in action*. Bloomsbury Academic.

Heifetz, R. A., Grashow, A., & Linsky, M. (2009). *The practice of adaptive leadership: Tools and tactics for changing your organization and the world*. Harvard Business Press.

Hijfte, S. V. (2020). *Make your organization a center of innovation: Tools and concepts to solve problems and generate ideas*. Apress.

Hofstede, G., Hofstede, G. J., & Minkov, M. (2017). *Cultures and organizations software of the mind: Intercultural cooperation and its importance for survival*. MTM.

Kegan, R., & Lahey, L. L. (2009). *Immunity to change: How to overcome it and unlock the potential in yourself and your organization*. Harvard Business Press.

Kofman, F., Scoss, M., & Mendoza, I. (2004). *Metamanagement: O sucesso além do sucesso*. Elsevier.

Kofman, F. (2014). *Conscious business: How to build value through value*. Sounds True.

Korzybski, A. (1933). *Science and sanity: An introduction to non-Aristotelian systems and general semantics*. International Non-Aristotelian Library Publishing Company.

Kraaijenbrink, J. (2018, December 19). *What does VUCA really mean?* Forbes. https://www.forbes.com/sites/jeroenkraaijenbrink/2018/12/19/what-does-vuca-really-mean/?sh=2810380717d6

Lipton, B. H. (2016). *The biology of belief 10th anniversary edition: Unleashing the power of consciousness, matter & miracles.* Hay House Inc.

Latour, B. (2005). *Reassembling the social: An introduction to actor-network-theory.* Oxford University Press.

Mari, A. (2020, January 10). *The Brazil tech and innovation roundup: We have a new unicorn.* Forbes. https://www.forbes.com/sites/angelicamarideoliveira/2020/01/10/brazil-tech--innovation-roundup-11020-we-have-a-new-unicorn/?sh=6376f5614f2e.

Maturana, H. R., & Varela, F. J. (2008). *The tree of knowledge: The biological roots of human understanding.* Shambhala.

Meyer, E. (2014). *The culture map: Breaking through the invisible boundaries of global business.* Public Affairs.

Nonaka, I. (2008). *The knowledge-creating company.* Harvard Business Review Press.

Palmer, P. J. (2000). *Let your life speak: Listening for the voice of vocation.* Jossey-Bass.

Palmer, P. (2007). *The courage to teach: Exploring the inner landscape of a teacher's life.* Jossey-Bass.

Rogers, C. R. (1969). *Freedom to learn: A view of what education might become.* Charles E. Merrill.

Scharmer, C. O. (2009). *Theory U: Leading from the future as it emerges: The social theory of presencing.* Berrett-Koehler Publishers.

Senge, P. M., Scharmer, C. O., Jaworski, J., & Flowers, B. S. (2008). *Presence: Exploring profound change in people, organizations, and society.* Doubleday.

Senge, P. M. (2006). *The fifth discipline.* Random House Business.

Wolk, L. (2008). *Coaching: A arte de soprar brasas.* Qualitymark.

16 Applications of Adaptive Leadership in Central and Eastern European Contexts

Tomas Hancil and Matthew Rich-Tolsma

Very little has been written about the practice of adaptive leadership in the Central and Eastern European context. We, the authors, have been influenced by adaptive leadership as organizational leaders and as consultants attempting to support leaders in a wide range of international contexts. We have encountered mixed success in our attempts to bring adaptive leadership practices to our work in Central and Eastern Europe, however, and find ourselves experimenting with how these practices might be adapted to become more suitable to the unique cultural context in that region. In this chapter we begin by offering a brief overview of the development of leadership practices in the Czech context, drawing on recent research as well as our own experience. In this section, we draw attention to Czech cultural and historical trends, many of which are generalizable to the region as a whole. We will also bring a developmental lens to making sense of these trends. We then explore a number of vignettes drawn from our own experience to demonstrate the complexity of working with adaptive leadership in this context. We explain the approaches that supported our work concerning our clients' capacity to practice adaptive leadership. In this chapter, we challenge a systemic understanding of organizations (which is, in our opinion, adopted by the adaptive leadership orthodoxy) in favor of a processual understanding drawing on Elias and others to make sense of our experience. We argue based on our experience that organizations are not systems, but can better be understood as complex emerging social processes. This chapter explores what some of the implications of taking this ontological distinction seriously may be for the practice of organizational consulting.

Understanding Leadership in the Czech Context

More than thirty years have passed since the Velvet Revolution, the non-violent transition of power in what was then Czechoslovakia, and the fall of the Berlin Wall. Yet the Czech Republic (much like its Central and Eastern European neighbors) still struggles to define an efficient leadership culture. Initially, a strong heroic leadership approach engulfed the region

DOI: 10.4324/9781003099109-16

only to be supplanted by a fascination with charismatic leadership (Crevani et al., 2010; Cunliffe & Coupland, 2012). Whereas heroic leadership, in general, is centered on the performance of the leader as an individual and their capacity to take charge and get things done, charismatic leaders' performances of leadership are focused on their own personality and ability to affect a crowd. This distinction has been keenly felt in the rise of populist leadership in the region (Buštíková & Guasti, 2019). This shift in how leaders were perceived and valued was prompted by the mass importation of Western expatriate executives to lead the region's transition from a planned to a free market economy. Soulsby and Clark (1996) point out that following the revolution "everything from [the] previous was thrown out and everything from the West was seen as good" (Soulsby & Clark, 1996, p. 227). This transition was accelerated by the European Union's aggressive Eastern enlargement, which brought with it a prestigious new national identity (Petrovic & Solingen, 2005).

Auer-Rizzi and Reber (2013) provide an analysis of the development of leadership in the Czech Republic based on the situational trait-based Vroom-Yetton-Jago model (Vroom & Jago, 2007; Vroom & Yetton, 1973). They argue for an empirical comparison of organizations in Germany and the Czech Republic between 1991 and 2011 as in both countries the business environment and the social conditions have changed considerably, yet leadership styles essentially have not. Leadership styles have remained authoritarian and non-collaborative, they claim, with a tendency towards leaders who find themselves situationally out of place to be unconsciously drawn to perpetuate this pattern. For instance, they note that leaders are slightly more likely to enforce decisions when subordinates disagree with them (Auer-Rizzi & Reber, 2013). This seems to accord with the research on the governance and management of Czech family-owned businesses conducted by Odehnalová (2014). Odehnalová argues that the majority of Czech family businesses have a risk-averse approach which tends towards directive leadership with a positive orientation towards staff motivated by care (Sundaramurthy, 2008). In general, German and Czech leaders are struggling to transition towards greater professionalization and delegation (Greiner, 1997; Kets de Vries, 1993).

At the same time, we have observed increasingly in our practice that the idealization of heroic leadership is slowly being questioned, especially by younger leaders in the Czech Republic. There is a growing spirit of innovation, a maturing confidence in the sophistication, knowledge, and capability of the workforce, and a burgeoning need for shared purpose and respect across the leaders in the organization (Sobotka et al., 2003; Soulsby & Clark, 1996). This, claim Sobotka et al. (2003), is a result of an internalization of Western leadership and management values and the influence of the milieu that began with the Prague Spring of 1968 and the Velvet Revolution in 1989, both of which emphasized aspirational values of benevolence and self-transcendence.

We argue that one characteristic that has remained very central to the Czech conception of leadership is the idea of the charismatic leader. Under communism, the state relied on mechanisms of propaganda, whereas the dissident movement developed a narrative of artistic, intellectual, and cultural renewal. Shortly after the end of the communist regime, there was a strong focus on economic liberalization and growth, exemplified by the technocrat Vaclav Klaus, who served on different occasions as finance minister, prime minister, and president (Hanley, 1999; Saxonberg, 1999). More recently, Czech politics have witnessed a return to its populist and authoritarian history, best exemplified by the present prime minister Andrej Babiš (Buštíková & Guasti, 2019). Babiš exudes the charisma and media obsession with self-promotion, offering an approach to leadership that is highly "personal and aims at the radical transformation of an established institutional order" (Pappas, 2016, p. 380). In some ways, this sense of a return to the authoritarian roots of communism (Buštíková & Guasti, 2019), seems to support the idea of the durability and inertia of culturally defined leadership traits (Auer-Rizzi & Reber, 2013). Although it seems that the last three decades have been something of an ideological rollercoaster in the Czech political arena, we argue that the idealization of the charismatic leader and strong attraction to authoritarian leadership has been a consistent trend connecting these different approaches not only in Czech Republic but all over central Europe.

One of the authors, Tomas, belongs to the last generation that still remembers living under communism. He was a student activist during the late 1980s leading up to the Velvet Revolution. At that time any leadership position was necessarily tainted with connection to the communist party. Leaders were generally feared, but at the same time, they were targets of suspicion and silent contempt, although some may have understood the role as self-sacrifice to protect others from the system. Following the revolution, Tomas pursued graduate education in the West during the 1990s, allowing him to experience and ultimately embrace a range of alternative approaches to leadership. This unique combination of perspectives has allowed him to map several vital forces shaping the current struggle to find appropriate leadership in the volatile, uncertain, complex, and ambiguous socio-political and organizational landscape of the Czech Republic (Horney et al., 2010; Nicolaides & McCallum, 2013). In response, Tomas' consulting practice, like Matthew's (the other author's), has been shaped by concepts of adaptive leadership (Heifetz, 1994; Heifetz et al., 2009; Heifetz & Linsky, 2017).

This has not always been easy. During our time working in management consultancy in the Czech Republic, we have frequently experienced clashes between the basic tenets of adaptive leadership and the dominant leadership culture. For example, leadership in Czech culture is often associated with decisiveness and decision-making power. Leaders are expected to know what to do. Consequently, consulting with others, searching for different perspectives, or even tolerating ambiguity is often seen as a weakness. Decisions are usually expected to be made in a directive way through hierarchical structures and are not participatory (Auer-Rizzi & Reber, 2013; Danis et al., 2011).

In many ways, these cultural conditions appear to be antithetical to the practice of adaptive leadership. However, in our view, it is not only cultural differences that need to be taken into account when we attempt to apply the adaptive leadership model to different environments. Our experience working with adaptive leadership in Czech culture raises questions about assumptions and conditions that are presupposed by the dominant stream of thinking in adaptive leadership (for a discussion of some of the assumptions of adaptive leadership, see Chapter 11). When we look at organizations where adaptive leadership appears to have taken root, we see several developmental characteristics of leaders who created conditions for success. These characteristics are not culturally dependent; while some cultural differences might contribute to applying adaptive leadership in Czech organizations, it is also helpful to look at the developmental presuppositions of adaptive leadership.

As a young and fairly inexperienced consultant working in the Czech Republic, Tomas noticed some years ago that leaders made sense of specific pieces of theory differently. It did not take long to see that it was not helpful to explain such differences as functions of personality type, style, or preferences, nor simply as cultural conditions. Rather, Thomas was witnessing the consequences of differences in reasoning capability and meaning-making: ways of knowing and the complexity of thought. He reached a conclusion that different leaders understood the situational challenges in radically different ways because they were operating from different developmental stages (Day & Dragoni, 2015; Jaques, 2006; Kegan, 1998; Rooke & Torbert, 1998).

The Ambrose Pilot

Ambrose Autocorp is a Swiss manufacturer of components for the trucking and heavy machinery industry. It is a privately owned family business with major manufacturing plants in North America, China, Northern Europe, and Central and Eastern Europe. Tomas' relationship with Ambrose went back several years. He had facilitated strategy sessions with the Eastern European senior leadership team and a number of skill development workshops. In 2018, we launched an ambitious new talent development program focused on preparing a new generation of plant managers as leaders. The vignettes provided in this chapter are drawn from our pilot with eight young (aged 25–35) leaders, all of whom held middle management positions, responsible for a number of functions. The backgrounds of the participants spanned Western and

Eastern Europe and Russia. This hybrid 18-month program included four 2-day in-person retreats held in the Czech Republic, supplemented with monthly group coaching clinics.

Box 16.1   Vignette 1: Ambrose

Before convening the Ambrose pilot group, we were told that we might not be able to get the participants to speak about anything of substance. After general introductions and orientation, we asked the group to talk about their struggles in their roles. It was a wide-ranging conversation, a survey of experience in breakdown—experiences that did not seem to make sense, where normal, habitual ways of working no longer seemed to suffice. For what seemed an excruciatingly long time, the conversation drifted abstractly and politely, punctuated by protracted, awkward pauses. Eventually, Matthew drew attention to this pattern. "What was it," he mused out loud, "that we might be avoiding talking about? Was there truly nothing of consequence for us to examine together? Or was there something so terribly anxiety-provoking about the prospect of unveiling our uncertainties that it was unbearable to do so?"

One of the Czech managers, a process efficiency expert named Jiri, boldly took this up as an invitation. He started to share his deep frustration with his role, with an endless demand to generate data and meet key performance indicators; generating abstract lists of numbers had become the core of his job. "Processes are about people," he lamented, but his role seemed to have become completely dehumanized. This confession from Jiri opened the floodgates, leading to similar stories about how other participants had found themselves stymied in aspects of their roles.

Tomas pointed out that it appeared that the participants needed to put up with a lot of bullshit in their roles. "What might the function of this bullshit be?" he asked. "How are we all playing a role in perpetuating it and who is it serving?"

The Consultant Role in Adaptive Leadership

Consulting is inherently performative, a process of persuasion and rhetoric, always seeking to represent the consultants in a flattering light (Berglund & Werr, 2000; Spicer, 2013). As a result, a consultant's appetite to face the messiness of their own practice is generally limited (Czarniawska, 2001). Power (2010) points out:

> All practices give accounts of themselves which are aspirational rather than descriptive ... what has been left out must be brought back in, even at the expense of the official account itself. The obviousness of practitioner common sense must be questioned by revealing the process by which that common sense was formed. (pp. 7–8)

We propose that as consultants offering a model such as adaptive leadership, we might easily fall prey to this tendency to offer idealized and reified accounts of our practice, as if it is a complete solution in an attempt to truncate the anxiety clients feel when they are facing uncertainty—as well as our own. As consultants, we also seek relief from the interminability of discomfort. Power (2010) points out that, "an intellectually attractive program [can be] a source of irritation to practitioners" (p. 8). It may prove to be self-defeating by lowering the sense of trust in what consultants are doing. This helps explains why consultants are sometimes regarded with a degree of suspicion and even derision, despite the fact that the dominant *habitus* fosters a certain degree of dependence on their services and the sense of soothing they might provide. In a similar vein, it makes sense that managers raised in this sort of milieu might take up a similar approach in their leadership practice. The Czech leadership style has a tendency towards a focus on charisma (as rhetorical skill) and the situations in which leaders have found themselves working, historically, that tended to rely on dehumanizing and overly bureaucratic rationalities that were disembedded from the complex social realities of the day-to-day task of leadership (Townley, 2008) allowing for clear decisions or even orders. This has been the case whether strategy has been enacted bureaucratically (as was the case under the communist regime), economically, (as was the case in the 1990s and early 2000s), or technocratically (as seems to increasingly be the case). What we observed at Ambrose is that middle managers found themselves asked to do things that appeared very "fancy" and complicated, but did not really make sense. They felt they were wasting time and yet proceeded in a relatively unreflective way. The participants in our program were generally not performing "bullshit" roles—they performed very practical and material tasks that directly impacted the production process and others with whom they worked. At the same time, they found themselves confronted by a vision of leadership, promoted by their superiors and consultants, that was very divorced from their actual experiences. In developmental terms, they were experiencing a gap between the complexity of thinking needed to tackle the situation and their current developmental stage. These individuals reported feelings of alienation and anxiety, punctuated by confusion and re-sistance. They seemed to spend much of their time in a state of dis-gruntled helplessness, believing that they had little influence upon the status quo in their organization. The generally unreflective way in which participants take this on, despite their reservations, is reminiscent of what Alvesson and Spicer (2012) describe as functional stupidity, a phenomenon characterized by an "unwillingness or inability to mobilize three aspects of cognitive capacity: reflexivity, justification, and sub-stantive reasoning" (Alvesson & Spicer, 2012, p. 1199). They argue that functional stupidity serves multiple functions, chiefly, the reduction of anxiety; compliance is often rewarded through promotions, pay raises, and smooth organizational functioning. We argue that functional stu-pidity equates to the apparent functionality of organizational bullshit (Spicer, 2013; 2018; 2020; Curtis, 2018; Graeber, 2018).

Of course, functional stupidity also has risks. The lack of reflexivity that characterizes functional stupidity means that there is significant potential for avoidable risks to not be adequately anticipated and in-sidious organizational problems to be overlooked. Curtis (2018) relates this to his idea of functional collusion. He explains that,

> Collusion is a social phenomenon in which patterns of relating emerge as interdependent people interact with one another to maintain their ways of being together. It is important to point out that I am proposing that such collusion takes place without prior discussion or planning by those involved, and may also be outside of their awareness, and so is different from what one would understand as deliberate cooperation or conspiracy. (p. 58)

In adaptive leadership, we might understand this as a strategy of work avoidance. However, we would contend, in light of Curtis's argument above, that this may be a slightly reductionistic way of making sense of our bullshitting processes. The processes of organizational bullshit are functional; they are simultaneously an avoidance of and process of work. The term work avoidance proposes that we could know the right thing to do ahead of time and that we can consciously choose whether or not to engage. Some proponents of adaptive leadership may argue that work avoidance is a natural but unconscious response to the discomfort as-sociated with adaptive work, yet once again this presumes that we could know what the right thing to do is ahead of time (i.e., that we could know which work is "adaptive" or not before we have done it). So, while we would certainly agree that people engage in a range of defensive behaviors (both conscious and unconscious) to resist change and adap-tion, we contend that the black and white splitting of work into the categories of adaptive work (good) and work avoidance (bad) does not accord with our experience. (Work avoidance can be a strategic leadership move to reduce anxiety.) And bullshit work is still work; we cannot know what the meaning or outcomes of our activities will be when we are engaged in them, and the reality is that most work is enabling and constraining at the same time. Work is an emergent social process, which is about far more than just the superficial business outcomes which it purports to deliver. Elias (2001) drew attention to the fact that humans are not self-contained individuals but rather exist as part of a social process and that life is thus inherently political. It is inevitable that groups of people will come together and begin to form a "we" identity. The possibility of then being excluded from a group with which one identifies can be incredibly anxiety-provoking, as one becomes dependent upon others in the group. In their study of dynamics of inclusion and exclusion in a small English town, Elias and Scotson (1994) draw attention to the ways in which "we identities" are formed around a common ideology and sustained by processes, such as gossip occurring in the group. Reflecting on Elias and Scotson (1994), Stacey (2003) points out that

> Ideology ... preserves the current order by making that current order seem natural. In this way ideological themes organise [*sic*] the communicative interactions of individuals and groups. As a form of communication, as an aspect of the power relations in the group, ideology is taken up in that private role-play, that silent conversation, which is mind in individuals. (p. 125)

Stacey's insight offers some explanation as to why patterns of bullshit might be sustained in organizations. Intelligent people such as those in our group, including ourselves—are frequently induced to perpetuate patterns of behavior that are manifestly nonsensical, not just as a collusion to truncate anxiety, but also because of the profound risk to identity implied by the amplification of difference. Difference, and hence by extension conflict, creates possibility for the emergence of novelty; it also runs the risk of exclusion. It is also true that not all ideologies focus on conservation, some might, as examples, idealize transcendence or emancipation.

With our own flaws as consultants and potential co-creators of organizational bullshit firmly established—as humans, we are susceptible to many of the same propensities as our clients, we now turn our attention to considering how the techniques that we found ourselves using with this group might relate to some of the core ideas of adaptive leadership.

Mobilizing the System and its Stakeholders

We have highlighted tendencies in the Central Eastern European culture to promote authoritarian leaders and wait for orders from on high. We have attempted to perturb this understanding by drawing attention to

the complex patterning of social processes through which all participating individuals are shaping the group whilst simultaneously being
shaped through group association. Drawing attention to the emergent
patterning of relationships as a social process problematizes the idea of
the organization as a system, or a system of multiple interconnected
systems, as generally posited in adaptive leadership where individuals are
viewed as systems interacting in a larger social system. This way of
thinking about organizations draws predominantly on the discourse of
complex adaptive systems (e.g., Marion, 1999; Wheatley, 1999). This is
potentially problematic because organizations are not biological organisms any more than they are machines; rather they are a dynamic patterning of processes of relaying between interdependent human
individuals. We will shortly go on to explain why we think that this
distinction is fundamentally important (for more details on complexity
leadership and complex adaptive systems in relation to adaptive leadership, see Chapter 1).

Diagnosing the System and the Adaptive Challenge

We chose to engage the members of the group using an abductive approach, giving primacy to experience through attending to breakdowns
(Alvesson & Kärreman, 2011), specifically situations where surprise and
doubt problematize one's current explanation of their lifeworld
(Martela, 2015). Allowing different explanations and engagement with
different perspectives is at the same time providing developmental opportunities for those involved. What we discovered through this process,
however, is that there was no "system" to be diagnosed. What was
troubling participants as they started to make sense of the challenges of
working together in an organizational context, is that the challenges
were not about them and their individual skills and behaviors, nor was it
about the behaviors of the organization as an object or a system. Rather
we found ourselves paying attention to the emergent patterning of relationships that participants were forming in that moment, while simultaneously being formed by them. These patterns have some
diagnostic relevance because, as Elias (2001) points out, they exhibit
some degree of stability—they pattern (largely unconsciously) as stable
and emergent while, paradoxically, predictably unpredictable. On the
surface it may seem that this perspective is similar to complexity leadership as theorized by Uhl-Bien et al. (2007), a perspective that aligns
with adaptive leadership. We argue, however, that the processual perspective which Elias is advocating is ontologically different to the systemic notion of complexity leadership. Organizations are not things at
all. While there may be limited usefulness in thinking about organizations *as if* they were systems, believing that they actually are systemic
wholes is something quite different to understanding them as complex

patterning of relational processes between interdependent individuals. As Griffin (2002) points out,

> The suggestion that an organization is a living system reflects a holistic philosophy. It sets up a whole outside of the experience of interaction between people, a whole to which they are required to submit if their behavior is to be judged ethical. This distances us from our actual experience and makes it feel natural to blame something outside of our actual interaction for what happens to us. It encourages the belief that we are victims of a system, on the one hand, and allows us to escape feeling responsible for our own actions, on the other. Or, it alienates people. They come to feel that they are insignificant parts of some greater whole and that there is nothing much they can do about it. (p. 84)

So, participants may, through a process of discussion, become aware of how their engagement in a process of collusion has sustained existing patterns of power-relating in the organization. This disturbing realization may help participants to imagine new choices that they might make, but it is impossible to predict what the responses to these different choices might be, and to know whether they would necessarily prove helpful. Attending to this diagnostic therefore requires a vigilant, experimental state of mind (Loren, 2005) and the application of practical wisdom (Shotter & Tsoukas, 2014). Whereas adaptive leadership does, in general, advocate an experimental approach, the rational causality that underpins an experimental approach presupposes that such experimentation could lead to some relatively certain way of discovering the right way to go forward.

A Descent into the Maelstrom

Bauer Bookkeeping is a global software service company that produces accounting software for the transport and logistics industry. Although the Czech Republic contributes just 6% of Bauer's global revenue, it is the dominant player in the local market. The leadership of the local subsidiary, particularly its managing director, Petr, is held in high regard by Bauer's international board. Tomas first started working with Petr, an accountant by background, as an executive coach more than five years ago when Petr served as Bauer's regional financial director. Two years into his role as managing director, Petr described a growing distance between his team and himself. He had the sense that, although highly respected, he felt very much alone in his leadership and that all of his reports were preoccupied with their functional roles. He engaged us to work with him and his senior leadership team to understand why they were struggling to collaborate and to build a more effective "one team."

Box 16.2   Vignette 2: Bauer Bookkeeping

It was the second afternoon of our first 2-day meeting with the leadership team. Fifteen people (including Tomas and Matthew) were sitting silently in a circle. The tone of the meeting had become increasingly sullen as the day progressed and a mood of apathy seemed to have settled over the group. We had attempted to broach several planned strategic topics, but as soon as we started to get anywhere interesting or productive in our conversation, the energy would rapidly dissipate and everyone would turn to us with a look of bored desperation.

Tomas decided to call out the pattern he was seeing. "It seems to me", he said, "that it is somehow difficult for us to talk about what is happening in this group. Why is that? What makes it difficult?"

No one actively took initiative, but several people shuffled in their seats and a few furtive glances were exchanged. Tomas continued, "It seems like it is pretty uncomfortable to even begin to draw attention to this." At this point, Milos (head of regional sales) let out an audible groan, he shook his head and put his palms over his eyes. Petr was suddenly incensed. "What is it? Speak up. If you have a problem, then spit it out".

Milos leaned forward in his chair facing Petr head-on. He spoke in a low voice, but his slowly-forming words were charged with rancor. "What's the point? This is all a waste of time! You act like we are supposed to be a team, like we can actually influence things, but it's not like that... We don't get a say, not really. Those jerks in Hamburg don't understand our market, and they don't care... and you..." -he was wagging his finger at Petr now and seemed on the verge of tears—"...you never stand up to them. We all just have to do what we're told."

Petr was flushed. "I am so sick of your excuses," he spat, casting his gaze around the room. "All of you. I know that the Hamburg office is a pain. I have to deal with that too. I am constantly dealing with them on your behalf. But, at the end of the day, we are the people who *need to run this business. We need to find a way to work together in the face of whatever challenges come our way."* Petr crossed his arms and sat back in his chair.

After a few minutes of silence, we broke for coffee. When everyone returned to the circle, Matthew changed his tactic slightly and told the group he would like to share the story of Edgar Allan Poe's (2012) A

Descent into the Maelstrom. It recounts how the protagonist survived a shipwreck and was able to detach himself from the emotional turmoil of being tossed about by the currents to notice the patterns that were occurring in the storm ... that some objects were being drawn into a whirlpool, while others were pushed to its periphery. As a result, he was able to take decisive action to save his life. His two brothers, however, were overwhelmed by panic and consequently died in the storm.

   Matthew's point to the group was that in a threatening situation, it is easy to be overwhelmed by anxiety and panic. One might respond through logic, seeking the right model or tool to solve the problem or one might become lost in a panic, perhaps striking out at others or ourselves. Like Poe's story of the fisherman and his unfortunate brothers, our emotions do not control reality, but they can control us. The question then becomes, how can we contain our emotions sufficiently to get some distance, to track the patterns emerging in the group?

Norbert Elias made use of Poe's story to illustrate his idea of the paradox of involvement and detachment (Elias, 1956; 2007). Matthew turned to this story in that moment because of the way in which it points to the simultaneity of involvement *and* detachment. Elias describes this paradox in the following way:

> The fisherman ... found himself involved in a critical process, which at first appeared wholly beyond his control. For a time, he may have clutched at some imaginary hopes. Fantasies of a miracle, of help from some unseen persons, may have crossed his mind. After a while, however, he calmed down. He began to think more coolly; and by standing back, by controlling his fear, by seeing himself, as it were, from a distance... he managed to turn his thoughts away from himself to the situation in which he was caught up. It was then that he recognised [*sic*] the elements in the uncontrollable process, which he could use in order to control its condition sufficiently for his own survival. (Elias, 2007, p. 109)

Referencing Elias, Mowles (2015) argues that paying attention simultaneously to our involvement and detachment enables greater reflexivity in our practice. If one considers organizational life as a process through which its members interdependently form and are formed by each other, reflexivity-how one thinks about what one is doing-becomes a useful skill to make sense of the uncertainty that inhabits most organizations. The historical context that Czechs share with other Central and Eastern European countries makes this kind of reflexivity very painful. The collective experience of being simultaneously a victim of the system and its constitutive collaborator (Havel, 1985) fuels an unspoken unwillingness to confront parallel situations such as the one described in the Bauer vignette: working in a multinational corporation with deficient regard for local specifics.

Stacey (2006) and Stacey and Mowles (2016) argue that the rise of systems thinking in the social sciences is dependent upon an autonomous theory of change, a neoliberal identity that provides a theoretical basis for models such as adaptive leadership. Adaptive leadership draws attention to the ways in which an individual is simultaneously shaped by internal and external forces. This spatial way of thinking reveals the underlying systemic suppositions of the model. The individual is a bounded system yet shaped through interactions with other (external) bounded systems which collectively make up larger bounded systems. With reason and perspective, sufficient insight can be gained to understand other self-systems to diagnose and predict the behavioral patterns of others, including decision-making. While it may be argued that this interpretation of adaptive leadership depends on the level of development of the adaptive leader, and that it may be possible to hold a transrational interpretation of the ideas presented by adaptive leadership (a position with which we would by and large agree), we would still maintain that the above interpretation is not purely a misrepresentation, because many of the assumptions it draws on are rooted in the rhetoric of the model.

The dominant discourse of consulting situates the consultant as being outside of an organizational system (Stacey, 2012; Stacey & Mowles, 2016). From this vantage point, they can critique the general work of the organization, draw attention to abstract themes, and recommend abstract cures to abstract maladies. Of course, there are a number of authors who directly challenge this way of thinking (e.g., Shaw, 2002), but they are certainly on the periphery of the mainstream discourse. In the dominant discourse, there is an appearance of remoteness, a supposition that the consultant is epistemically removed from the object of their inquiry, yet at the same time, consultants find themselves fundamentally entangled in the complex figurations of power-relating that comprise the organizations they intend to serve (Elias, 1978). This is always the case in human social interactions. The epistemological challenges presented by the metaphor of the balcony are discussed by Reams (Chapter 5); Reams argues that our understanding of this metaphor is shaped by our worldview which (we would add) is formed through our experience of social participation. Based on our experience we propose that the idea of the balcony, as described by Heifetz and others (Heifetz et al., 2009;

Heifetz & Linsky, 2017) should be understood in a particular way. While Heifetz et al. present several practices to overcome one's blind spots and overcome habitually constraining unconscious habits, their recommendation and practices are often viewed from an individualistic point of view that implies individual rational agency and hence over-looks the ways in which humans are habitually constrained by un-conscious habits and interdependent relational bonds. Secondly, we argue that we must avoid splitting the paradox of involvement and de-tachment. Adaptive leadership suggests that as a leader becomes more skilled in moving between the dance floor and the balcony, they develop the capacity to do both simultaneously (an idea similar to Schön's [1983] "reflection-in-action"). Going to the balcony implies that one can leave the dance floor and somehow observe it from the outside. Elias (2007), however, argues that we are always in both places at the same time and that we can never be either completely involved or completely detached, but rather paradoxically simultaneously on the dance floor and the balcony, which is critical to navigating the types of challenges illustrated in the Bauer vignette. With practice and sufficient perspicacity leaders can cultivate a quality of reflexivity that enables them to pay more conscious attention to this emergent reality. Again, this is an ability that is closely linked to the level of individual development and complexity of thinking of the leader.

Gossip and Feedback

Box 16.3   Vignette 3: Lumpen Kavarna

At a subsequent retreat with the Bauer Bookkeeping leadership team, most of the participants seemed to be in a more reflective mood. Perhaps, we hoped, they had been practicing the awareness skills we talked about the last time we were together. The shift towards more thoughtful and tentative self-disclosure was noticeable. After a while, a sense of heaviness descended upon the room.

Radek, one of the senior people, said after a theatrical sigh, "Well I have to say that I am really tired of this fake politeness. I know you are talking about me and others behind our backs. We are all doing it; making fun of each other, maligning each other. Then when we get together in a group we are all polite ... Come on!" His words were followed by an agonizing pause.

Eventually, when the silence broke it was with an apologetic tone. Some colleagues attempted to deny Radek's accusations. But then another director gave the phenomenon a name: lumpen kavárna—the name used for the secretive coffee house meetings where dissidents would meet. At Bauer, she suggested, those who felt that they did not have access to power and significance met to vent frustration instead of confronting it openly in the moment. These gossip sessions resulted in feelings of inclusion for those involved and exclusion for those talked about.

Gossip might have negative effects, but we believed it neither possible nor desirable to attempt to prevent people from meeting with each other. Matthew joined the conversation. "You are obviously able to see the negative impact gossip has on the organization and on you as a group. Yet you are engaging in such a behavior anyway. So... Why are you doing this? What are the benefits of such a behavior? These meetings carry risks, as you well know—but also serve a function. What function is that?"

This acknowledging shifted the conversation from one of protective self-awareness to an exploration of behaviors that are human and can be healing. People began to recognize that it was important to be able to vent frustrations, but soon began to question why it was so difficult to give direct feedback to each other instead of taking their grievances to the *lumpen kavarna*.

Elias and Scotson (1994) discovered that gossip often serves as a powerful and effective act of cohesion in groups. It is a relatively universal behavior that bonds groups, both enabling and constraining their interactions; no one individual can control the interplay of interactions where processes of inclusion and exclusion play out in predictably unpredictable ways. There is something unique, however, about the process of the *lumpen kavarna*. It is a place where neither individual nor group take precedence; rather both are simultaneously brought into view. In essence, this serves to affirm identity, enabling socially conditioned norms for a group. It is a place where acts of conformity and resistance begin to define the images we cherish of ourselves and wish to present to others. Once again, this process simultaneously enables and constrains our presentation of self.

Whereas it is often quite difficult for groups to recognize that gossip can serve legitimate and useful purposes, it is easy to start cultivating. It actively, once it is understood as behavior, normalizes rather than vilifies. This shift, in turn, nurtures a quality of authenticity in conversation, a quality often lacking in the Central and Eastern European organizational context. The ability to freely express one's opinion is a cherished achievement connected with the toppling of the communist oppression. Balancing an idealization of expression as freedom with shared responsibility for team cohesion, organizational effectiveness, and overall good relations remains an ongoing challenge.

Shifting attention from the negative consequences of gossip into questioning the functions gossip serves in organizations allowed us to give the work back to the participants. On the one hand, participants were exculpated; they were also given full responsibility for the impact of their choice to participate in this way. These conditions created a holding environment for the group to engage in a discussion about their behavior from a different perspective. As a result, participants were no longer preoccupied by their differences and felt greater freedom to explore why these differences existed and assumptions about those differences. The gossip that created the cohesion of a particular subgroup turned into open discussion of group norms and intentions. It became increasingly clear that the questions the group was asking were bigger than the past experiences of any one individual and instead that meaning-making was a complex emergent process that belonged to the group. They were able to see the reciprocity of their experience: The process was formed by the participating individuals while, at the same time, the individuals were formed by the process itself. This shift in the group's understanding of the nature of development and learning had profound implications for their work together.

Conclusions

It is clear from the examples provided here that the Central and Eastern European contexts constitute an environment in which adaptive leadership is both timely and relevant. At the same time, the unique sociopolitical milieu and the developmental center of gravity from which most leaders are operating means that some adaptation and translation of ideas is required. We have noted success with a pragmatic, breakdown-oriented approach, where our engagement was led by our clients' problematization of their own experience. Increasing conscientization emerges in response to a problem-posing praxis (see Freire, 2000). This approach has revealed that some ideas of adaptive leadership can be generalized from a particular cultural experience but may not be immediately applicable in other contexts. Our experience emphasizes once again the importance of involved detachment (Elias, 2007) and keeping the global and local simultaneously in view. Further, our experience points to the importance of a developmental lens that explains why some ideas are not accepted regardless of cultural fit. What we realized in this work is yet another invitation to take experience seriously (Stacey & Griffin, 2005) rather than adhering uncritically to a method regardless of how clever it may be.

Our experience led us to the conclusion that the ideas that underpin adaptive leadership need to be critically re-examined. We argue that a better understanding of the complex social processes of relating through which individuals are simultaneously forming and being formed by each other will help consultants to more effectively use adaptive leadership in their practice. Along these lines, we have drawn attention to the ways in which one's interdependent interactions tend to be simultaneously enabling and constraining and that often one's apparently bullshit behaviors are not what they initially seem, taking on a quality of functional collusion. While it might be tempting to diagnose behaviors that one considers to be merely bullshit and approach them as work avoidance, with some detachment these processes can be seen as purposeful and their aims quite different than how they initially appear. Adopting a paradoxical and processual perspective offers a more plausible account of our experiences of working with clients and reveals that practical judgment is required in order to judiciously deploy tools and techniques of adaptive leadership in ways that takes the contextual peculiarities of their leadership more adequately into account.

References

Alvesson, M., & Kärreman, D. (2011). *Qualitative research and theory development: Mystery as method.* SAGE.

Alvesson, M., & Spicer, A. (2012). A stupidity-based theory of organizations. *Journal of Management Studies, 49*(7), 1194–1220. 10.1111/j.1467-6486.2012.01072.x

Auer-Rizzi, W., & Reber, G. (2013). Leadership styles: Inertia and changes in the Czech Republic. *Journal of Eastern and European Management Studies, 18*(1), 9–35.

Berglund, J., & Werr, A. (2000). The invincible character of management consulting rhetoric: How one blends incommensurates while keeping them apart. *Organization, 7*(4), 633–655. 10.1177/135050840074008

Buštíková, L., & Guasti, P. (2019). The state as a firm: Understanding the autocratic roots of technocratic populism. *East European Politics and Societies: And Cultures, 33*(2), 302–330. 10.1177/0888325418791723

Carter, P., & Jackson, N. (2004). For the sake of argument: Towards an understanding of rhetoric as process. *Journal of Management Studies, 41*(3), 469–491. 10.1111/j.1467-6486.2004.00441.x

Crevani, L., Lindgren, M., & Packendorff, J. (2010). Leadership, not leaders: On the study of leadership as practices and interactions. *Scandinavian Journal of Management, 26*(1), 77–86. 10.1016/j.scaman.2009.12.003

Cunliffe, A., & Coupland, C. (2012). From hero to villain to hero: Making experience sensible through embodied narrative sensemaking. *Human Relations, 65*(1), 63–88. 10.1177/0018726711424321

Curtis, G. (2018). *Functional collusion in a UK non-governmental organisation: Processes of shame and exclusion from the perspective of an organisational development practitioner* [Unpublished doctoral dissertation]. University of Hertfordshire.

Czarniawska, B. (2001). Is it possible to be a constructionist consultant? *Management Learning, 32*(2), 253–266. 10.1177/1350507601322006

Danis, W. M., Liu, L. A., & Vacek, J. (2011). Values and upward influence strategies in transition: Evidence from the Czech Republic. *Cultural Psychology, 42*(2), 288–306. 10.1177/0022022110396924

Day, D. V., & Dragoni, L. (2015). Leadership development: An outcome-oriented review based on time and levels of analyses. *Annual Review of Organizational Psychology and Organizational Behavior, 2*(1), 133–156. 10.1146/annurev-orgpsych-032414-111328

Elias, N. (1956). Problems of involvement and detachment. *The British Journal of Sociology, 7*(3), 226–252. 10.2307/587994

Elias, N. (1978). *What is sociology?* Hutchinson.

Elias, N. (2001). *The society of individuals* (M. Schröter, Trans.). Continuum.

Elias, N. (2007). *Involvement and detachment*. University College Dublin Press.

Elias, N., & Scotson, J. L. (1994). *The established and the outsiders: A sociological enquiry into community problems* (2. ed). SAGE Publications Ltd.

Freire, P. (2000). *Pedagogy of the oppressed* (30th anniversary ed.). Continuum.

Graeber, D. (2018). *Bullshit jobs*. Simon & Schuster.

Greiner, L. E. (1997). Evolution and revolution as organizations grow: A company's past has clues for management that are critical to future success. *Family Business Review, 20*(4), 397–409.

Griffin, D. (2002). *The emergence of leadership: Linking self-organization and ethics*. Routledge.

Hanley, S. (1999). The new right in the new Europe? Unravelling the ideology of Czech Thatcherism'. *Journal of Political Ideologies, 4*(2), 163–189. 10.1080/13569319908420794

Havel, V. (1985). The power of the powerless. *International Journal of Politics, 15*(3/4), 23–96.

Heifetz, R. (1994). *Leadership without easy answers*. Harvard University Press.

Heifetz, R. A., & Linsky, M. (2017). *Leadership on the line, with a new preface: Staying alive through the dangers of change*. Harvard Business Press.

Heifetz, R. A., Linsky, M., & Grashow, A. (2009). *The practice of adaptive leadership: Tools and tactics for changing your organization and the world*. Harvard Business Press.

Horney, N., Pasmore, B., & O'Shea, T. (2010). Leadership agility: A business imperative for a VUCA World. *People & Strategy, 33*(4), 32–38.

Jaques, E. (2006). *Requisite organization: A total system for effective managerial organization and managerial leadership for the 21st century* (Rev. 2. ed. memorial). Cason Hall.

Kegan, R. (1998). *In over our heads: The mental demands of modern life*. Harvard University Press.

Kegan, R., & Lahey, L. (2002). *How the way we talk can change the way we work: Seven languages for transformation*. Jossey-Bass.

Kegan, R. & Lahey, L. (2009). *Immunity to change: How to overcome it and unlock potential in yourself and your organization*. Harvard Business Press.

Kets de Vries, M. F. R. (1993). The dynamics of family controlled firms: The good and the bad news. *Organizational Dynamics, 21*(3), 59–71. 10.1016/ 0090-2616(93)90071-8

Loren, G. (2005). Thought leadership: Ronald Heifetz-the challenge of adaptive leadership. *New Zealand Management, 52*(7), 46–48.

Marion, R. (1999). *The edge of organization: Chaos and complexity theories of formal social systems.* Sage.

Martela, F. (2015). Fallible inquiry with ethical ends-in-view: A pragmatist philosophy of science for organizational research. *Organization Studies, 36*(4), 537–563. 10.1177/0170840614559257

Mowles, C. (2015). *Managing in uncertainty: Complexity and the paradoxes of everyday organizational life.* Routledge.

Nicolaides, A., & McCallum, D. C. (2013). Inquiry in action for leadership in turbulent times: Exploring the connections between transformative learning and adaptive leadership. *Journal of Transformative Education, 11*(4), 246–260. 10.1177/1541344614540333

Odehnalová, P. (2014, November). Family-business governance in the Czech Republic. In *European conference on management, leadership & governance* (pp. 206–211). Academic Conferences International Limited.

Pappas, T. S. (2016). Are populist leaders "charismatic"? The evidence from Europe. *Constellations, 23*(3), 378–390. 10.1111/1467-8675.12233

Petrovic, B., & Solingen, E. (2005). Europeanisation and internationalisation: The case of the Czech Republic. *New Political Economy, 10*(3), 281–303. 10.1080/13563460500203391

Poe, E. A. (2012). *Descent into the maelstrom.* Read Books.

Power, M. (2010). *The audit society: Rituals of verification* (Reprinted). Oxford Univ. Press.

Rooke, D., & Torbert, W. R. (1998). Organizational transformation as a function of CEO's developmental stage. *Organization Development Journal, 16*(1), 11–28.

Saxonberg, S. (1999). Václav Klaus: The rise and fall and re-emergence of a charismatic leader. *East European Politics and Societies: And Cultures, 13*(2), 391–418.

Schön, D. (1983). *The reflective practitioner: How professionals think in action.* Basic Books.

Shaw, P. (2002). *Changing conversations in organizations: A complexity approach to change.* Routledge.

Shotter, J., & Tsoukas, H. (2014). In search of phronesis: Leadership and the art of judgment. *Academy of Management Learning & Education, 13*(2), 224–243. 10.5465/amle.2013.0201

Sobotka, T., Zeman, K., & Kantorová, V. (2003). Demographic shifts in the Czech Republic after 1989: A second demographic transition view. *European Journal of Population/Revue Européenne de Démographie, 19*(3), 249–277. 10.1023/A:1024913321935

Soulsby, A., & Clark, E. (1996). The emergence of post-communist management in the Czech Republic. *Organization Studies, 17*(2), 227–247. 10.1177/ 017084069601700205

Spicer, A. (2013). Shooting the shit: The role of bullshit in organisations. *M@n@gement, 16*(5), 653–666. 10.3917/mana.165.0653

Spicer, A. (2018). *Business bullshit*. Routledge.

Spicer, A. (2020). Playing the bullshit game: How empty and misleading communication takes over organisations. *Organisational Theory, 1*, 1–26. 10.1177/2631787720929704

Stacey, R. (2006). Theories of change in therapeutic work. *Clinical Child Psychology and Psychiatry, 11*(2), 191–203. 10.1177/1359104506061446

Stacey, R. D. (2003). *Complexity and group processes: A radically social understanding of individuals*. Routledge. http://public.ebookcentral.proquest.com/choice/publicfullrecord.aspx?p=199340

Stacey, R. D. (2012). *Tools and techniques of leadership and management: Meeting the challenge of complexity*. Routledge.

Stacey, R. D., & Griffin, D. (Eds.). (2005). *A complexity perspective on researching organizations: Taking experience seriously*. Routledge.

Stacey, R. D., & Mowles, C. (2016). *Strategic management and organisational dynamics: The challenge of complexity to ways of thinking about organisations* (7th ed.). Pearson Education.

Sundaramurthy, C. (2008). Sustaining trust within family businesses. *Family Business Review, 21*(1), 89–102. 10.1111/j.1741-6248.2007.00110.x

Townley, B. (2008). *Reason's neglect: Rationality and organizing*. Oxford University Press.

Uhl-Bien, M., Marion, R., & McKelvey, B. (2007). Complexity leadership theory: Shifting leadership from the industrial age to the knowledge era. *The Leadership Quarterly, 18*(4), 298–318. https://doi-org.ezproxy.herts.ac.uk/10.1016/j.leaqua.2007.04.002

Vroom, V. H., & Jago, A. G. (2007). The role of the situation in leadership. *American Psychologist, 62*(1), 17–24. 10.1037/0003-066X.62.1.17

Vroom, V. H., & Yetton, P. W. (1973). *Leadership and decision-making*. University of Pittsburgh Press.

Wheatley, M. J. (1999). *Leadership and the new science: Discovering order in a chaotic world* (2nd ed.). Berrett-Koehler Publishers

Index

Milton Keynes UK
Ingram Content Group UK Ltd.
UKHW022044070923
428265UK00013B/118